Appealing to the Crowd

Appealing to the Crowd

The Ethical, Political, and Practical Dimensions of Donation-Based Crowdfunding

JEREMY SNYDER

OXFORD
UNIVERSITY PRESS

OXFORD
UNIVERSITY PRESS

Oxford University Press is a department of the University of Oxford. It furthers
the University's objective of excellence in research, scholarship, and education
by publishing worldwide. Oxford is a registered trade mark of Oxford University
Press in the UK and certain other countries.

Published in the United States of America by Oxford University Press
198 Madison Avenue, New York, NY 10016, United States of America.

Library of Congress Cataloging-in-Publication Data
Names: Snyder, Jeremy, author.
Title: Appealing to the crowd : the ethical, political, and practical
dimensions of donation-based crowdfunding / Jeremy Snyder.
Description: New York, NY : Oxford University Press, [2024] |
Includes bibliographical references and index.
Identifiers: LCCN 2023017330 (print) | LCCN 2023017331 (ebook) |
ISBN 9780197658130 (hardback) | ISBN 9780197658154 (epub) |
ISBN 9780197658161
Subjects: LCSH: Crowd funding—Moral and ethical aspects. | Electronic fund
raising—Moral and ethical aspects. | Crowd funding—Social aspects. |
Electronic fund raising—Social aspects.
Classification: LCC HG4751 .C628 2017 (print) | LCC HG4751 (ebook) |
DDC 658.15/224—dc23/eng/20230526
LC record available at https://lccn.loc.gov/2023017330
LC ebook record available at https://lccn.loc.gov/2023017331

DOI: 10.1093/oso/9780197658130.001.0001

Printed by Integrated Books International, United States of America

Contents

Acknowledgments

Leigh Palmer read and commented on the entire manuscript of this book and helped my research on crowdfunding during countless conversations over the past few years. Iva Cheung edited this manuscript and pushed me to make it better. Thank you to a wide range of audiences who have listened to different facets of my research on crowdfunding over the past few years and helped to clarify and improve my work. Some of the research I drew on in this book was supported by the Greenwall Foundation, the Canadian Institutes of Health Research, and the Social Sciences and Humanities Research Council of Canada. My thinking on crowdfunding was shaped by conversations with people who have used crowdfunding for themselves and their loved ones and by people working in the crowdfunding industry. My work has also benefitted by reading countless crowdfunding campaigns, many of which contain devastating stories of unmet needs. Finally, my wonderful family has always supported me without question, with their only reward being hearing about this topic far more than they would like—thank you and I love you Leigh, Jude, and Merit.

Introduction

Asking for and giving financial help is a normal part of life for most people. A few days before writing this, both of my children emptied their backpacks on the kitchen counter and presented me with forms for their elementary school walkathon. If I agreed to donate to the fundraiser, my kids would join their classmates in walking a certain number of times around their school's track. The money they earned would go to buying library books and musical instruments for the school. I was happy to make a pledge, and my kids went on to request the same thing from their grandparents. Their grandparents probably remembered when my wife and I had participated in similar fundraisers for our schools and pledged their support, too.

For my kids, the tradition of the school fundraiser this year was made a little more complicated by the COVID-19 pandemic. There was less going around in person to friends and neighbors to seek pledges, and there was a strict requirement that all donations be transferred to the school electronically. The pandemic is probably part of the reason fundraisers among my university colleagues have increasingly moved online as well. Instead of passing around an envelope at an in-person faculty meeting or leaving a collection box out at the front office, recent requests to help a professor fleeing the Taliban takeover of Afghanistan or to pay for the legal fees of a climate change protest took the form of "starting a GoFundMe."

Online crowdfunding campaigns like these—which in my and many other communities have become synonymous with the GoFundMe brand—have increasingly taken over from offline giving activities. In the recent past, someone needing help to pay for medical treatment might have put a description of their need and a collection tin at the front counter of the local gas station. This kind of community-based crowdfunding is now commonly supplemented or replaced by online forms. While both offline and online crowdfunding involve appealing to community members for donations to directly support an individual or specific cause, the online version of this practice uses social networks to promote the campaign, thus greatly increasing its potential exposure. The online nature of this form of crowdfunding makes

Appealing to the Crowd. Jeremy Snyder, Oxford University Press. © Oxford University Press 2024.
DOI: 10.1093/oso/9780197658130.003.0001

it easier to transfer funds and makes it more likely that people beyond one's geographically proximate community of acquaintances will learn of the campaign and be moved to donate to support it.

Precise figures on the global scope of crowdfunding can be difficult to find given limited reporting by the platforms that host them. That said, it is clear that this practice has a large and quickly growing global presence. In the United Kingdom, a quarter of all people donated to a crowdfunding campaign between mid-2020 and mid-2021, and younger donors are more likely to participate in this form of giving than older donors.[1] The crowdfunding platform GoFundMe, with users across the English-speaking world and much of the European Union, collected $625 million in donations from 9 million donors for COVID-19–related needs between March 1 and August 31, 2020.[2] Eighteen percent of Americans donated to health-related crowdfunding campaigns alone in the year leading up to April 2021, and nearly a third of Americans donate to crowdfunding campaigns yearly.[3,4] Donation-based crowdfunding (as opposed to reward-based crowdfunding for start-up companies or other enterprises) is increasing in Brazil, China, India, Indonesia, and elsewhere.[5,6] In upper- and lower-middle-income countries where institutionalized giving is less well established, crowdfunding for individuals is increasing overall participation in giving practices.[7]

The reasons for this growth in crowdfunding are numerous and to some degree complicated. But the basic appeal is simple: as with other online technologies, it makes a long-standing practice—in this case, fundraising—more convenient. Instead of organizing the transfer of funds in person, crowdfunding takes advantage of electronic funds transfers to make helping out incredibly easy. In the case of the crowdfunding campaign my colleague organized for an Afghan professor, the online nature of the campaign meant that the campaign organizer could easily provide updates on the professor's journey, including escaping Afghanistan, navigating the Canadian visa process, and, eventually, arriving in their new country safely. Not incidentally, these updates were a good way to encourage continued giving and provide donors with a sense of meaning and accomplishment.

Crowdfunding, then, is in many respects a continuation of long traditions of offline fundraising while taking advantage of online technologies. It makes both giving and receiving easier, streamlining existing giving patterns. Boosters of this form of fundraising have also hyped it as having a transformative effect—including, in tech-sector parlance, "disrupting" traditional giving so that "when you layer asking for help with social media, it turns one donor into hundreds, even thousands of donors."[8] Former GoFundMe CEO Rob Solomon describes charitable crowdfunding as making up the "giving layer of the internet," a phenomenon that for the first time combines "e-commerce and social sharing, into something far more democratic and altruistic."[9] Journalists covering this practice report that the technology enabling online crowdfunding extends traditional, analog forms of giving, becoming "the miracle of interconnectedness leading to globalized compassion."[10] This shift online means that campaigners are no longer limited to soliciting help from only their immediate social networks and communities. Instead, campaigns "become unbound" from where campaigners live and "who they knew."[11] As a result, crowdfunding is "turning us all into Good Samaritans."[12]

While mainstream philanthropic organizations are also increasingly using online crowdfunding to raise money, the individualized and relatively democratic nature of crowdfunding is framed as being something new and distinct from giving by and through large institutions. Crowdfunding empowers donors to connect directly with individuals they care about. As one crowdfunding executive describes it, "you're not just giving to an organization that then decides how it's going to use the funds. [Donors] can say 'I'm giving to this specific person, I identify with their need.' "[13] These philanthropic organizations are framed by crowdfunding enthusiasts as being too slow and inflexible, letting down many people in need. Crowdfunding, by comparison, allows campaigners to quickly create a campaign suited to their own needs and use online technologies and social media, tools with which they are already familiar and comfortable. Thus, crowdfunding campaigns, integrated into existing social media platforms, can serve as the "take-action button for the internet"[14] or a "digital safety net."[15] Through these online pathways, campaigners can connect with friends, family, and even strangers who might not have participated significantly in giving to traditional philanthropies but are motivated to help specific crowdfunding campaigners.

Online crowdfunding can transform traditional giving practices into something that is easier, faster, more personalized, and more democratic. But the popular press is full of stories charging that crowdfunding's transformative effects can also be profoundly negative. These include headlines presenting crowdfunding as having a "hidden cost"[16] and "dark side,"[17] being sometimes "ugly,"[18] and acknowledging that crowdfunding has "revolutionized how we give" but questioning whether that is "a good thing?"[19]

The concerns expressed about crowdfunding vary. In some cases, they aren't targeted at the practice of crowdfunding specifically but rather at the necessity of asking the public for help with basic needs. In this view, crowdfunding is a helpful and even lifesaving but necessary evil, symptomatic of the failures of the government, market mechanisms, and even philanthropic institutions to help provide for these needs.

Other criticisms of donation-based crowdfunding target the practice itself, focusing on the observation that making a successful public appeal for support requires making oneself appealing to the crowd. Campaigners must perform for the public to establish their deservingness for financial support. As with other forms of social media, crowdfunding has the "effect of publicizing private struggles."[20] This can include parading vulnerability and need in uncomfortable ways and "revealing intimate details of their life for a chance at having strangers pay their bills."[21] By the logic of this popularity contest for public support, those who do not receive any or enough support are not deserving. This outcome can be deflating for campaigners on top of the suffering that motivated their campaign in the first place. As one campaigner put it, "I suppose if I'd been one of those people who found an abandoned hedgehog and created a backyard sanctuary for hedgehogs and asked for $50 and got $100,000, I'd be super happy with GoFundMe. But all I've done is expose myself."[22]

While crowdfunding can be enormously helpful for some people, it also does little for many and generally fails to address the underlying causes of these needs. So-called viral campaigns get a great deal of publicity and are promoted as uplifting public interest stories demonstrating the goodness of people who come together to help someone in need. In reality, most crowdfunding campaigns fail to meet their goals, and many do not receive any donations at all. Distributing funding in this way creates a "marketplace of compassion, which is what crowdfunding sites amount to," and which "produces winners and losers like any other marketplace," meaning that "everyone must beg to survive, and most will not beg well enough."[23]

People with large and wealthy social networks have an advantage in the interconnected environment of online crowdfunding. While people with smaller or poorer networks can also go viral in online crowdfunding, factors like telling a sympathetic story or catching the eye of an online influencer help determine success such that "whoever has the most heartrending story wins."[24] Campaigns typically focus on immediate and superficial needs rather than their underlying causes. As such, campaigns can be "well-intentioned" but "cringeworthy" when raising funds, ignoring structural causes of need while positioning the campaigner as a "white savior" stepping in to help those in need.[25] As the CEO of the Canadian crowdfunding platform FundRazr acknowledged, "Crisis stories work so much better than chronic stories," meaning that some kinds of needs are more likely to receive public support than others.[26]

The online nature of crowdfunding reduces barriers to creating campaigns and allows donors greater decision-making over which individuals and causes they fund. This democratic aspect of crowdfunding is positive in many ways but also raises concerns that harmful and fraudulent campaigns will be funded as a result. This harm can include fundraising for campaigns that rely on hateful attitudes toward others or illiberal political goals, like anti-immigrant political campaigns and efforts to end marriage equality. Anti-science misinformation is also promoted on these platforms, including anti-vaccine misinformation that is popular on social media channels and, via crowdfunding, backed with financial support. Although crowdfunding platforms vet campaigns to some extent, campaigners are free from the typically more rigorous vetting by state institutions and philanthropic institutions and can simply lie about their needs. As a result, crowdfunding is accused of enabling "scams on a massive scale."[27]

Aims and plan for the book

My focus in this book is on crowdfunding for basic needs like housing, food, medical care, and education. While donation-based crowdfunding is also used to raise money for honeymoons and religious mission trips, among many other things, these kinds of activities generally fall outside the scope of the book. My first aim for this book is to look critically at the ethical, political, and practical dimensions of donation-based online crowdfunding against a backdrop of traditional giving practices. These traditional practices include giving directly to individuals and indirect giving through intermediaries such as nonprofit organizations. Crowdfunding has genuine advantages over some aspects of these traditional forms of giving. At the same time, it reproduces and deepens some of the shortcomings of traditional forms of giving while also introducing new concerns.

My second aim for this book is to suggest ways to shape and engage with donation-based crowdfunding more responsibly. In doing this, I situate crowdfunding as a practice that has a strong appeal to many people and is growing worldwide. While we might prefer that people's basic needs be met as entitlements through the state or philanthropic institutions that focus on long-term social reforms, crowdfunding is and will remain part of the fabric of giving practices. Crucially, crowdfunding does provide genuine benefits, particularly in the absence of fully just political and social institutions. But, as currently practiced, crowdfunding is deeply problematic in how it supports giving.

In achieving these aims, we will encounter a range of challenging philosophical questions, including "What is the role of the state in meeting basic needs?," "How should we conceive of the values of privacy and dignity?," and "How should individuals set priorities in giving to others in need?" In this book, I introduce these debates in terms of how they relate to giving practices, but I avoid taking a deep dive into or defending a particular position within these debates. I'm choosing this approach because, first, I want to focus on the many ethical, political, and practical dimensions of crowdfunding specifically rather than individual giving more generally. Second, this approach will help me develop a widely acceptable argument about the most responsible uses of crowdfunding by establishing areas of broad consensus about, for example, the value of personal privacy and need for individual giving under conditions of injustice. Finally, I hope that this book has a wide audience including academic philosophers, applied ethicists, and social scientists, but also the wider public working in the fundraising and philanthropy sectors or simply interested in the practice of crowdfunding. I believe that this shallower discussion of philosophical debates in favor of a deeper discussion of the pragmatics of crowdfunding can engage and serve all of these audiences.

In Chapter 1, I place donation-based crowdfunding in the context of traditional giving practices. I give an overview of the development of donation-based crowdfunding and the advantages it provides for donors and campaigners. These advantages are particularly due to crowdfunding's integration into online social media environments, which empowers campaigners to direct their own fundraising activities and to reach a much wider audience of potential donors than is generally the case through off-line fundraising. This expansion and democratization of giving through crowdfunding supports a line of critique against institutional intermediaries like philanthropic organizations. Whereas crowdfunding seemingly allows campaigners to identify their own needs and individual donors to choose individuals to help, philanthropic intermediaries are often slow to act, are dominated by wealthy and otherwise advantaged community members, and create barriers to individuals' ability to receive help.

Despite these advantages of crowdfunding over traditional forms of giving, the bulk of this book examines the new and expanded ethical, political, and practical issues created by crowdfunding. Many of these concerns are connected to the online nature of crowdfunding, which impacts the privacy of campaign recipients (Chapter 2) and puts these recipients in the position of having to establish their worthiness to receive help (Chapter 3). Online crowdfunding does democratize giving, but there is also strong evidence that the public chooses to support recipients who are already relatively advantaged in terms of wealth, education, racial privilege, and other factors (Chapter 4). This individualization of giving further pulls the public's attention from systemic causes of need, instead focusing on individuals and presenting crowdfunding campaigns as a solution to systemic need and social injustice (Chapter 5). The removal of intermediaries from giving also creates new opportunities to engage in fraudulent campaigning (Chapter 6) and spread misinformation, promote hateful causes, and engage in other harmful fundraising activities (Chapter 7). Chapter 8 demonstrates how these concerns were made vivid during the COVID-19 pandemic, a period of rapid growth in crowdfunding activity while also an illustration of its many shortcomings.

These chapters take largely for granted that, for better and for worse, donation-based crowdfunding removes intermediaries from giving, thus devolving oversight and decision-making to donors and campaigners. Chapter 9 complicates that picture by examining how crowdfunding platforms like GoFundMe serve as intermediaries between donors and recipients, shaping which campaigns rise to the public's attention and how campaigns must be presented to be successful. At the same time, crowdfunding platforms are increasingly providing the infrastructure for philanthropic organizations to raise money online. Thus, the advantage of crowdfunding over indirect giving through intermediaries is largely overstated and declining. In the conclusion of this book, I draw lessons from this observation and the other chapters to argue for guiding values for crowdfunding and practical steps to promote the genuine benefits of this practice while reducing some of its many negatives. Although we don't have to accept or engage with crowdfunding as it is, we do need to take seriously the growing size and appeal of this practice to engage more responsibly with crowdfunding.

One note on the excerpts of crowdfunding campaigns quoted in the book: where these excerpts are taken directly from crowdfunding campaigns, including at the beginning of Chapters 1 through 8, I don't include a citation to that campaign to protect the privacy of campaigners who may feel compelled to share their stories with the public—an ethical issue I describe in Chapter 2. An exception to this approach is citations of different versions of a specific campaign that I describe in Chapter 8 and that received extensive media exposure. In other cases, quotations are taken from news media and scholarly outputs, and citations are given in these cases.

When I first began writing on donation-based crowdfunding in 2016, very little had been published on this topic, especially around its ethical and political dimensions. This is not surprising, given the relative recency of online crowdfunding and the timeline for capturing the attention of scholars and producing and publishing research on any topic. Since then, however, scholarship on donation-based crowdfunding has taken off, drawing insights from a wide variety of disciplines. This book synthesizes and advances much of that output, giving an overview of the advantages and perils of the rapidly growing online crowdfunding sector.

Crowdfunding as a practice will continue to evolve and expand worldwide, as its more recent turn toward intermediated giving demonstrates. While individual, platform, and public policy responses to these changes will need to evolve as well, the suggestions offered here serve as a starting point for shaping a rapidly growing practice that will continue to influence how giving takes place worldwide.

1

Giving and the rise of crowdfunding

THANK YOU everyone for your generosity. Every dollar has made
a difference and is greatly appreciated. . . . Three different times I was
certain I would need to redirect funds to Mom's burial expenses, but
then at the last moment she would rebound. Three times. That was
not fun. However, as I said, being able to take care of a few issues for
them, without having to deal with financial stress over it, was a god-
send for everyone.

The giving practices of people who aim to support others' basic needs have
varied across cultures and throughout history. Understanding the arguments
for and against some of these traditional giving practices can offer context for the recent development of online donation-based crowdfunding.
Crowdfunding mirrors many of the benefits, limitations, and drawbacks of
these other giving practices. At the same time, crowdfunding includes distinctive advantages and shortcomings that can only be understood through
the context of other giving practices.

Throughout the book I draw a broad distinction between (1) giving by
individuals *directly* to those in need or to their agents and caregivers with the
aim of addressing their basic needs and (2) giving by individuals *indirectly*,
to groups or organizations that act as intermediaries to distribute these resources to those in need. In the first category of direct giving, I include direct gifts to people for their benefit, such as giving spare change to a person
experiencing homelessness to buy lunch or purchasing tickets for a con-
cert benefiting a specific person who needs money for a medical treatment.
On this understanding, direct giving overlaps with religious practices of
almsgiving to poor people. The second category of indirect giving includes,
for example, donations to support a soup kitchen that feeds many hungry
people in a specific area or giving to a nonprofit organization promoting
democratic reforms in a foreign country. Giving indirectly through an

Appealing to the Crowd. Jeremy Snyder, Oxford University Press. © Oxford University Press 2024.
DOI: 10.1093/oso/9780197658130.003.0002

intermediary can address immediate needs or longer-term, structural changes that focus on the underlying causes of these needs.

Giving by individuals may not always fall easily into these two categories of direct and indirect giving; some cases could arguably fit into either or neither category. That said, for the purposes of this book, the distinction between giving directly to individuals versus giving through intermediaries marks different practices that raise different ethical, political, and practical concerns. As I argue in Chapter 9, online donation-based crowdfunding has been treated largely as direct giving. However, crowdfunding platforms are increasingly serving as intermediaries as well. This evolution is crucial to understanding the ethical dimensions of crowdfunding and suggesting ways to address problems within the practice of crowdfunding.

Ethical arguments for giving

There is a wide consensus in Western philosophical ethics that giving to others to support their basic needs is at least morally praiseworthy and to a large extent morally required. Ancient and contemporary accounts of virtue typically include discussions of how to approach our own wealth, including giving a portion of it to support others. For Aristotle, the virtue of liberality describes a *mean*, understood as acting in the right way, with regard to the practice of giving and getting wealth. Virtues, on this account, are deeply ingrained character traits that are given shape through our actions and responses to the world. The virtue of liberality is bookended by two vices or extremes with regard to giving and receiving wealth: prodigality, or excess giving, and stinginess, or deficiency in giving. A liberal or virtuous person, according to Aristotle, gives for "the nobility of giving" or for its own sake rather than for the praise, thanks, or other benefits of giving. The mean in giving our wealth to others can be found in the person who gives "to the right people, the right amount, and at the right time."[1] The right amount of giving will depend in part on the resources of the giver. For Aristotle, a liberal or virtuous person will tend not to be rich as they will give their wealth to others regularly and value wealth for the ability to give it to others rather than for its own sake. Giving to the "right people" is not simply a matter of giving to the poor indiscriminately, for the prodigal person will "make men rich who ought to be poor, and will not give anything to the worthy, while heaping gifts on flatterers and others who minister to their pleasures."[2] For Aristotle, reducing poverty is not in itself the aim of liberality, then; rather, liberality is a matter of giving to those who are worthy of receiving wealth. While differing in the details of what forms of giving count as achieving the mean, contemporary or neo-Aristotelian accounts of virtue ethics similarly consider how we should use our resources to help others.[3,4]

David Hume picks up on the centrality of human character to morality in virtue ethics but in a significantly different way from Aristotle. Hume argues that benevolence, understood as concern with the welfare of others, is fundamental to both human nature and morality. This connection to human nature allows for universality in how we respond to certain events and objects—what Hume calls virtues. Hume catalogues virtues according to their usefulness and agreeableness to ourselves and others. This catalogue includes a category of virtues centering on mental qualities that are useful to others, among which is the virtue of charity. As Hume states, "Giving alms to common beggars is naturally praised; because it seems to carry relief to the distressed and indigent: But when we observe the encouragement thence arising to idleness and debauchery, we regard that species of charity rather as a weakness than a virtue."[5] Thus, giving to those in need is virtuous insofar as it is useful in relieving suffering. When such giving encourages the recipient to turn down income from working or to feed substance use, it is not useful to the recipient or society and is thus not a virtue.

For Hume, the usefulness of giving speaks in large part to our sentimental reaction to these actions. Efficacy is at the heart of utilitarian arguments around giving as well in that the value of helping others should be judged by the outcomes of the gift, with emphasis on creating the best or most effective outcomes possible in terms of relieving suffering or improving welfare. The canonical utilitarian approach to assessing the value of gifts is given by John Stuart Mill, who argues that the value of actions should be assessed by their outcomes. Creating goodness in the world, understood as increased welfare, is the single principle of right and wrong. This understanding of the value of giving can be highly demanding in that it requires that we do the most good through our actions, with less beneficial actions deemed morally inferior.[6]

More recently, this utilitarian approach has given rise to the *effective altruism* movement. Effective altruism urges people to assess the value of giving to others based on the outcomes of these gifts. Effective altruism is particularly associated with Peter Singer, who has articulated a range of stronger and more moderate versions of a broadly utilitarian view that we ought to give our excess resources to others, with a focus on doing the most good possible through these transfers.[7] For Singer and others in this vein, giving to this extreme and with the focus on the efficient use of resources is not a simple kindness to others or an optional matter of choice; rather, it is a basic requirement of morality. Significant disagreements exist over which forms of giving are most effective, including whether to prioritize giving to charitable organizations offering various forms of poverty relief or political and policy organizations aiming to reform unjust international institutions.[8] Nonetheless, the general emphasis is on maximizing good for others through giving with a focus on outcomes. Assessments of these outcomes are generally impartial as to which individuals receive these benefits, including when and where they are received, instead focusing on the quantifiable good done by the action.

While utilitarianism and related ethical traditions focus on outcomes, others put greater emphasis on the motivation behind giving. Immanuel Kant argues that we all have duties to others, which include duties of practical love, understood as promoting others' happiness. This duty takes the form of promoting the *permissible ends* of others, which can be achieved in various ways depending on others' ends. Given the basic needs of humans for survival, pain-free living, and good health, supporting these basic needs will nearly always be a form of supporting others' permissible ends.[9] Supporting others' basic needs is not the only way to discharge this duty of beneficence, but where others lack basic supports, helping to support them generally counts as a means of acting in accordance with this duty.

A Kantian duty of beneficence is generally understood as an *imperfect duty*, meaning that one has some discretion in terms of who, when, and to what degree to help others. While there is some choice as to whom one gives aid, Kant is clear that giving to others is a requirement and not simply optional when assessed over the full course of one's life. As he describes it, "[b]eneficence to others must rather be commended as a debt we owe, than as a piece of kindness and generosity; and so it is in fact; for all acts of kindness are but small repayments for our indebtedness."[10] One's context can help to specify this general duty of beneficence. For example, disregarding those in immediate need of help for survival where one is specially or uniquely positioned to help can demonstrate disregard for their humanity. At the same time, Kant is generally understood as allowing partiality to the happiness and needs of friends and family insofar as one can wish for others' happiness universally but act specifically to support the happiness of those of most concern to oneself.[11]

In practice, these broad approaches to the duty to give to others differ enormously over how much, when, and to whom we must give. Virtue-based approaches emphasize a median in giving in the "right" amount and to the "right" people, while broadly Kantian traditions emphasize the intention behind giving, in contrast to effective altruists' focus on best outcomes. These camps agree, however, that some giving to meet others' basic needs is required of us. Some particularly strong liberty- and property-based accounts of ethics make control over one's resources absolute and giving to others purely optional, but these accounts are largely outliers within Western philosophical ethics—and, even in those cases, giving is generally discussed as a personal obligation that should be free from state coercion rather than something that is purely optional.[12]

While there is disagreement about the scope and targets of giving in Western philosophical ethics, in practice a range of factors help to determine where people tend to focus their giving. Donors typically view their giving as more akin to an imperfect Kantian duty in that they have discretion as to when, how, and whom to help.[13] In other cases, giving is viewed as supererogatory—something that is praiseworthy but not morally required.[14] In high-income countries, people tend to prefer giving to local rather than international charities, even when these international charities are in low-income settings where donations are likely to have a greater positive impact.[15] Personal connections and empathy with potential recipients help to direct giving, as when the donor or a loved one has experienced the same medical condition as the recipients.[16] Even when donors are given information about the likely outcomes of different giving options, people tend to prioritize giving based on personal preference and connections rather than the efficacy of the gift.[17]

In short, there is significant diversity in ethical arguments about why one ought to give to others and a wide gulf between most of these arguments and the actual practice of giving. Online crowdfunding can accommodate any of these approaches. An effective altruist, for example, can choose to use a crowdfunding platform to support a philanthropic organization that efficiently uses these donations to address long-term threats to humanity's well-being. In practice, however, crowdfunding has typically emphasized giving to individuals in ways that are ill suited to the requirements of effective altruism and other outcome-focused ethical approaches. This might suggest a more relational approach to giving in the practice of crowdfunding. However, as I show in later chapters of this book, giving in crowdfunding often does not follow any of these ethical approaches but is typically more impulse-based.

Direct giving

When individuals give directly to other individuals, recipients can include the person in need or their caregivers or agents acting on their behalf, such as a friend or parent. In this section I include examples of some religiously mediated practices of giving, focusing on giving directly to individuals (though these practices also motivate giving to institutions, including religious institutions, for poverty relief). My aim is not to give a comprehensive overview of giving practices worldwide or throughout history. Instead, I offer a broad sampling of giving practices and their motivations in order to contextualize criticisms of direct giving. These criticisms have encouraged a shift to more institutionalized practices of indirect giving.

Among many Indigenous communities, giving to others is shaped primarily by relationships of reciprocity rather than through the aim of relieving poverty. Giving in these contexts is not primarily an expression of selfless altruism but part of a web of mutual obligations and relationships.[18] In Indigenous South African communities, for example, giving to others is treated as a more equitable or horizontal practice rather than a hierarchical interaction between rich and poor. In these communities, giving is often governed by norms of solidarity, caring, and shared humanity. This form of giving takes place among both relatively rich and less wealthy individuals. In part, given the material constraints of less wealthy people, these giving practices can include giving nonmaterial goods, such as donating one's time to look after a sick neighbor.[19] To take another example, giving practices among many First Nations peoples in North America often emphasize community connectedness and de-emphasize the needs of specific individuals in favor of stressing a larger cosmological and historical story of their people.[20] Thus, these giving practices may not emphasize or create status differences within these communities.

This nonhierarchical and reciprocal conception of giving in some Indigenous communities is also framed in terms of a drive toward *mutual aid*.[21] A key element of mutual aid is captured in the slogan "solidarity not charity." On this view, giving in the form of charity is typically guided by the priorities of wealthy people or the government rather than people in need of aid. Furthermore, charity tends not to address the systemic causes of poverty, violence, and inequality. By comparison, giving as a form of mutual aid seeks a shared understanding of why some people are struggling to meet their basic needs while others have much more than they require. Mutual aid takes this knowledge about root causes of need and channels them into political movements to change social systems. Rather than dividing people into deserving and underserving groups when addressing these needs, the value of solidarity in this context stresses universal connection and participation in social movements. Social movements connected to mutual aid are intended to be widely participatory and include people in need rather than taking on a more passive form controlled by relatively privileged donors.[22] In these ways, mutual aid activities take on the nonhierarchical nature of some Indigenous giving practices while also taking on a deeply political and reform-based ethos.

Among elites in ancient Greek and Roman communities, giving was generally tied to expressions of citizenship—for example, paying for public works and the entertainment of fellow citizens. When giving took place between individuals, this practice could focus on how giving bound them together and created relationships of reciprocity.[23] The Roman philosopher Seneca, for example, writes that giving creates an ongoing relationship of equality. A loan from a creditor can simply be repaid and the relationship of obligation ended. However, with a gift or benefit "even when I have repaid his kindness we remain connected, for when I have paid my debt I ought again to renew it, while our friendship endures unbroken." As a result, Seneca argues, we must be careful in choosing from whom we receive gifts and to whom we give them. Because these gifts give rise to friendship and love, he says, it is "wretched . . . to feel it to be his duty to love one whom it does not please him to love."[24] On these views, worthiness in giving or receiving a gift is not based on the good that gift will do or the suffering it will relieve but rather on the obligations and relationships it will generate.

Religious traditions, of course, also have had an enormous impact on shaping norms around direct forms of giving. Within Judaism, there are numerous provisions requiring giving to the poor. These include requirements to leave the edges and gleanings of fields for the poor to gather,[25] which is justified in part on the basis that the Jewish people were once destitute slaves in Egypt in need of aid.[26] Other commands of giving to the poor include giving a tithe or 10% of one's produce every three years to foreigners, the fatherless, and widows.[27] More generally, how much to give to others in the Jewish tradition depends on how much is needed, with a broad requirement to meet others' needs.[28]

Later interpretations of the Hebrew Bible expanded the concept of *tzedakah,* or justice, which included giving by individuals to aid the poor. In addition to regular, obligatory payments of *tzedakah* akin to tax payments, giving directly to individuals was typically seen as required. One interpretation of this form of giving derives from Moses Maimonides's description of eight degrees of *tzedakah,* which differentiate between more and less praiseworthy forms of giving. At the top of this ladder is giving that enables another person to find work or otherwise no longer need aid. Lower on this ladder, giving where the giver and receiver do not know one another's identity is still valued. Direct giving of this kind can help protect against disreputable charitable organizations wasting funds and protect recipients from what Maimonides views as the humiliation of receiving charity. Lower forms of giving speak to the problematic motivations of the giver, including giving only after being asked to do so, giving less than needed, and giving reluctantly.[29]

Many early Christian thinkers stressed giving to others by virtue of their shared humanity and common creator.[30] This understanding of the role of direct giving among early Christians broadly echoes the lessons of Christ in the Gospels: Christ was said to have been born into poverty and, in the words of his disciples, connected sin to wealth and goodness to giving funds to the poor. In particular, the Christian practice of giving alms created a longstanding expectation that all Christians would use their wealth to relieve the suffering of the poor. To make this point, Saint Augustine of Hippo wrote that it was acceptable for there to be rich people, but only if they are generous to and share their wealth with the poor around them.[31]

Other early Christian thinkers advocated for discrimination in terms of which people should receive gifts of alms. Saint Ambrose of Milan, writing in the fourth century, warned against giving to those who make a show of being poor: "people who are in perfectly good health—and they come along with no good reason other than the fact that they spend their lives wandering from place to place, and their intention is to use up the supplies intended for the poor."[32] People deserving help included those who cannot work because of ill health or who lack their freedom—for example, prisoners of war. Ambrose justified this discrimination in largely practical terms, warning against giving too little but also being overly wasteful or generous with resources such that the poor who come later cannot be helped. Later Christian thinkers built on

Ambrose, suggesting that priority should be given to helping one's family and those known to the almsgiver. Helping strangers was permitted, but only if it would not harm them. Helping nondisabled strangers who could work was viewed as a harm of almsgiving as it would encourage idleness and dependency on charity.[33] Early Reformation thinkers put giving in the context of stewardship of property, viewing material wealth as a gift from God for one's own enjoyment but also for the purpose of healing one's neighbors.[34] For Calvin, giving to others was an expression of love for them as "in regard to everything which God has bestowed upon us, and by which we can aid our neighbour, we are his stewards, and are bound to give account of our stewardship."[35]

For Muslims, the Quran commands that the faithful be good to their parents and kin, orphans, and the needy.[36] Among the five pillars or core obligations of Islam is *zakat*, the giving of alms calculated by the individual's wealth. *Zakat* is understood as an act of purification of the sins of the giver; failure to discharge this obligation merits punishment. This act of giving can be targeted to help the poor, relieve debts, ransom slaves, support travelers, and urge conversions to Islam. During Ramadan, obligatory *Zakat al-Fitr* supports poor Muslims in celebrating Eid al-Fitr. Beyond the obligations of *zakat*, Islam encourages voluntary giving or *sadaqa* over and above the obligations of *zakat*. These gifts can target the same recipients as *zakat* and also serve to remove sin.[37] These forms of giving are justified in part because one's ability to earn a living and very life are due to God's goodness. Just as God has shown generosity, each person owes a reciprocal duty to share with others so that they may live well.[38]

In Hindu, Buddhist, and Jain traditions, *dāna* is a religiously mediated practice of giving away one's wealth. In general, the practice of charity in these traditions is unilateral in the sense of not including an expectation of reciprocity. For example, the Bhagavad Gita differentiates between giving without expectation of a return and less praiseworthy forms of giving, including when reciprocation is expected or the gift is given grudgingly, with disdain, or to unworthy people.[39] Giving to one's benefactor would thus tend to violate the ideal of giving in these traditions. Instead, the best forms of giving demonstrate disinterest in the potential material advantages of giving even though the act itself may give pleasure. Giving to others may also express meritorious disregard for material goods and serve as a means of unburdening oneself from these goods. Deservingness on the part of the recipient of a gift is typically tied to religious merit. Thus, Brahmans, monks, nuns, and other religious devotees are particularly worthy targets of giving because they have relinquished material goods. Importantly, these figures are typically unable to reciprocate a gift in material ways. Thus, giving to them avoids tainting the gift with expectations of reciprocity and affirms the pure intentions of the giver.[40]

These traditions of giving directly to others, along with many other practices, aim at some mix of helping those in the giver's community, establishing or avoiding relations of reciprocity, and discharging religious and ethical obligations. Through these gifts, countless lives have been saved and enormous suffering has been reduced. However, these traditions of giving have also been a target of criticism, often by those who advocate different norms around or practices of charitable giving.

As seen above, giving traditions differ in whether the relationship between giver and recipient is relatively horizontal or hierarchical. Particularly in highly hierarchical giving relationships, direct giving can treat the recipient in harmful or disrespectful ways. For example, Kant argues that direct giving can in some cases be demeaning to the poor and act more as an expression of the giver's pride rather than as a true act of beneficence. In these cases, the recipients of alms "are demeaned by it. It would be better to think out some other way of assisting such poverty, so that men are not brought so low as to accept alms."[41] This concern that charity is humiliating to the receiver is echoed in Maimonides's praise of forms of charity where the giver does not know the identity of the receiver so that the receiver can be protected from humiliation.[42] We can reasonably ask whether recipients of charity *ought* to feel humiliated by these practices and note that norms around self-sufficiency are problematic, mask social injustices, and favor nondisabled people and other relatively socially advantaged groups. Nonetheless, forms of charity that reinforce direct contact between the giver and recipient can harm the recipient. This is particularly true in communities where receiving help is seen as humbling, recipients are sorted into deserving and undeserving groups, and direct giving reinforces deep asymmetries in power and social position.

As Kant's focus on the giver's pride shows, the intention behind giving can itself be problematic as well. This concern is reflected in giving traditions that favor anonymity between the giver and receiver or make reciprocity between giver and receiver impossible. In these traditions, the act of giving should be selfless and an expression of the value of giving or some other ethically acceptable intention rather than of hope for personal benefit. Thus, extravagant public giving with an eye toward receiving praise and recognition is contrary to giving for its own sake. This valuation of giving stands in contrast to more reciprocal traditions such as those found in ancient Greece and Rome, where the point of giving is in part tied to the concrete and personal relationships it creates. Notably, however, these reciprocal traditions are meant to create bonds between community members and are often less hierarchical. Thus, concerns with the intention behind giving are typically located in expressions of the superiority of the giver over the receiver or a disregard for the receiver's good in favor of personal aggrandizement.

Direct giving can also be criticized for its outcomes, including making giving seem optional, not requiring sufficient amounts of giving, and not making efficient use of gifts. This is broadly Peter Singer's critique when he argues that because "giving money is regarded as an act of charity, it is not thought that there is anything wrong with not giving. The charitable man may be praised, but the man who is not charitable is not condemned."[43] When one is thanked or praised for giving to others, it's implied that they might reasonably have declined to give without condemnation. Importantly, in many of the arguments for and practices of giving described above, giving to others is not seen as optional. Nonetheless, a critic in Singer's vein might argue that many practices of charity do not demand enough of us and that our language around giving tends to reinforce the idea that giving on the scale that Singer supports is not obligatory. Similarly in this regard, direct giving can be focused on existing relationships with individuals or based on the whims and preferences of the giver. While doing some good, giving in this way may do less good than a more institutionalized and intentional form of giving. In particular, giving that is unfocused and not driven by achieving maximally good outcomes may focus on the most visible and sympathetic displays of need rather than sustainably addressing the most substantial and pressing needs.

Indirect giving

Cultural and religious traditions encourage various forms of giving directly to individuals. Giving also regularly takes the form of supporting institutions that act as intermediaries to help address the public's basic needs. In part due to the criticisms against direct giving summarized above, giving within religious and secular traditions has also emphasized supporting institutions because of their potential for greater and more sustainable positive impacts.

Giving mediated through philanthropic institutions could address at least some of the concerns with direct giving, particularly that giving creates degrading relationships and does not focus on achieving long-lasting, positive effects.

Religious institutions have historically served as philanthropic intermediaries between givers and receivers. Among Christians, while alms were often given directly to those in need, wealthy landowners during the medieval period in Europe also frequently gave to monasteries, religious orders, and other institutions that would use this income to carry out their missions of aiding the poor.[44] The Late Middle Ages in Europe saw increased giving to fund institutions aimed at poverty relief generally and helping specific impoverished groups. This shift was in part due to the greater use of wills and last testaments, motivated by dying people seeking redemption for their sins. Institutions supported through wills and other gifts included hospitals aimed at housing and caring for the poor and leper houses for those suffering from leprosy; later, institutions for other specific disease types would be more commonly funded.[45] Among Jews in Europe during the medieval and early modern periods, restrictions on owning property and supporting Christian charitable organizations encouraged giving to a range of private Jewish philanthropic organizations to aid the poor, ransom captives, and support Zionist resettlement projects. In some cases, these institutions paralleled Christian facilities such as hospitals, almshouses, and orphanages but targeted Jewish residents.[46] For Muslims, while *zakat* payments can be given directly to individuals, this religious obligation is commonly discharged by establishing or giving indirectly through philanthropic institutions. Moreover, *sadaqa,* or voluntary giving beyond the requirements of *zakat*, can be performed by endowing philanthropic entities known as *waqfs* that use the revenue from property to benefit others. *Waqfs* can be used to benefit people, buildings, or institutions, and they can last over generations. In many cases *waqfs* have explicitly religious goals, like when they endow religious institutions or activities. In other cases, educational or health benefits for the community are the aim.[47]

Economic changes have encouraged indirect giving practices as well. The Industrial Revolution created massive wealth in the hands of a small group of industrialists while also encouraging inequality and urban poverty. Many of these industrialists sought to establish philanthropic foundations out of a sense of religious mission, to improve their reputations during their own lives and after their deaths, and to ward off regulatory actions and other responses to the concentration of wealth and power in their hands. More recently, tech entrepreneurs have continued this practice, donating to existing philanthropies and financing new foundations to carry out a variety of broadly philanthropic missions, including conducting basic research, providing healthcare, building housing, funding the arts, and conserving the natural environment.[48] These are not purely Western developments, as industrialization, the rise of the tech sector, and increased wealth have seen wealthy entrepreneurs form philanthropic foundations in China, South Asia, and elsewhere globally.[49] While giving to and establishing philanthropic foundations are in many cases motivated by religion, these foundations may also offer a secular alternative to religious philanthropic institutions and pursue a humanist mission rather than a religious mandate. Similarly, these foundations can offer an alternative to state support for basic needs, even in the context of the social welfare state, by addressing perceived gaps in state support domestically, helping those in need in less wealthy nations, and funding needs and activities not supported by the state.[50]

Aiding others indirectly through philanthropies, given their scope, longevity, and institutional expertise, could address some of the chief shortcomings of direct giving. Whereas giving directly to others can be intermittent, unfocused, and humiliating, philanthropic institutions can be administered on a more systematic basis that allows funding to be used more efficiently, impersonally, and equitably. This is in part because it enables funds to be spread to a larger community of people on a sustained basis, directed by interests in maximizing the good produced by this funding, and leveraged to encourage longer-term policy changes that reduce the need for philanthropic giving over the long term.

However, giving mediated through philanthropic institutions raises its own problems. One perceived advantage of private philanthropy over the public provision of basic entitlements is that it allows for individual donors to exercise their free choice over how to dispose of their property and, potentially, to meet the public's basic needs more efficiently than can the public sector. But even if this were the case, Eric Beerbohm argues for the necessity of public involvement in carrying out the requirements of justice. Beerbohm argues that distributive obligations are *agent relative*, meaning that they can't simply be outsourced to philanthropists. Collective action by democratic citizens has an expressive value, including an expression of solidarity, that is lost if philanthropic institutions take on the work of distributive justice without the participation of the public citizenry. Put simply, justice doesn't simply require that entitlements to basic education, healthcare, housing, and nutrition be met, but that the "provider must be all of the citizens, acting together."[51] Beerbohm notes that the agent relativity of justice does not mean that philanthropists should retreat from giving in the absence of just distributive institutions. Rather, philanthropic giving is not an endpoint of justice and must be coupled with supporting democratic engagement.

While indirect giving through philanthropic institutions can act as a stopgap in conditions of injustice, in practice, modern philanthropies often act in ways that undermine the goals of distributive justice. Rob Reich notes two ways in which philanthropy can harm the aims of equality, drawing on the specific legal context of philanthropic giving in the United States.[52] First, generally only wealthy donors are incentivized to give through the system of tax deductions for donations in the US tax code because itemizing these deductions is worthwhile for only the wealthiest taxpayers. While the large majority of Americans give to others, both directly and through intermediaries, only those who itemize their deductions are rewarded by the tax system for doing so. Moreover, these deductions are of greater value to the wealthiest who inhabit the highest tax brackets because these donors pay relatively higher marginal rates on their income, and it is this income that is deducted through giving for the purposes of taxation.

Second, inequalities exist in terms of which people receive the benefits of giving to philanthropies. These include geographic inequalities that reflect concentrations of where wealthy people live. Moreover, although a wide array of philanthropic organizations receive tax-deductible donations and tax-exempt status in the United States, religious organizations still dominate among institutional recipients of giving. While these organizations redirect some of their donations to people in need, they also use donations to build and operate facilities, hire religious staff, and carry out religious activities. After religious groups, giving to educational and medical institutions is most common. These donations may help those most in need of education and healthcare but also commonly support institutions with whom wealthy donors have connections, including their alma maters and medical institutions that gave them or their loved ones care in the past. For example, parents who are able to raise funds for their children's local schools in wealthy communities can widen inequalities and diminish support for increased funding for chronically underfunded public schools.[53]

In general, the activities of philanthropic institutions are often inferior to those of the government in reducing inequality and, in many cases, doing so is not part of the institution's mission.[54] As Reich sums it up, "charitable giving seems to be more frequently about the pursuit of individual projects, a mechanism for the public expression of one's values or preferences, rather than a mechanism for redistribution."[55] In these cases, indirect giving, like direct giving, can fail to address basic needs, serve primarily to benefit the giver, and disregard the needs of recipients, all while undermining democratic oversight over providing basic entitlements.

The rise of crowdfunding

Just as the prominence of the tech sector has created a new class of extremely wealthy people endowing and supporting philanthropic institutions, this sector has also created new means for individuals to engage in giving online. Specifically, online platforms now allow people to create appeals for financial support and give donors the means to easily find, share, and support them.

Online crowdfunding for charitable purposes, understood as pooling donations for individual recipients, has a number of offline antecedents. These include microfinance institutions ranging from the Irish loan funds of the early eighteenth century to Bangladesh's Grameen Bank, begun in the 1970s, which combines donations to make loans to poor individuals with the aim of promoting economic independence.[56] More recently, charitable microfinance platforms like Kiva have moved online as well to receive and distribute donations as microloans.

Initially, online crowdfunding was largely associated with fundraising for entrepreneurial purposes, now commonly known as *reward-based* or *equity crowdfunding*. While many of these early crowdfunding platforms were used to fund business start-ups, others helped fund artists and other cultural projects that included rewards for donors. The term *crowdfunding* itself was coined in 2006 by Michael Sullivan to describe his video blog-funding platform. Before that, the cultural crowdfunding platform ArtistShare, founded in 2000, is thought to be the first online crowdfunding platform.[57,58] The Great Recession of 2008 encouraged alternative means of financing for start-ups, as was seen in new, and still hugely influential, reward-based crowdfunding platforms like Indiegogo in 2008 and Kickstarter in 2009.[59,60]

In North America, a number of donation-based crowdfunding platforms were started in the late 2000s and early 2010s, with direct inspiration from reward-based crowdfunding platforms. Thus, in referring to the then largely unknown GoFundMe platform in 2012, TechCrunch called it "like KickStarter for the rest of us."[61] GoFundMe's predecessor, CreateAFund, was started in 2008 by Brad Damphousse and Andrew Ballester. CreateAFund itself grew out of Coin Piggy, a personal savings website with the same founders. While Coin Piggy failed because of the high costs of debit card transaction fees, it included an option to request a gift from others that was used as the basis for CreateAFund. CreateAFund initially sought to make money by enrolling charities onto its online platform in exchange for a subscription fee. This business model had little success, but a free option for individuals saw significant interest. For that reason, Damphousse and Ballester rebranded CreateAFund as GoFundMe in 2010, to focus entirely on crowdfunding for individuals. This tighter focus on individual crowdfunding was enabled in part by a change in the financial processing site PayPal that allowed transactions to be split between individuals. This change meant that GoFundMe could now retain 5% of the donation given to the crowdfunding campaigner as a platform fee.[62]

With its focus on charitable crowdfunding for individuals, GoFundMe began seeing rapid growth. This included 500% more in donations in 2012 and an additional 300% more donations in the first half of 2013. The company also grew from the initial two cofounders to eighteen employees during that time.[63] In 2012, medical-related campaigns made up 17% of activity on GoFundMe, followed by 11% for school tuition and volunteer trips at 10%.[64] In 2012, it reported raising $37 million per year, rising from $2 million per month to $3 million monthly.[65] By May 2016, GoFundMe reported that it had raised $2 billion from 25 million donors and then $3 billion by October of that year and $4 billion from 40 million donors by mid-2017.[66–68]

In 2016, Damphousse and Ballester sold a controlling stake of GoFundMe to Accel Partners and Technology Crossover Ventures, a pair of private venture capital groups, for $600 million. While the two founders remained on the board of GoFundMe after the sale, Rob Solomon, the former president of the online coupon and event site Groupon, was hired as CEO. By that time, GoFundMe had grown to fifty employees.[69] GoFundMe initially focused largely on English-speaking countries, including the United States, United Kingdom, Canada, and Australia. Under its new management, in 2017, it expanded into France, Spain, and other European countries to include eighteen countries where campaigns could be hosted.[70] Notably, GoFundMe's founders and leadership team have all come from the marketing rather than the philanthropy world. Damphousse and Ballester met at a start-up marketing viral content, former CEO Solomon was in charge of a company that used online coupons to market businesses, and current CEO Tim Cadogan has a background in advertising.[71]

While GoFundMe has assumed a dominant position among Western donation-based crowdfunding platforms, it is not the only nor the first such company. The UK's JustGiving had one of the earliest starts among donation-based crowdfunding platforms, with a focus on providing online fundraising tools to charities in 2001. By 2008, it had helped raise £250 million for these charities.[72] An option to allow crowdfunding by individuals was added in 2015, and, by 2016, their fundraising total had increased to $4 billion raised (half of which came during the previous two years) from 26 million donations, including 43,000 campaigns for individuals.[73] In 2017, JustGiving was purchased for £95 million by the US-based software company Blackbaud, which merged JustGiving with Everydayhero, another crowdfunding platform it had previously purchased.[74] By 2022, JustGiving reported a total of £5 billion raised globally through 152 million donations for 450,000 charities and 95,000 individual campaigners.[75] Elsewhere, Chicago-based GiveForward predated GoFundMe when it was founded in 2008 with a focus on health-related campaigns.[76] Vancouver's FundRazr also opened in 2008, as a Facebook app that then became a standalone website.[77] YouCaring was started in San Francisco in 2011 by three friends who had spent the previous two years on religious missions. This platform initially aimed to help raise money for education, but a year and a half later was hosting largely medical campaigns and bringing in $180,000 daily in donations. By 2018, they had received more than $900 million in donations for health-related campaigns alone.[78]

GoFundMe's rapid growth and current dominance was enabled in part by its acquisition of many of these competitors. In January 2017, GoFundMe purchased CrowdRise, a charitable crowdfunding platform that specialized in supporting crowdfunding campaigns for charities and nonprofits, though it hosted campaigns for individuals as well.[79] In 2018, GoFundMe bought its largest US competitor, YouCaring (which itself had purchased the crowdfunding platform Generosity.com earlier in the year and GiveForward the year before).[80] Through these acquisitions, GoFundMe was able to absorb most of its competitors and dominate the US crowdfunding market over the first ten years of its existence. By the end of 2022, GoFundMe reported that it had raised $25 billion over its life, including 28 million people sending or receiving funding that year alone.[81]

Charitable crowdfunding has grown rapidly worldwide as well. In India, charitable crowdfunding platforms emerged at around the same time as their North American counterparts. The founder of Ketto, Varun Sheth, has stated that the prospect of charitable crowdfunding in India was initially seen as daunting, given a common belief that "Indians are not giving by nature." Sheth disputes this view: "People give in India. Just very differently. They give to temples, to people around like maids and drivers, or the guy on the street. We just need to walk 10 metres to find poverty in India, unlike the West." According to Sheth, crowdfunding in India needed to convince Indians to give in a more organized way through campaigns with "a receipt, to give updates, to engage people with causes, show them the history of what they have done."[82] Ketto initially targeted entrepreneurial crowdfunding when it opened in 2012. It got little traction in that area but did see interest in charitable campaigns instead. It has raised more than $65 million through the campaigns it hosts, and over half of these campaigns are for health-related needs.[83] By 2020, it employed more than 150 people.[84] The company is now diversifying to support more of the languages used in India and reach out to people in more rural communities.[85]

Another Indian donation-based crowdfunding platform, Milaap, started in 2010, with a focus on microlending for rural entrepreneurial projects; later, this platform shifted to include giving for personal needs.[86] Almost half of these campaigns originate outside of the seven largest Indian cities, and about half of donors use mobile phones when transferring money to campaigns. This platform had raised more than $100 million for 100,000 campaigns by March 2020, and health-related campaigns now make up 85% of campaigns overall.[87] ImpactGuru is currently the largest of the Indian donation-based crowdfunding platforms and focuses on medical campaigns as well. Started in 2014 by Piyush Jain, a US-educated Indian entrepreneur, it reports hosting more than 10,000 campaigns that have collectively received $200 million from 1 million donations.[88,89]

Online charitable crowdfunding has become increasingly popular in China as well. Giving online to charitable causes was recently assessed to be infrequent in China as only 6% of the population engaged in charitable giving online in 2015, compared with 31% globally.[90] At this time, the three largest charitable crowdfunding platforms in China are Tencent Gong Yi, Ant Group Gong Yi, and Taobao Gong Yi. These three platforms raised $148 million in 2015, half of which was intended for health-related needs. By 2017, charitable crowdfunding was bringing in $3.83 billion and made up

1.6% of charitable donations in China. The Tencent Gong Yi crowdfunding platform alone raised $2.6 billion in 2017.[91]

Donation-based crowdfunding platforms are generally, though not always, for-profit companies. Initially, many charged a 5% fee for their services that was subtracted from the donated amount. These fees were typically combined with an additional 2.9% charge for donations made with credit cards. As charitable crowdfunding became more visible, brought in larger total donation amounts, and saw more competition among platforms, some critics charged that these companies were making potentially massive profits on the backs of people in desperate need and the donors seeking to help them. For example, in 2017, JustGiving charged the then-standard flat 5% fee from donated totals, allowing it to gross £20 million in fees that year.[92] However, privately run charitable crowdfunding platforms like GoFundMe and JustGiving now generally follow a tip-based model of voluntary payments by donors. These tips, which are assessed on top of what is given to the campaign recipient, often default to 10–15% of the donated amount, but the donor can reduce them to zero if they choose.[93] This change has helped deflect some of the concern that crowdfunding platforms are taking away donated money from campaigners while also obscuring these platforms' overall revenues.

Crowdfunding's appeal

Online crowdfunding makes up a fraction of overall giving, but its rapid growth demonstrates that it has considerable appeal to both donors and people in need. GoFundMe describes several advantages to crowdfunding when "funding from the government and nonprofits falls short." These advantages include removing "traditional barriers" by having no application process, not requiring a waiting period for receiving funding, taking the fear out of asking for help from friends and family, and making it easy to reach beyond one's social network.[94] Thus, donation-based crowdfunding is presented as a disruptive technology, helping users to harness online social networks to more directly connect with potential donors.

The speed with which crowdfunding allows users to start a campaign and receive funds is a consistent selling point for this practice. The crowdfunding platform Fundly tells its users that the ease of setting up a campaign means that "you can start raising funds as soon as you hit 'publish.' When correctly promoted on social media, your campaign has the potential to go viral. In fact, most campaigns are able to reach their goals within 4 weeks!"[95] The speed advantage of crowdfunding applies to donors as well, who are able to see the immediate impact of their gifts and, often, receive feedback and thanks from the recipient.[96] This immediacy may in turn encourage higher overall donation rates when compared with the weaker connections between donors and recipients in institutionally mediated philanthropic giving.

The speed of giving through crowdfunding is created in part by the ease of giving through these online platforms.[97] Ketto notes that while giving to philanthropies is a long-standing tradition in India and elsewhere, "simplicity and ease of operation often make people look towards crowdfunding when they urgently need to meet medical treatment costs for family or friends."[98] While individuals can and do still give to one another in person and through traditional means, the online nature of crowdfunding removes some barriers to doing so. Moreover, crowdfunding has minimal barriers to participation by donors, campaigners, and recipients. As crowdfunding is self-directed, it allows users to start the campaign they want for the benefits they desire without the need for an application and review process or any mediation by the government or philanthropic institutions. Thus, Fundly notes that with crowdfunding there are "no restrictions on what projects, life events, or causes you can fundraise for."[99]

Online crowdfunding also supports a close connection between donor and recipient. Whereas giving charity to strangers may be a one-off interaction that may leave questions about how the money is being used, crowdfunding campaigns allow the donor to monitor what the recipient does with their donation and track the impact of the gift. This ongoing relationship through the crowdfunding campaign potentially creates an emotional connection that both encourages giving and is valuable in itself. On this point, GoFundMe's CEO Tim Cadogan notes that he does not see crowdfunding as a replacement for social safety nets funded by the state and through insurance programs. However, he argues that the "thing that we do as well, which is very, very different, is the emotional support that a GoFundMe campaign offers. It's the fact that your family, your friends, some people in your community that you don't know, some strangers who aren't even in your community, would rally around and say: 'I'm really sorry this happened. We just want to help you.' We provide a place to convey that."[100] An institutionalized process of giving, whether through the state or through private philanthropy, may struggle to recreate this emotional bond and communicate messages of support that can clearly be enormously meaningful to recipients and validating to donors.

The low barrier to entry into crowdfunding for donors creates a democratizing potential within giving in line with the mutual aid slogan of "solidarity not charity." This potential stands in contrast to the antidemocratic tendencies of institutional philanthropy. Whereas indirect giving through philanthropies is dominated by wealthy donors who are able to dictate giving priorities and aspects of public policy, crowdfunding allows smaller donors to pool their contributions to make a larger impact and help to shape priorities in giving.[101] People who donate to crowdfunding campaigns in the United States tend to be younger and are more likely to be people of color than in traditional giving, further supporting the idea that crowdfunding democratizes giving.[102] Crowdfunding further empowers individuals by "giving the beneficiaries the oversight over where the money goes and changes the narrative about what donations can accomplish," thus empowering recipients to lead the fundraising process.[103] In this way, crowdfunding "democratizes" giving because "Anyone can seek funds through crowdfunding" because "you don't need to know venture capitalists or philanthropists" to succeed in your campaign.[104] Perhaps as a reflection of this younger and more racially diverse donor base, crowdfunding campaigners are more likely to donate to support social justice causes than are traditional donors, further suggesting the more representative and democratic nature of this form of giving.[105]

These benefits, particularly around the ease and speed of giving, are undeniable. It is extremely easy to find stories of people whose lives have been changed through crowdfunding campaigns, including by being able to access education, receive life-saving surgeries, and obtain housing supports, among many other needs. For example, young adults seeking help paying for cancer treatments described crowdfunding as "a life saver" and emphasized that they would not have been able to get this treatment without the help of crowdfunding.[106] And, in aggregate, these campaigns can have measurable impacts on access to entitlements. In the United States, every 10% increase in the amount of health-related funding raised through crowdfunding has been found to lead to 0.04% fewer bankruptcies due to medical debt. At the same time, money raised for health-related needs has a direct impact on access to medical care.[107] In short, the sheer growth and overall size of donation-based crowdfunding combined with the stories of need in these campaigns speak for themselves.

Conclusion

Giving practices—both giving directly or through philanthropic foundations—are highly varied and represent geographic, cultural, religious, and temporal differences. Giving can be hierarchical or horizontal in terms of how asymmetries in wealth and power are exhibited. It can be governed by norms of reciprocity or altruism around how giving creates obligations on the part of the receiver. Giving is secular and religiously motivated, aimed at all in need or only a subset of those deemed worthy, and directed at the people closest to us or those for whom the most good can be done. And, of course, giving practices demonstrate many other, finer distinctions in their many forms.

That said, some common concerns around practices of giving to address others' basic needs apply across the many manifestations of giving, including direct and indirect giving generally. First, giving can focus on the needs and interests of the giver rather than the recipient. This type of giving can be seen in reciprocal giving directly to those in need, giving for the sake of public perception or religious benefit, and indirect giving as a means of promoting our own priorities and image rather than those of the public or the requirements of justice. In these various forms, giving forefronts the desires of the giver, making the needs of the receiver a lower priority, if they are given any consideration at all.

Second, giving can demand too little of givers. While ethical and religious accounts of giving differ on this point, some amount of giving is generally seen as obligatory, and this obligation may be very demanding. Considering any amount of giving as praiseworthy may shield givers from criticism that they have not done enough to help those in need. This is especially the case if giving fails to address the underlying causes of need or, worse, undercuts the kinds of policy changes required to address these needs.

Moreover, giving can humiliate or disrespect the recipient. Direct giving may be especially prone to this if asymmetries in the power and wealth of the giver and recipient are used to emphasize differences in status and devalue the humanity of the recipient relative to the giver. While indirect giving somewhat protects the receiver from these experiences, when philanthropic institutions sort recipients based on their deservingness to receive help, as when the nondisabled poor are refused aid, would-be recipients are devalued.

Finally, giving can be highly inequitable and undemocratic in terms of how aid is distributed and who benefits from it. Direct giving may focus on relationships, reciprocity, and perceived worthiness rather than need, efficiency, or fairness. This is true of philanthropic foundations as well, particularly as they are often governed by the values and priorities of their supporters, which may not reflect those of their communities or the values of justice. Thus, giving practices may not create a fair playing field in terms of who can benefit from these gifts.

Crowdfunding does not avoid all of these concerns, as I demonstrate in the remainder of this book. However, it does have a number of benefits over other giving practices, including facilitating speed in fundraising, removing barriers to making an appeal for help to the wider public, and directly connecting campaigners and donors without philanthropic intermediaries. This last benefit in particular has the potential to democratize giving and respond to criticisms of philanthropic giving practices. However, as I will argue, in practice donation-based crowdfunding continues many of the previous ethical problems with giving while introducing new concerns. Moreover, the development of this giving practice is increasingly starting to reflect indirect, mediated giving as crowdfunding platforms become more involved in picking winners and losers among campaigns.

2

Crowding out privacy

Most of you reading this probably don't know my sister, and those that do may not even be aware of her story. My sister is a very private person, and I would only ever disrupt that privacy if it was warranted. Unfortunately, I believe the situation warrants a small disturbance to her privacy. So let me give you a brief history.

Crowdfunding is designed to allow people to appeal to the public for financial support. Some people use these campaigns primarily to coordinate giving by close friends and family. But, by its nature, online crowdfunding is public facing and accessible beyond one's close contacts. This is no accident: crowdfunding platforms typically include embedded options to link campaigns to wider social networks through Facebook posts, tweets, email, and other means. Public awareness of crowdfunding efforts also often comes through news coverage of would-be viral campaigns. These forms of wider visibility are often actively pursued for their potential to generate much greater financial support than one's immediate contacts are able to provide.

Through the public nature of online crowdfunding, the campaign recipient's private life is put on display. This includes information about the cause of the recipient's needs, such as a severe medical condition, job loss, or a family tragedy. Explaining this need often requires telling a story about the recipient's history that can expose their current emotional state, past traumas, family members' stories, and other intimate details. Thus, crowdfunding, and especially successful crowdfunding, sits in tension with keeping the campaign recipient's personal information private.

The public nature of crowdfunding can cause significant stress and emotional difficulty. For example, Richard, a crowdfunding campaigner seeking support for his wife Laila's pancreas transplant, felt that the campaign would be more likely to receive donations if his family was seen as sympathetic and worthy of support. For this reason, Richard added photographs of his family,

Appealing to the Crowd. Jeremy Snyder, Oxford University Press. © Oxford University Press 2024.
DOI: 10.1093/oso/9780197658130.003.0003

including his children, and a video of Laila speaking openly about her medical diagnosis and financial need on his campaign page. But, as Laila put it, "I'm very private, so doing that video was really difficult."[1] Laila did go ahead with the campaign and the video, however, and was able to receive nearly $6,000 of support for her transplant and aftercare.

Insofar as crowdfunding comes at a cost to privacy, it is a cost hundreds of thousands of people like Richard and Laila are willing to pay in exchange for increased financial help. In this chapter, I examine why privacy matters, how it has been impacted by giving practices in the past, how it is impacted by crowdfunding, and how much control crowdfunding campaigners and recipients really have over what private information they share in crowdfunding campaigns.

Why does privacy matter?

The importance of privacy can be divided into its more abstract and practical aspects. As an abstract value, privacy is linked to the concept of integrity. As applied to people, integrity can be understood as a quality of the wholeness and unity of a person and is deeply tied to notions of respect. This concept extends to the bodily integrity of people, which includes self-determination, the right to exclude others from access to oneself, and self-ownership of one's body. The concept of integrity can extend to mental or psychological integrity as well, including the capacity to have a fully integrated conception of the self or a cohesive self-narrative, and, on some accounts, can also extend to moral integrity, understood as principled adherence to an ethical system or code. Taken together, integrity is being able to be a whole self, bodily and psychologically, with a cohesive set of personal boundaries and narrative identity. In practice, maintaining integrity has been understood to require, among other things, control over access to aspects of oneself.[2]

Understood in this way, privacy is linked to integrity as entailing a claim to determine who should have access to oneself, including information about oneself. Personal information, including images, experiences, medical data, thoughts, and emotions, are not bodily aspects of the self but do make up aspects of a cohesive identity or whole self. Lack of control over these aspects of the self can threaten the capacity of a person to develop and maintain their distinct and whole self. Early legal arguments on informational privacy and the impact of new technologies reflect this view. Photographs taken without permission, for example, could undermine the "more general right to the immunity of the person—the right to one's personality."[3] More generally, the value of controlling one's personal information can be linked to the value of autonomy and liberal principles that grant individuals control over aspects of the self, including information about oneself.[4]

Control over information about and access to oneself may also be valued more concretely in terms of what this control does for people and what losing it can mean. Privacy has a role in creating and maintaining the possibility of certain relationships, including intimate relationships of romantic love and friendship.[5] Loss of control over potentially embarrassing or compromising information can leave a person vulnerable to blackmail or other forms of exploitation. When people engage in behaviors or hold views that are devalued or ridiculed in their society, privacy can help protect individual dignity and the ability to engage in ways of living outside of the social mainstream.

Social norms over what kind of information is private and potentially sensitive or otherwise deserving of heightened scrutiny vary over time and communities. A Victorian's attitude about how much skin is appropriate to display in public may be very different from that of a modern European's at the beach. Rapid technological shifts and the development of social media have made many people more comfortable with sharing information, images, and video of themselves publicly than would have been the case in the recent past. These shifts in privacy norms driven by technological change, however, do not drift inevitably in the direction of more openness. As the consequences of this openness, such as having one's ill-advised teenage tweets surface at a job interview, become more apparent, norms around openness can shift back to more closely guarding personal information.[6]

In communities where poverty or the need to ask for help is stigmatized, making this need public can be harmful. The shame or stigma associated with the need to ask for help can vary based on cultural norms and other factors such as class. In medieval Europe, for example, the "shamefaced poor" (nobles and formerly wealthy and powerful people who had fallen into need) were viewed as more vulnerable to humiliation from needing assistance. For this reason, they were in some cases shielded from public view when receiving aid.[7] More generally, Maimonides's ladder of charitable giving particularly values donations where the giver does not know the identity of the recipient, to protect the recipient from feelings of shame.[8] In contemporary societies, people having to ask for assistance for the first time—for example middle-class people facing catastrophic loss after a natural disaster—may particularly perceive stigma and humiliation in making their need public.[9]

Expressions of power are also at the heart of why privacy matters. John Gilliom notes that people receiving state welfare assistance, at least, do not necessarily view state surveillance as specifically violating a right to privacy.[10] Concern with privacy, in Gilliom's study of mothers receiving welfare in Appalachia, is not linked to a "right to be let alone," as with some of the earliest legal scholarship on privacy.[11] In this community, the values of care and mutual dependence are dominant, as opposed to the hyper-individuality often seen in academic discourse on privacy and surveillance. Gilliom argues that what these women tend to find objectionable about being subjected to surveillance in exchange for welfare support is the asymmetrical relationship of power and dominance that shapes this support and creates conflict with those in a position to determine whether they meet the criteria for assistance. State support for basic needs is a different relationship from philanthropy and charity, of course, but relationships of dominance and highly asymmetrical power can take place in a variety of giving relationships, particularly where receiving help is contingent on the recipient's personal life, history, resources, and needs.

What unites these attitudes about the value and role of privacy is a sense of the central importance of control over who has access to personal information. This control should be given to individuals who may then determine for themselves when, how, and to whom their private information should be disclosed. Privacy understood in this way is not absolute—for example, a tax fraud investigator may legitimately require access to bank accounts or other personal information, given the social goods encouraged by a just tax regime. Putting conflicts with other values aside, there is a general value to control over one's private information.

Investigating the poor

Receiving financial help to meet one's basic needs can result in a loss of privacy. This loss can occur when would-be recipients of financial help are compelled to share information to establish their eligibility or deservingness for support. Assistance from the state in the form of poverty relief and social welfare payments has long included measures to verify the qualifications of those receiving this aid, particularly when the state discriminates between those able and those unable to work.[12] These forms of investigation and surveillance can be highly invasive and have included midnight home raids by the police, moral fitness tests, genetic testing of offspring, drug testing, fingerprinting, and probes into recipients' intimate relationships.[13] Often these investigations into the lives and finances of recipients can increase stigma toward receiving aid from the state, as with the oft-used trope of the "welfare queen" in US politics.[14]

In the context of nonstate aid, eligibility and priority-setting rules used by philanthropic institutions serve a similar purpose to those in state institutions—and can be similarly invasive. Josephine Shaw Lowell, the founder of the New York City Charity Organization Society, viewed the invasion of aid recipients' privacy to be a necessary evil. As she described it in the late 1800s, the only "excuse for trespassing upon the privacy of other human beings, for trying to learn facts in their lives which they prefer should not be known, for seeking to discover the weak spots in their characters, for trying to find out what pitiful personal sorrows their nearest and dearest have brought upon them" is that you have been asked to help that person and "you cannot help him unless you know all about him."[15] On the one hand, these visits and ongoing surveillance aimed to ensure that resources were used efficiently and would enable potential recipients to gain or retain independence from philanthropic aid. However, this surveillance was achieved through close investigation of the lives of would-be recipients by powerful agents able to determine whether they would have their basic needs met.

For some philanthropies, the decision of whether potential recipients should be supported is based on the perceived impacts of giving. The *scientific charity movement* in the United States, for example, was motivated in part by the common concern that religious traditions of direct almsgiving could encourage indigence among the so-called able-bodied poor. One key element of this movement was the home visit, where volunteers would investigate potential aid recipients to determine their deservingness.[16] For example, the philanthropic activities of the Society of Saint Vincent de Paul accepted some of these criticisms of almsgiving as encouraging idleness and adopted home visits. These visits were designed to determine the deservingness of aid recipients, and some potential recipients were subjected to labor tests where their physical capacity to engage in work was examined. People with alcohol dependency were also excluded from receiving help during these visits on the theory that aid would only encourage continued substance use.[17]

The physical structure of philanthropic supports for the poor can have a major impact on the privacy of recipients as well. Almshouses, workhouses, hospitals, and other structures have been used historically to provide relief to the poor and move them from a system of receiving alms in public to being housed and cared for indoors. In some cases, as with workhouses during the Victorian era in the United Kingdom, these structures were designed so that recipients of aid could provide value for the help they received in the form of industrial outputs. Conditions were intentionally squalid so that those able to work outside of these institutions would prefer to do so and therefore not fall into dependency on aid. In these various forms, philanthropic institutions housing and feeding the poor often do so communally and so reduce the physical privacy of those being supported. Facilities that are more supportive of physical privacy existed during these periods as well, but often were seen as less desirable because of increased cost or because of the intended punitive design of poverty relief.[18]

Beyond examining recipients' lives to ensure that gifts are used efficiently and do not encourage dependence, both direct and indirect giving can be predicated on establishing whether the recipient is morally worthy of support. Standards of worthiness can privilege those whose need is seen as not tied to their own actions or who are viewed as particularly vulnerable or helpless. In the present context, establishing this worthiness often requires relinquishing privacy and subjecting oneself to examination by relatively powerful donors. For example, newspapers in Hong Kong often maintain philanthropic funds used to help local community members in need. These newspapers include sections in which individuals can appeal for donations from the papers' readers. A study of two of these newspapers found that successful recipients had to portray themselves as socially inferior to potential donors and disclose detailed personal information including their full names, work history, family background, and a personal photograph. Groups that were most often able to present themselves as deserving of aid were disabled people, older adults, and widows—people able to meet social expectations about genuine neediness and helplessness.[19]

Trading privacy for financial help

Crowdfunding campaigners receive many signals about the need to be open about their lives, histories, and needs in order to encourage giving and meet their campaign goals. Often, these signals take the form of explicit advice from crowdfunding platforms, blogs, and patient advocacy groups, among others.

Crowdfunding platforms typically require that some personally identifying details be included in the crowdfunding campaigns they host. This disclosure is justified by the need to convince potential donors that they are not contributing to a fraudulent campaign. Most commonly, this means that the campaign organizer must use their real name to create a campaign and that this name is visible to potential donors as well. GoFundMe, for example, prohibits "Lying or being misleading about your identity as an organizer or your relationship to the ultimate recipient of the funds."[20] Donors are given advice on how to avoid contributing to fraudulent campaigns that includes confirming the recipient's name, "researching" the recipient, asking what the funds will be used for, and communicating with the campaigner to determine who will have access to campaign funds, where they will be stored, and how their use will be verified for donors.[21]

Beyond these basic antifraud requirements, crowdfunding campaign organizers are told to be as open as possible when campaigning in order to encourage donations. Campaigners are urged to "Be clear about your needs. Give an outline of how much money you need to raise and what the funds will be used for, including how it will help you."[22] GoFundMe acknowledges that when a tragedy has led to one's need for support, it can be difficult to share details online. Nonetheless, "telling one's story requires courage and honesty."[23] Oprah.com tells its readers that "effective campaigns are detailed and personally compelling" and that campaigners for health-related needs should present a "thorough description of the recipient's health status with an explanation of how the money will be spent, and update your supporters regularly."[24] GoFundMe advises campaigners to write their "fundraiser story honestly and thoroughly" because doing so will help potential donors understand "the reality of your medical situation."[25] Campaigners are told that successful campaigns will avoid the common mistakes of being "too short" or "lacking important details about the beneficiary's condition."[26] Similarly, these campaigns should "be specific" in what they are using the money for, including "your current situation, the reason why you're fundraising, and your desired outcome," noting that donors "appreciate transparency."[27]

Campaigners are advised that sharing copious personal details in their crowdfunding campaigns shouldn't be limited to just the campaign text. According to GoFundMe, "photos are powerful fundraising tools and can take your fundraiser to the next level."[28] One reason personal and identifying photos are said to be important is because "Most people will feel more comfortable donating to a cause when they can see photos of the person their funds will be going to. Be sure to use high-quality images that show you or your beneficiary."[29] Videos, as well, are meant to be highly revealing about the campaign beneficiary and those people around them: "If possible, record the beneficiary at home, in the community, and/or with loved ones. Record family and friends speaking about their relationship with the beneficiary and what makes them so special."[30] These images are not solely meant for consumption on the campaign page but are themselves meant to be shared more widely on social media: "The more beautiful and varied your images are, the more people will want to share them on social media."[31]

When assembling videos for their campaigns, campaigners are reminded to "Include the beneficiary, nonprofit or cause's name in your video title to make the video easily searchable."[32] Similarly, GoFundMe encourages campaigners to put the recipient's name and the hardship they are experiencing in the title of the campaign.[33] Campaigners are told that their campaign should be spread broadly on social media to friends of their parents, friends of their children, the parents of their children's friends, members of groups related to their cause, and current and former classmates, colleagues, and acquaintances.[34] Another tip is to move beyond your network of personal connections: "Post your fundraiser link on your city's Facebook page. This is a great way to reach out to local folks you may not know."[35] Media exposure is also described as very important, as coverage by just one media outlet can mean "your cause gets valuable exposure to thousands of people."[36] To succeed with their fundraising goals, campaigners are encouraged to maintain a "constant presence" on social media.[37]

This advice to share early, widely, and often is given to people across a wide range of fundraiser types, including those very likely to touch on areas of particular sensitivity. For people seeking to raise money for gender-affirming surgeries, GoFundMe suggests campaigners "use plenty of photos and video. . . . In addition to using photos and videos on your fundraiser page, be sure to include them in the updates you post for donors throughout your gender confirmation surgery fundraiser."[38] For people raising money for cancer treatment, other information that campaigners should provide includes "your history," "what treatments will you be going through," and "the highs and lows of treatment or recovery."[39]

In addition to communicating the legitimacy of the campaign and informing potential donors about how their money will be used, this transparency is intended to generate sympathy from the public. Campaigners are urged to "Tell it from the heart. Be honest and direct with your supporters. Vulnerability goes a long way"[40] and are encouraged to think of their campaign as a storytelling exercise with an eye to encouraging empathy in their reader. To do this, campaigners should give details about their history, including how they have attempted to overcome their hardship, what barriers they have faced, and "how have they changed you as a person." This storytelling is not limited to the recipient but also those around them, as they are told to "describe the effect of your struggle on your family, your local community, or society as a whole."[41] In this vein, the Rare Genomics Institute tells its community members that when crowdfunding for medical care, "It's important to be transparent and believable. People respond to emotion, so the campaign should state the need earnestly (so potential donors believe in it) and visually (so they can better understand how difficult the issue is)."[42] Vulnerability is part of what sells a story to potential donors, and so campaigners shouldn't "be afraid to be vulnerable when you share details."[43]

The transactional nature of providing personally identifying photos is made clear as "It can be difficult to be vulnerable in this way, but this kind of vulnerability is also what can touch people and inspire them to support you during this difficult time."[44] Campaigners are also told that the volume of photos matters, as "fundraisers with at least five photos raise more than those with one. The fact is donors love seeing multiple images."[45] Photos that are "compelling" and "media-worthy" can also help with getting media coverage and therefore more people to visit your fundraising page.[46] GoFundMe acknowledges the costs created by sharing personal details online but makes the case that doing so is necessary to achieve fundraising goals. As they put it, "It can be difficult to post photos of yourself when going through such a difficult time, but photos can draw people into your world and allow them to empathize with your story." While they caution that images of medical bills should be obscured to remove "sensitive information," the general tenor is to emphasize the necessity of opening one's life up to potential donors.[47]

The data bear out the advice given to crowdfunding campaigners: if you want to meet your crowdfunding goals, then protecting your privacy is not an option. Several potentially invasive forms of sharing personal information have been cited as helping to establish the legitimacy of medical crowdfunding campaigns, including details about the recipient's financial supports other than crowdfunding; details about the recipient's medical situation; multimedia sources including photographs, videos, and news stories; regular updates; and comments to donors.[48] A study of 200 US-based medical crowdfunding campaigns found a positive correlation between campaign success and the numbers of campaign updates, photos, videos, and social media shares.[49] Similarly, an analysis of Chinese medical crowdfunding campaigns found that communicating information about the recipient's family members, income, and financial need were positively correlated with meeting campaign goals.[50] In campaigns seeking funding for the healthcare needs of trans people, the number of times a campaign was shared on Facebook was positively correlated with campaign success.[51]

Interviews with crowdfunding campaigners show that they do not always see participating in these campaigns as a challenge to their privacy. They may see the information shared in these campaigns as in line with what they already share on other social media platforms and thus a way to help connect with other people experiencing pain and deprivation in their everyday lives. In other cases, campaigners feel that they had to share personal information to receive help, whether or not they were comfortable doing so. Privacy is seen as a trade-off with publicity, leaving one campaigner to choose between "everyone knowing [the recipient's] business" and losing "our house."[52] These campaigners specifically note potential harms of sharing information about their health and financial needs online, including scaring off potential employers and other professional contacts during a job search or receiving criticism from friends and family for asking for help publicly and not putting enough faith in God for a cure to their disease.

Crowdfunding campaigners report feeling pressure to describe their financial and medical situation in great detail to establish their honesty and the authenticity of their need to potential donors. The transactional nature of this exchange of private information for donations can be felt explicitly, as with one campaigner saying that they felt they had to "let people know everything that's happening. [Then,] maybe people who thought I was cheating in the beginning will read more updates, details, and pictures."[53] These disclosures not only impact the campaign recipient but also draw in family members who may disagree about having their financial information shared online and have different attitudes about this exchange of private information for financial support.

Crowdfunding campaigners report fearing social stigma when revealing personal information in their campaigns. This includes stigma around asking the public for financial help, which could invite judgments about the legitimacy of their financial need and the life and spending choices that led to this need. Personal details and the nature of the need can invite social stigma as well. In one case, a family disagreed about whether to share the cause of death in a crowdfunding campaign for funeral expenses for a family member who died from a poisoning from unregulated drugs. This family was torn between preferring to keep those details private and feeling the need to be open about the cause of death to encourage giving.[54] Among people crowdfunding for addiction treatment, many expressed reservations about being open about their history with substance use and addiction. The stigma often associated with addiction and substance use made asking for public help embarrassing for some people and raised the risk of publicly associating their name with a history of addiction. Others noted reservations by family members who did not wish to be publicly associated with the campaigner's substance use.[55] While difficult to track, this fear of stigma and public exposure certainly leads some people who would have benefitted from crowdfunding to choose not to seek support in this way.

Not surprisingly, privacy concerns can vary according to the type of need being addressed. An analysis of trans people crowdfunding for top surgery found that they had to choose how much to discuss about their experience of coming to identify as trans and whether and how to discuss and display their bodies, including unwanted body parts. These concerns can be especially heightened for members of marginalized communities, including trans people, who have historically been subjected to discrimination, verbal abuse, and physical violence because of their identity. In one study of campaigns for gender-affirming mastectomies, 16.2% of campaigners expressed concerns in the campaign about having to crowdfund their surgeries, including concerns about forgoing their privacy. One campaigner noted their fear about "outing myself to folks or worse" but decided the campaign was necessary to "step further into my true self."[56] Even within categories of specific types of need, context shapes the trade-off between maintaining privacy and crowdfunding success. A person who is very open and celebratory about their trans identity, for example, may face lower disclosure costs than a person who has only been open about their identity and desire for gender-affirming surgery to a more intimate group of people.[57] By comparison, someone who has been a victim of violence or faced other threats to their safety may be particularly wary of publicizing their personal details through a crowdfunding campaign.[58]

Donors to crowdfunding campaigns can face privacy concerns as well. In the case of campaigns for stigmatized needs or politically divisive causes, donors can potentially face negative personal and professional repercussions from having their name associated with a cause. Donors do generally have the option of remaining anonymous on most crowdfunding platforms, a protection that is generally not available to campaigners and recipients. However, a donor may not fully consider the consequences of publicly supporting a crowdfunding campaign with their name or not consider a campaign goal to be divisive at the time of their donation. Even when donors choose not to share their names publicly, crowdfunding platforms will typically retain information about their identities to process their payments to the campaigner. This information is vulnerable to exposure, as with a leak of supporters of a politically divisive campaign on the GiveSendGo crowdfunding platform that led to some donors facing dismissal from employment and other personal consequences.[59]

Crowdfunding for others

When a person is running their own crowdfunding campaign, they at least have the advantage of being able to decide what personal details, photos, videos, and other aspects of their lives to make public. However, the crowdfunding campaigner and recipient are often not the same person, which further complicates decision-making around trading privacy for donations. Although adult recipients in these cases could presumably give consent to what details of their private lives will be included in the campaign, it isn't always clear that consent has been given or that the recipient has been consulted in detail about the campaign.

GoFundMe explicitly suggests having others take over your medical fundraiser, noting several advantages of doing so: "Asking for help takes pressure off the patient, who should be focused on healing not raising money. You may find that someone else can often tell your story better than you. Having an outside perspective of what you're going through can be beneficial when writing a fundraiser story."[60] GoFundMe suggests that a team approach to fundraising can include multiple people in different roles, including a public relations manager who focuses on media outreach, a social media manager, a writer who puts together campaign text, a photographer and videographer, and an overall campaign manager.[61] Needless to say, maintaining clarity about consent to publicly disclose personal information will be complicated with a diverse team and a seriously ill recipient.

This suggested team approach to crowdfunding is visible in practice as well. One study of medical crowdfunding campaigns found that well over half of all campaigns were not initiated by the intended recipient for the funding.[62] Another analysis of crowdfunding campaigns for people with kidney cancer found that 28.8% of these campaigns were run by friends of the recipient and 14.8% by family members (not including parents of a child).[63] More than half of campaigns for the treatment of addiction and substance use were initiated by someone other than the intended recipient, in another study.[64] Similarly, two-thirds of campaigns for young adults needing help with cancer treatment were organized by someone else—typically a friend or family member.[65] The reasons for handing off the campaign can vary but include well-intentioned desires to conduct a campaign to help someone who has difficulty accepting help from others, to protect the recipient's identity, or to relieve the recipient of the burden of conducting the campaign.

However well intentioned, these campaigns can be problematic if campaigners do not have permission to share the recipient's—and potentially their family's—personal information. Lack of consultation and consent raises important ethical issues around whether the privacy of the recipient is being undermined to help them financially. But at least adult campaign recipients can generally be consulted about having their private information shared with the public in principle if not in fact.

In other cases, the very possibility of consent is lacking. Most notably in this category, crowdfunding campaigns seeking help for minors to pay for essential needs are not uncommon. In one review of campaigns for recipients with kidney cancer, 17% of the campaigns reviewed were for pediatric patients.[66] A study of the Chinese crowdfunding platform Tencent Gong Yi found that 40% of campaigns for medical needs had children as recipients,[67] and a separate study of Chinese medical crowdfunding campaigns identified 70% of recipients as children.[68] As an example of what it takes to write a successful crowdfunding campaign, GoFundMe cites the example of a child raising money for a friend's wheelchair.

With his parents' help, 8-year-old Paul started a GoFundMe titled Get Kamden Rollin' again so his friend Kamden could get a new wheelchair. In 10 months, Paul has posted 25 updates with photos, videos, important developments and links. He's shared good news and bad, but every update is filled with gratitude and optimism. His from-the-heart updates keep donors emotionally involved in their story and let them know where their money is going.[69]

In this case, the fundraiser is organized by, or at least written in the voice of, Kamden's friend Paul, a similarly aged child. The advice given by GoFundMe is that campaigns for children should be emotionally gripping and highly detailed. Similarly, the Rare Genomics Institute tells its community that "If a family is trying to raise money for a sick child who has a rare disease, explain how this illness affects their normal, everyday activities. Tell them what the life of this child is like. You want your audience to walk in your shoes and think, 'Imagine if that hit me.' "[70] Campaigners are told that creating empathy with potential donors and "pulling on their heartstrings" is key when appealing for financial help for children, including by using videos featuring the child and their illness. "Ideally you will show a brief yet poignant 'snapshot' of the way this child's life is—one that shows the viewer the problem in a compelling way so they will want to help. If the medical campaign is for a child, and the child is in the position to actually speak and explain their situation, that may also prompt deep empathy in others."[71]

As with campaigns by adults, crowdfunding campaigns for children that share intimate details seem to have an advantage in receiving donations. The most successful campaigns raising money for medical treatments for four diseases affecting infants and small children had more images, updates, and shares on Facebook than less successful campaigns. These campaigns also regularly shared images of other family members, including other minors, as well as information about the recipient's first and last name, birthdate, medical history, medical treatment, personal history, and daily struggles.[72]

Crowdfunding campaigns for children can be further complicated when parents have different attitudes about what kinds of private information should be shared. In one instance, a divorced mother began a crowdfunding campaign for a wheelchair ramp for her child and participated in media interviews raising public awareness about the campaign. Her ex-husband became aware of the campaign through this media coverage and angrily called the mother, objecting that "it made him look cheap. Like he didn't care for his daughter, wasn't providing for her." This experience left the mother feeling relieved that she had received financial support but also finding that "My ex-husband's so angry at me, and I don't know what to do."[73] This example shows how crowdfunding can take existing family stresses and disagreements about the care of children and move them into the public sphere.

Crowdfunding campaigns for adults with cognitive limitations are common as well. A study of crowdfunding campaigns for stem cell interventions for people with neurological conditions found that 5% of the campaigns reviewed were for people who experienced a stroke and 2.6% for people with a brain injury, both of which can lead to severe cognitive limitations. Other campaigns in this study were to help people with Alzheimer's disease and other forms of dementia, which can lead to progressive loss of cognitive ability.[74] Similarly, a study of medical crowdfunding campaigns in Germany found that the third most common category of need was for people with mental disorders, and the seventh most common was for people experiencing dementia.[75]

As with campaigns for young children, the diminished mental capacity of some adult recipients will complicate the process of informing the recipients about what information is being provided in these campaigns and receiving consent for providing this information. Whereas extended campaigns for young children may allow for increased capacity to consent as the child matures, campaigns for adults in these circumstances may face increased challenges around receiving informed consent to sharing information if the recipient experiences progressive cognitive decline. In other instances, a person with a significant medical issue may be fully able to consent to sharing information at the start of a campaign but lose that capacity because of a severe medical event involving loss of consciousness or extended periods of hospitalization with limited contact with the campaign organizer.

Conclusion

Sharing private information through online crowdfunding campaigns can harm campaigners and campaign recipients. In some circumstances, this information can be difficult to share, creating an emotional burden for campaigners and recipients. This information can be stigmatizing, associating the donor with behaviors like substance use that are discriminated against or diseases that are linked to socially undesirable lifestyles. People who are not yet publicly open about an illness or life-changing decisions such as undergoing gender-affirming surgery may be compelled to share information before they feel comfortable doing so and to people they would have preferred not to know at that time. Asking for financial help opens the recipient up to judgment about their life choices, spending habits, employment history, and savings. These discussions can create and publicize family rifts about medical decisions, financial choices, and the degree to which they should disclose normally closely held, personal information.

Certainly, the invasiveness of crowdfunding campaigns will depend on the campaigner and the needs underlying the campaign. Moreover, sharing this information online is not nearly as invasive as some of the worst historical practices in giving, where homes, histories, and bodies have been subjected to scrutiny by those overseeing philanthropic activities. That said, crowdfunding is distinctively costly to personal privacy in ways that traditional giving practices have generally not been. Private details in crowdfunding campaigns are not disclosed to a few philanthropic administrators or individual donors to verify the genuineness of the recipients' need. Rather, these details are made widely public and potentially in perpetuity as part of the campaigner's appeal for donations. Personal details are not incidental to the campaign but central to how potential donors are motivated to contribute. This information is most effective when it is shared widely through the campaign itself and social media platforms and traditional news media outlets. Wider dispersal of personal details means more financial support, and so normally private information becomes a commodity to be laid out to donors and mere bystanders alike to encourage financial support.

Crucially, decisions about what personal information to share online are often not made by those most impacted by these decisions, as campaigners often don't have the recipient's consent to share their private information with the public. This is most apparent when the recipient is a young child or an adult with severe dementia or other cognitive limitations. In other cases, adults crowdfunding on behalf of other adults do not consult fully or at all with these recipients about what information to disclose publicly. In these instances, treating privacy as a right can help to explain the wrongness of putting this information into the public sphere without permission to do so. While a parent or legal guardian will in some cases have the authority to share this information on behalf of others, in many other cases this permission—and therefore the right to share this information—is lacking.

Moreover, treating privacy simply as a right that individuals can choose to forgo misses major aspects of what is problematic about choosing to exchange privacy for financial support. We can question how voluntary these exchanges are, especially when the recipient's options are between, for example, becoming homeless and hoping that a soul-baring plea to the public will encourage donations. Thus, power—or the lack of it—is behind what is problematic about trading privacy for necessary supports as well. Although there is not a powerful state or philanthropic group dictating invasive surveillance of crowdfunders, crowdfunding donors, as a collective, have the power to determine which campaigns succeed and fail. Moreover, crowdfunding platforms, by creating an ecosystem that urges campaigners to trade their privacy for support, exert enormous pressure on campaigners to disclose not just financial needs but also recipients' histories, emotional states, images, and testimonials, all supported by regular updates. While the power used by state and philanthropic institutions to compel recipients to give up their privacy is overt, the power of potential donors and crowdfunding platforms is more subtle. As a result, it's harder for crowdfunding campaigners to make the case that they had little or no choice but to exchange their privacy for financial support.

Some openness about the personal circumstances of the recipients of giving can be justified by the need to prevent fraud and distribute financial resources fairly and effectively. This is true with crowdfunding campaigns as well, where fraudulent or misleading campaigns are not uncommon. However, the openness demanded for crowdfunding success goes well beyond these justifications. Private information is shared not simply to prove that the recipient is genuinely in need and will use the resources as described but also to play on the public's sympathies and motivate giving. This need to invite the public into the recipient's life is made explicit in the advice that crowdfunders receive and in the evidence on crowdfunding success. Not every crowdfunder wants to go viral and receive substantial donations from the general public. However, the structure of crowdfunding campaigns and incentives built around this practice are to make the private public to the largest extent campaigners are willing to do so.

Privacy, and its loss, in the context of crowdfunding is not simply a matter of nonconsent, rights violations, and permissions, then. It should also be examined in terms of who has power over what crowdfunding campaigns are likely to receive support, how this power is exerted to require crowdfunding recipients to perform as sympathetic targets for donors, and what privacy costs are felt by relatively powerless crowdfunding campaigners and recipients. As I have shown in this chapter, privacy is often sacrificed in crowdfunding campaigns to make the case for the deservingness of recipients for aid. In the next chapter, I examine how deservingness is at the forefront of crowdfunding narratives and how this problematically turns online giving into a popularity contest among would-be recipients.

3

Proving your worth

So I want to start this fundraising for her so she doesn't has to worry too much about the bills and money, and so she could focus on her mental health. She's always the first one to help anybody, especially her friends and family and she never asks anything in return. But she never ever asks help for herself, and I really think she deserves to receive some help and support this time. She really is a good person and deserves to be happy again.

In late 2018, a pair of Republican operatives initiated a GoFundMe campaign to pay to build a wall on the United State's southern border with Mexico after Congress refused to fund its construction. The *New York Daily News* picked up on this story, noting that the fundraiser was one of the most successful crowdfunding campaigns of all time, outraising a fundraiser for victims of a mass shooting at a Florida high school. Rather than contributing to the wall fundraiser, the *Daily News* suggested several other, arguably more "worthwhile" campaigns. These included funding for a four-year-old's cancer treatment so that the family could focus on being together; contributing to the family of a man shot by the police where the money would be used for diapers and college tuition and would "make a significant difference in the lives of Kyle's wife, son, and daughter"; and support for a woman set on fire during a domestic abuse incident where the donations would support the victim and her children.[1]

One other campaign flagged by the *Daily News* as worthy of its readers' support was for the Ilinetsky family. Soon after the birth of their twins, the Ilinetskys saw that the twins were not developing normally. After repeated trips to their family physician and medical specialists, they learned that their infant twins had Canavan disease, a neurodegenerative genetic condition that usually results in death in childhood. Although a physical therapy program helped to combat some of the effects of the disease, the twins' only hope

Appealing to the Crowd. Jeremy Snyder, Oxford University Press. © Oxford University Press 2024.
DOI: 10.1093/oso/9780197658130.003.0004

for a cure was through a scientifically unproven gene therapy that would re-place the twins' mutated genes. However, paying for a clinical trial for the gene therapy that would include the twins would cost $3.5 million. Even the twins' physical therapy was not covered by the Ilinetskys' medical insurance, and insurance coverage for participating in the clinical trial was also out of the question.

For this reason, the Ilinetskys started a crowdfunding campaign with the goal of raising $2 million. They saw crowdfunding medical treatment for their children as a last resort, feeling that their twins deserved med-ical help. The twins' father, Zohar, noted that they were hard-working: "we are *not* poor people. We are not out of work. I started working three days after I came to America. Ask in our community!"[2] News coverage of their campaign noted the great good that could come of the proposed clinical trial, not only saving the lives of the twins and other children enrolled in the trial but also possibly helping to "save future generations of Jews."[3] The Ilinetskys also appealed to the local and international Jewish community, particularly as Canavan disease primarily affects Ashkenazi Jews. They went as far as to consider employing a public relations company to "sell *us*" and show the public they were deserving of help.[4] While the campaign raised more than $300,000 from 3,300 donors, it has not been enough to pay for treatment for the twins.[5]

One effect of crowdfunding is that campaigners must compete with one another to show that they deserve support from the crowd of potential donors. This is true particularly for campaigners like the Ilinetskys who seek large sums of money and need to depend on the support of strangers through viral campaigns. Online crowdfunding creates opportunities to reach large numbers of potential donors, which would have been vastly more diffi-cult before the advent of these fundraising platforms. At the same time, the Ilinetskys have felt the intense pressure to tell the public a story about why their infant children deserve to be supported. Zohar Ilinetsky described his response as feeling helpless: "What do you want me to do? How can I prove to you that my kids are sick? It's just another story. That's what the social-network world is doing—it makes everything just another story."[6] It is hardly new that people in need are pressured to show potential donors—whether individuals or institutions—that they are worthy of support. But, as the Ilinetskys show, the shift to crowdfunding via online social networks creates new opportunities and new costs to demonstrating the deservingness of their loved ones for help from friends and strangers alike.

Patterns of worthiness

In many religious and ethical traditions, giving to others is viewed as an ob-ligation that is not tied to the perceived worthiness of the recipient. Rather, the simple fact that a person is in need or requests aid is sufficient reason to help. This is particularly true in the case of traditional forms of direct giving or almsgiving where giving is immediate, the recipient is proximate, and the focus is on the act of giving rather than the characteristics of the re-cipient. For example, within the Hindu tradition of *dāna*, giving to those in need does not entail reciprocity or accountability to the donor, and much of the value of the gift is seen in the giver's renunciation of material wealth.[7] Early Christian thinkers tended to focus on almsgiving as an obligation of the rich, viewing property as something to be shared with all and not a re-source that those in need had to justify receiving.[8] Where giving traditions are more horizontal or communal in nature, as in traditional giving practices in South Africa, the focus in giving is often on the need of our neighbors rather than their seeming deservingness for receiving aid. This is the case as well with many other Indigenous giving practices in North American and Africa where mutual aid and communal support are emphasized.[9] In these circumstances, there is both less focus on the character of the recipient and relatively little infrastructure with which to investigate the lives and worthi-ness of those in need.

By comparison, relatively hierarchical giving traditions and contexts where resources are largely controlled by elites are more likely to focus on the deservingness of recipients. For example, ancient Greek and Roman notions of reciprocity in giving directed charitable aid to focus on those with whom one wanted to be associated. The hierarchical nature of these communities implied that one should be careful about giving to those who are not considered one's social equals. For example, Seneca's belief that giving creates reciprocal relationships akin to friendship led to clear warnings about the sorts of people one should give to. We should not accept gifts, he wrote, from people we "do not find congenial" or those we find "unworthy."[10] Seneca argues that because giving can lead to friendship and friendship creates new ties and obligations, we should exercise discretion about whom we should give help.

The distribution of resources within a community can change perceptions of who is worthy of receiving aid as well. Early Christians tended to focus on almsgiving as an obligation of the rich rather than something the poor had to prove their worthiness to receive. This practice was in part due to a perception that wealth belonged to all and a requirement to act in God's image by giving special favor and attention to the poor. This faith tradition later developed arguments for distinguishing between the so-called deserving and undeserving poor. In the medieval period, various religious scholars emphasized giving to those known to ourselves rather than strangers, the sick rather than the healthy, the humble and ashamed rather than aggressive beggars, and people seen to be innocent and respectable. This shift followed in part from elites repudiating the view of wealth as a communal resource and something to which the poor were entitled, instead requiring those in need to demonstrate their deservingness to be given resources justly held by the wealthy.[11]

In broad terms, arguments for giving only to certain people seen to be worthy of receiving these gifts take two forms. First, these arguments can be based on the perceived impacts of giving, making the case that giving to certain people will yield greater overall benefits and giving to others will result in wasted or less effective transfers. Alternatively, these arguments can turn on the perceived worthiness of some people to receive aid, arguing that past actions or present moral status make some people unworthy of aid regardless of whether that aid will do great good for that person or maximize the impact of giving overall.

Within this first group of arguments, emphasis on the worthiness of recipients grew in part out of critiques of the perceived unfocused and wasteful nature of direct giving. In both direct and indirect giving, the perceived worthiness of the recipient was influenced by scientific rationalization around maximizing the positive impacts of giving. In many instances, the perceived deservingness of charity recipients was tied to the larger goal of ensuring that direct giving did not encourage dependency. For example, descriptions of people in need of financial help in newspaper coverage in the early twentieth century focused on those who wanted to work or eschewed cash charity in favor of being offered additional work to help make ends meet.[12] Because of the perceived danger that aid would encourage dependence on help from others, having worked or wanting to continue working was a key sign of deservingness. Similarly, these news media campaigns tended to select people in need of short-term help, for whom aid was not a long-term need but rather a temporary boost to help the recipient "get back on their feet" and no longer require external support. Independence is largely seen as the end goal of those worthy of help, as with children who study hard for a brighter future and adults seeking employment, a new line of work, or a new home where work can be found.[13] More generally, giving movements such as *effective altruism* can make decisions about which individuals or groups should receive help based on creating the best long-term outcomes for all.

Within the second category of arguments for restricting giving, identifying recipients of giving as worthy or deserving of aid is often explicitly a moral judgment. Perceptions of what qualities shape the deservingness of people for aid change, of course, over time, place, religion, and culture. Nonetheless, common themes emerge, including treating some groups of people as particularly vulnerable or helpless and therefore morally worthy of help; holding people personally responsible for their need; assigning greater worth to those connected to oneself by ethnic, religious, or community ties; valuing selfless behavior; and expecting feelings of shame in response to needing help from others. Moreover, while restricting giving to those unable to work can be justified by concern with creating dependency and the aim of maximizing the benefits of giving, in other cases it is more explicitly tied to a moral judgment that those seeking aid in lieu of work are lazy, greedy, or otherwise morally unworthy of help.

Just as the perceived ability to find work and support oneself has frequently been used as a reason to deny people support, certain classes of people, including women, children, older adults, and disabled people, are typically selected as worthy of aid because of their perceived inability to help themselves. *The New York Times* ran a yearly campaign from 1912 to 1917 that identified the "one hundred neediest" people deserving donations from its readers. Typically, the people chosen for this mass-media campaign exhibited not only a depth of need but also moral worthiness of being helped. In these cases, worthiness was tied in part to the faultlessness of the recipient—that their need was not caused by their own actions and particularly not caused by what were seen as immoral behaviors. Being very young or very old made establishing faultlessness easier based on these recipients' perceived lack of agency and power. Children were presumed not to be able to provide for their own needs, and older adults could lose this ability through physical decline, especially when this decline led to losing the ability to work. For adults, illness that was not caused by behavioral choices was typically excused as well. A particular exception was made for adults whose illness was caused by hard work or other heroic efforts related to taking care of oneself or others. Stigmatized groups such as unwed mothers, people with alcohol dependency, and people with mental health disorders were never featured in these campaigns.[14] Similarly, in Europe, a continuum of perceived deservingness has typically existed based on the blameworthiness of the individual for their need, with older, sick, and disabled people seen as least blameworthy, unemployed people more blameworthy, and immigrants least deserving of all.[15]

As these examples show, a common factor that explains the distinction between who is and is not morally worthy of receiving help is perceived personal responsibility for one's need. Factors such as disability, illness, the inability to work due to youth or old age, loss of the primary earner in a family, and other factors make one's need beyond one's control and therefore the affected people blameless. Being perceived as able to work but choosing not to in favor of asking for help is seen as more clearly a choice. People seen as making this choice are therefore not deserving of help. Importantly, though, notions of personal responsibility for need extend to past choices as well. For instance, a history of substance use leading to the inability to work or failure to save funds for one's old age could both be viewed as causing one's own need and mark that person as being undeserving of aid. The language around giving also illustrates how perceived responsibility for need is used to assign deservingness. Language such as "through no fault of their own" and "circumstances beyond their control" is frequently used.[16]

As communities, economies, social systems, and understandings of human psychology change over time, what counts as responsible conduct changes as well. Over the course of the twentieth century, newspaper accounts in the United States of people in need adapted to the expansion of social supports by emphasizing people who fell through the cracks in these support systems or had some help from pensions and savings but not enough to get by. When the costs of medical treatment soar and social supports and private insurance are unable to keep up, these appeals focus on the inability of even hardworking people to make ends meet. During times of economic downturn, support is encouraged for people who wish to work but cannot find sufficient employment no matter how hard they try. These appeals also shifted from holding whole families accountable for the behavior and morality of their members to a more individualized approach, where an individual in need can be a worthy target of giving even if other family members are not. Over time these accounts began to note a distinction between thought and deed, recognizing worthiness in those with good intentions even if they did not act on them. Thus, a person in deep depression or psychological distress could be a worthy recipient of help if they *wanted* to be worthy through being a good parent or being employed; this was true even if they found it difficult or impossible to act on these good intentions. In these cases, giving was seen as a way of allowing the recipient to get into a position where they could be better able to act on these intentions. But even with these shifts in how worthiness was perceived, these newspaper accounts continued to identify some people as undeserving of help, particularly where their actions and intentions were both viewed as unworthy.[17]

Perceived moral worthiness for receiving aid can also be tied to the recipient's attitude and actions in the face of poverty. Individuals are often picked out for praise as appearing to be brave while experiencing hardships. Rather than simply accepting their situation, particularly worthy people continue to work even though their wages don't meet their needs or to seek work during unemployment, refusing to accept their situation passively.[18] People who are morally worthy of giving are also often seen as selfless, asking for aid not for themselves but only on behalf of others.[19] Thus, parents, primary income earners, and people providing for elderly parents or others in need can be seen as highly deserving of society's help. Attitudes around which people are worthy of help often demonstrate gendered ideals as well. Women and girls are praised for fighting to keep their household intact and caring for their family members as well as they can. Men and boys are commended for continuing to seek work and contributing financially to their families to the best of their ability.[20]

Other characteristics that have been associated with being morally worthy of aid are a sense of shame at having to ask for help. In early modern Europe, the poor were often seen as particularly deserving of support if they did not advertise their need, seeing it as dishonorable to do so. Associating the need for help with shame also helps to ensure that those people seeking aid truly need it, raising the cost of aid such that those who are able to work or find other means of support would do so.[21]

In practice, standards of who is worthy of help often include concerns about both the impacts of giving and the moral worthiness of the recipient. To take one example, the Charity Organisation Society (COS), a late-Victorian philanthropic organization, aimed to combat what it saw as the tendency of unorganized and unfocused direct giving that created a cycle of dependency on aid. By applying what were seen as scientific principles to giving, those seeking to help others could ensure that their giving was as effective as possible and would not have the perverse side effects of encouraging begging and discouraging work. When the COS gave direct aid, they reviewed applicants to divide them into deserving and undeserving groups. Reasons an applicant might be considered undeserving of aid included withholding information about present and past residences or having a primary earner within a family spend money on alcohol or have a prison record. But whereas distinctions were often made between those whose needs were caused by what were seen as personal choices and those who had no control over their needs, the COS went further in tying deservingness to the likely long-term impacts of giving. Thus, giving to those who had a temporary need and could then be brought back to work and independence was justified, whereas giving to those with little or no prospect of independence was less so.[22] The COS also used the perceived long-term impacts of giving to govern its aid to children, in some cases refusing to care for children where there were multiple offspring born outside of marriage. The rationale in these cases was that this behavior was immoral and a matter of choice, and supporting children born from such circumstances would only encourage more pregnancies by unwed mothers.[23]

There is good reason to criticize both tying deservingness to the efficacy of the gift and connecting it to the moral character of recipients. Restricting giving based on doing the most good can be defended, particularly where the resources of an individual or philanthropic organization are limited and they seek to make these resources as impactful as possible. But, even in these cases, there is reason for concern around the large-scale impacts of focusing exclusively on the efficacy of giving, particularly if doing so creates or widens inequities. This can happen if some groups require greater resources for marginally smaller gains than others—for example, if some medical needs are harder to treat than others or those facing mental health needs require greater support finding housing than those who do not have these needs. Inequities in who is easiest to help will be particularly concerning from the standpoint of justice if the ease of helping some groups is based on existing social structures that reflect racist or other discriminatory practices—for example, if racist norms make it harder for members of specific communities to find employment. Moreover, attitudes about what individuals or groups can most efficiently be helped can be based on insufficient evidence and reflect classist, racist, or other discriminatory norms. This can happen when specific people and groups are considered congenitally lazy and resistant to help, prone to substance use based on ethnicity, or beyond help because of mental illness.

While the practice of directing giving according to its impacts is vulnerable to problematic outcomes, restricting giving to those who are viewed as morally worthy is more intrinsically problematic. Giving only to those who are considered not personally responsible for their needs or who are unable to address their needs runs counter to treating goods like healthcare, education, and housing as entitlements or basic human rights. Moreover, these judgments of who is responsible for their needs frequently rest on factually incorrect understandings of the effects of, for example, mental illness and substance dependence, and the effects of systemic injustices such as racist housing policies. Furthermore, requiring deserving recipients to exhibit proper gratitude at receiving help and shame for being in need reinforces hierarchies and classism within communities and, again, shows too little understanding about the underlying causes of need and how they can reflect systemic injustices. Taken together, distinguishing between the morally worthy and unworthy among people in need often reinforces the attitudes and structures that create many of these needs in the first place.

Worthy advice for crowdfunders

As in other giving practices, crowdfunding campaigners need to consider how to present themselves to the public as deserving of their support. The advice that platforms give to crowdfunders typically includes platitudes that every cause and every person is worthy of support. In some instances, campaigners are advised to appeal to the universal deservingness of people. For example, in a column on how to campaign for debt relief, campaigners are told, "It's important to remember that nearly everyone experiences a time in their life when they have to deal with some kind of financial hardship. Your own experience might serve as a reminder to people that everyone deserves to receive help during tough times."[24] Deservingness can be tied to universal human rights or the universal requirements of justice as well. For example, people crowdfunding for gender-affirming surgery are reminded of the increase in anti-trans legislation and told "You deserve to receive medical care, especially gender-affirming surgeries. . . . [I]t's important to remember that there's no right or wrong way to receive this money. This is a medically necessary procedure that will make you feel more at home inside your body, and you're not any less worthy of it because of laws or health insurance coverage."[25]

At the same time, these guides tell campaigners that potential donors may not be motivated to support their campaigns and that there are steps campaigners can take to encourage donations. Thus, demonstrating and proving worthiness is crucial to succeeding in crowdfunding. GoFundMe is explicit about this in its guide to creating viral crowdfunding campaigns when it tells campaigners that "People will only share your post if they deem it worthy" before giving advice on how to capture the public's interest and engage with them emotionally.[26] Similarly, Australian crowdfunding platform Mycause tells campaigners that they should tell a compelling story to potential donors, including "Who is the beneficiary and why do they deserve the donations?"[27]

When the aim of the campaign is to go viral—that is, to receive wide support outside of one's immediate network of close friends and family—campaigners are told that media coverage of the campaign is essential. To achieve this coverage and expand the range of potential donors, campaigners must demonstrate to journalists that theirs is a story worth reporting. Campaigners are advised that "Stories that appeal to a local audience" are more likely to be picked up by local media. As part of establishing appeal to one's local community, campaigners are told that they should emphasize "What clubs, churches, synagogues, or local nonprofits are you or the beneficiary connected with" because "People like to donate to someone with a history of giving to the community." In a press release to local media, campaigners can also establish their worthiness for media coverage and donations by showing "that you're working hard to overcome obstacles—you just need a little help."[28]

GoFundMe acknowledges that asking for help can be difficult and cause embarrassment or shame for campaigners. While these feelings are sometimes dismissed as inappropriate, more generally they are seen as normal and natural—and even a way to prove one's worthiness of receiving help. These feelings can be addressed through the campaign in part by establishing that asking for help is a last resort, appropriate only after the campaigner has tried to help themselves without support or through any other means. For example, "If your fundraiser is to help with a difficult situation, explain how you've tried to overcome it yourself. Donors may feel more charitable if it seems like you've exhausted all other options."[29] In this way, deservingness is linked to individual effort and limited to those who are not at fault for their need.

Campaigners are also told to demonstrate their worthiness for receiving help from the general public by establishing that the donation will have a large, positive impact on their lives. In this regard, campaigners are told that having a plan for achieving self-sufficiency is key to gaining trust with potential donors and establishing worthiness to receive help. For example, in a column on how to ask for donations, GoFundMe suggests that campaigners should "lay out your plan to get back on track in as much detail as possible." Campaigners can also ask for financial counseling instead of or in addition to monetary donations so that "your network of friends and family members will see you're serious about taking charge of your future."[30]

Worthiness can also be expressed by telling stories about the campaign recipient. These stories can speak to the recipient's character or what they've done in the past to contribute to their community or to help others in need. This means of demonstrating worthiness for receiving donations is not strictly limited to those who are still able to contribute to their community. In some cases, past community contributions are highlighted so that the campaign becomes explicitly about paying back the good that the recipient has done in their life. For example, when crowdfunding for funeral expenses, campaigners are told to highlight how the deceased "made an impact, and share their goals, interests, or accomplishments."[31]

Special classes of people can be seen as especially deserving of help, something that can be highlighted in crowdfunding appeals. These groups include pregnant people who are crowdfunding for financial support and who are told by crowdfunding platforms that "You deserve to enjoy every moment of this important life event without worrying about impending medical bills or unpaid maternity leave."[32] The international fundraising platform GoGetFunding gives the example of a woman seeking safe housing after decades of domestic abuse in Brazil, asking that supporters help her "find the life which she truly deserves."[33] Similarly, the Indian crowdfunding platform ImpactGuru discusses the supports needed for children with autism and declares that "These children deserve all the medical support that they can possibly get" while children with cancer "deserve to have long, healthy lives."[34,35] More generally, perceived helplessness or vulnerability is also seen as a factor that will encourage giving by potential donors. Thus, campaigners are encouraged to be "vulnerable" through their storytelling, including sharing "the emotions associated with it, like fear or uncertainty."[36]

Even when the goal of a campaign is not to go viral or when the campaigner is focusing first on donations from friends or family who are familiar with the recipient, the recipient's worthiness for help comes into play. Campaigners are told that they deserve support from close friends and family and, for this reason, told to focus on these groups in their initial requests for help. GoFundMe notes that this focus can be personally affirming, demonstrating that "you or someone you love deserves support."[37] Personal connections with potential donors also can help establish that the recipient's need is genuine and deserves to be supported. Thus, GoFundMe suggests meeting in person in cases where there are "some friends or family members who have questions about your financial need."[38]

Whether the campaigner targets close friends and family or complete strangers, showing gratitude to donors is a consistent piece of advice given to fundraisers. Showing gratitude is polite and appropriate in the face of generosity from others, of course, but it also serves as a way to establish the character and deservingness of the recipient. GoFundMe suggests that when providing updates on campaigns, it is "critical to be grateful," which can help ensure that donors "feel valued" and encourage future giving.[39] GoFundMe suggests that crowdfunders write thank-you letters to donors not simply in recognition of their support but also out of self-interest, noting that 85% of donors have indicated that they would donate again if they received a personal thank-you letter. The importance of these letters is that they offer a way for campaigners to develop deeper relationships with donors and encourage giving by demonstrating the recipient's appropriate thankfulness for gifts.[40]

Demonstrating worthiness in practice

The advice given to crowdfunding campaigners on demonstrating worthiness to potential donors can be divided into four groups: (1) showing the potential good that can be done for the campaign recipient; (2) paying back the recipient for the good that they've done for others; (3) claiming membership in an especially worthy, innocent, or vulnerable group; and (4) affirming connections between the recipient and donor. In research on how crowdfunders appeal for donations in practice, these categories are well represented. Campaigners frequently point to the depth of the recipient's need and the great good that can be done by donating. Campaigners note the personal worthiness of the recipient, focusing on attributes such as how they are hard-working members of a family and what great good could be done for them personally and those around them by supporting their medical care.[41] For example, it is common to see campaigns for medical treatment with variations on the theme that treatment could be "life changing" or that it would "make a huge difference" in the recipient's life. This category of justification often includes children and young adults who are said to deserve special consideration because they should have many more years to live.[42] Campaigns that can point to needs with concrete and attainable solutions have the advantage of demonstrating to potential donors that their contribution will do great good for the recipient.[43] Showing this kind of tangible benefit can be seen, for example, in a campaign for a person with a criminal past who "deserves a fresh start" and needs help paying for housing to stay on probation while starting a new job.

Campaigners also frequently make the case that the recipient had done good for others in the past and so now it's time to "give back" to them by supporting their needs. These justifications can take the form of noting that the recipient has earned help because of their past good works or that they were the kind of person that would similarly help the prospective donor if the donor were in need.[44] In one characteristic campaign, a couple struggling with injury and hospitalization from COVID-19 are described as having "done so much for others who were in need and now they need help." The reliability and steadfastness of recipients who now need help is a common theme, as with a campaigner who is "a great friend to all of us and is always there when we need him." These campaigns often describe reciprocal obligations based on the good that they had done for their community, including descriptors of the recipients as being loyal, hard-working, and respectful.[45] In this vein, the children and grandchildren of those in need frequently point out what the recipient has done for them as a motivation for leading their crowdfunding campaigns.

In some instances, language is used to show that the recipient is not at fault for their need or is otherwise a member of what is perceived to be a particularly vulnerable, helpless, or otherwise innocent group. Young children receive particular attention in this regard, often described in terms of being brave, fighters, strong, or otherwise battling against their medical condition.[46] This approach can be seen in one campaign where a family on a religious mission in Uganda "found an energetic and fiercely happy three-year-old boy who needed a good home. So they embarked on what anyone would call a near 'Mission Impossible' to give him a chance at a good life." As with historical practices of distinguishing between the able-bodied poor and those unable to work, these campaigns regularly flag when a medical condition makes them unable to work and in need of help: "I've been without work and I'm just needing some help paying bills till I get back on my feet." Traditional gender norms in giving around the perceived helplessness of women and mothers appear as well, as with a mother and son now "left

alone" after the death of their spouse and father who "was their only emotional and financial support" while the mother "was home taking care of
their son and dealing with her own health issues."

Finally, campaigners demonstrate a relationship with the donor to show
that they should receive help. Campaigners frequently point to personal
connections with potential donors as justifying giving—for example, a duty
based on family connections or the love associated with close friendship.
Crucially, these campaigns are generally not trying to appeal to strangers
and people who did not already feel a connection to the recipient and thus
were not expecting viral success with their campaigns.[47] Similarly, a study
of crowdfunding campaigns for medical care on the Chinese crowdfunding
platform Tencent Gong Yi found that these campaigns emphasized family
bonds in their appeals.[48] These campaigns could include descriptions of why
the campaigner was helping the recipient but also how the recipient was a
loving family member who deserved support from their friends and family.
One representative campaign describes the recipient as "a mother, a sister, a
friend, a wife, an auntie and a daughter that is loved by all." Other common
themes in these campaigns include descriptions of the recipient's personal
character and overall worthiness, as well as the suffering of the recipient
and their family and how donations would help them. Relationships with
the recipient's wider community can be used to establish deservingness as
well. Some campaigns seek to position the recipient as a valued member of a
community from whom potential donors were approached. This community
could be immediate friends and family or a wider community, as in the case
of a well-known business owner in need of help.[49]

Conclusion

People in need have historically been categorized as deserving or undeserving of support by private individuals and philanthropic organizations.
This is still true today and often implicit or explicit in the advice given to
online crowdfunding campaigners and seen in the ways campaigners pitch
themselves to potential donors. In the context of crowdfunding, some people
are treated as more or less worthy of receiving aid based on the impact of
giving, including establishing that their need is episodic rather than part of
ongoing dependency. In other cases, people who are unable to earn a living
for themselves despite a desire to do so are seen as not responsible for being

in a position of need and therefore worthy of support. By this same logic, groups including women and children are often presented as helpless or especially vulnerable and deserving.

Campaigners with existing relationships with potential donors have an advantage in establishing their worthiness. This advantage exists not just through connections with close friends and family members but also with members of ethnic, religious, and civic communities. Deserving recipients are required to have a proper attitude toward receiving help, expressing it not as something they are entitled to but something they should be grateful to receive and somewhat ashamed to have to ask for. In this sense, the most deserving crowdfunding recipients, as with the most deserving recipients of direct and indirect giving more generally, are people who are familiar to donors and who have positioned themselves as social contributors who have now fallen on hard times or grateful people who are helpless through no fault of their own.

By mirroring past and existing practices of establishing deservingness for help, online crowdfunding is owed the same criticisms of these practices. These include concerns with the individualization of need, associating need with personal failings rather than systemic failures, and treating access to basic needs as optional rather than an entitlement or human right.[50] The individualization of need tends to stigmatize poverty and make it more socially acceptable to subject those in need to surveillance and loss of privacy (as discussed in the previous chapter). Moreover, tying giving to perceived deservingness tends to skew who gets help, often reproducing existing social inequities. As I discuss in more detail in the next two chapters, notions of deservingness are often tied to racial, ethnic, gender, and other social injustices; mask the systemic causes of unequal access to opportunities and income; and privilege people with strong local social ties over immigrants and outsiders.[51] People with the resources and skills to follow the advice and cues about how to tell a story about their deservingness for receiving help, especially from strangers, are therefore greatly advantaged over people who struggle to do so.

Tropes of deservingness and worthiness for receiving help in online crowdfunding shouldn't just be seen as a continuation of past practices and their harms. The public and networked aspects of crowdfunding have the potential to heighten the problems with these tropes in two ways. First, the online and highly visible nature of crowdfunding means that the harms of having to prove one's worth—whether in terms of undermining privacy, expressions of shame and embarrassment, and stigma associated with the nature of one's needs—are increased. This performance of worthiness is, by design, on public display and targeted particularly toward one's community, friends, and family—the people whose judgment of one's need will be most keenly felt.

Second, appealing to the crowd rather than to a few philanthropic organizations or local donors for help makes it harder to eliminate the practice of donation according to perceived worthiness. There is reason to think that professional philanthropies and perhaps more careful and regular individual donors are or can be made cognizant of the harms of forcing performances of deservingness. There is much less reason to think this is possible in online crowdfunding given the larger number of people involved and their potentially more tenuous connection to campaigners. Moreover, the pressure on campaigners to break through the crowd of other crowdfunders and tell a moving, viral story of deservingness is much more likely to reinforce these harmful practices. There have always been significant costs to making public appeals for help, but the public performances required for successful online crowdfunding will often amplify and entrench these costs.

4

Who gets funded?

I know I am not the only person struggling right now and that a lot of my circle are also artists hit by the pandemic. Anything you can give would be a great help, or even simply sharing the link with others (maybe you have some rich friends or a sugar daddy!) Thank you so much for reading and I hope the world gets better for all of us soon.

When a visitor arrives at GoFundMe's landing page, they're greeted with a selection of "Top fundraisers" based in part on the visitor's location. In my case, one morning in Burnaby, British Columbia, I'm shown three seemingly very successful campaigns from across Canada. One of these campaigns has raised 25% of its $200,000 goal in just five days, whereas another has exceeded its $30,000 goal in less than twenty-four hours. The campaigns selected for me are all intended to benefit people in desperate need of help. In the first campaign, the fundraisers are seeking help to pay for an air ambulance for their severely ill newborn son. Time is of the essence to relocate him to their home in Vancouver. In the second campaign, the family of a nurse killed in a tragic automobile accident seeks help to set up a trust fund for the nurse's three children. Reading these campaigns, their emotional updates, and the cheerful, encouraging comments by their many donors, I can't help being happy that these campaigners are getting at least some of the financial help that they seek, even if this funding won't address all of their problems.

At the same time, it isn't hard to find crowdfunding campaigns with similarly large and time-sensitive needs that are not as successful. Far away from GoFundMe's landing page and its list of top fundraisers, you will see a woman seeking help for transportation and medication for her husband who is ill with lung cancer and has "1 year to live." She received $250 of her $5,000 request in the first days of the campaign, but in the month since has received no donations and posted no updates. Another campaign seeks to help a single mother with a chronic illness who is facing eviction in the next

Appealing to the Crowd. Jeremy Snyder, Oxford University Press. © Oxford University Press 2024.
DOI: 10.1093/oso/9780197658130.003.0005

five days, along with her four children and a grandchild. The campaign organizer describes how her sister had been taken advantage of by her landlord and denied relief by the courts. This campaign received only $105 of its $8,000 goal. A month after being evicted, the campaigner states that her sister and her children are living with family members while they work to put together a deposit on a rental.

These stories, and many others like them, show that crowdfunding to pay for basic needs does not work for everyone. We often hear gratifying stories of communities coming together to help out people who are ill, in danger of becoming unhoused, or otherwise in desperate need. Crowdfunding platforms forefront these stories, and the news media are happy to share them. Not everyone gets to participate in this success, and that's not surprising. Giving to others is a means of relieving suffering, but individual giving does not carry a guarantee that everyone's needs will be addressed.

These differences in crowdfunding success are particularly ethically concerning in terms of who wins or loses and how the proceeds of crowdfunding are distributed. If we imagine that crowdfunding helps those most in need, makes the most efficient use of donations, or even acts as a random lottery for those in need, then we could defend this form of giving to others as at least not replicating injustices in terms of who does and does not get their basic needs met. However, if crowdfunding perpetuates or even worsens existing injustices in terms of who is able to have their basic needs met, this is more clearly morally problematic. Therefore, patterns of who is helped most and least by crowdfunding are important to identify, understand and, potentially, counteract.

Who benefits from giving?

Inequalities and injustices in terms of who benefits from giving are nothing new. In many cases, the outcomes of giving do not reflect values like equality in how people are treated, equality in the outcomes of giving, treating access to basic goods as an entitlement, and prioritizing those most in need irrespective of the cause of that need. To put this another way, giving practices often do not align with the requirements of distributive justice. I won't attempt to provide an account of distributive justice here, but the most plausible accounts of justice are driven by aims including prioritizing the needs of the worst-off members of a community, trying to help as many people as possible have their basic needs met, ensuring that resources used to help those lacking basic goods are used as efficiently as possible, and rectifying past injustices experienced by individuals and groups. Various plausible accounts of distributive justice have many serious disagreements and will endorse very different public policies and individual actions. That said, they do speak in favor of focusing on the absolute needs of individuals, using resources efficiently, and considering past experiences of injustice when determining whom individuals, organizations, and governments should support.

In practice, patterns of giving often favor people seen as most deserving of help. As discussed in the previous chapter, perceptions of deservingness are often tied to whether those in need are responsible for their need (e.g., through risky behavior) or are able to address their need themselves (e.g., through obtaining employment). Perceptions of deservingness may also depend on the recipient's membership in a group that is perceived to be vulnerable or innocent (e.g., children) and membership in one's own community (e.g., native born). In principle, some of these notions of deservingness can be ethically defensible. If, for example, a donor hopes to achieve the greatest positive impact through their giving, they may reasonably be concerned that some recipients will not be greatly aided by their gift or become trapped in a cycle of dependency. In such cases, favoring people actively seeking work or who are in treatment for substance use could have an ethical basis. However, in practice, many of these categories of deservingness are socially constructed based on an implication that different people have different moral worth and, as a result, are differentially entitled to having their basic needs met. These categories often reflect the assumptions and biases of their communities, including racism, problematic gender norms, and anti-immigrant attitudes. As a result, tying giving practices to perceptions of deservingness frequently creates new and worsens existing social inequities in who is able to have their basic needs met.

In aggregate, contemporary giving patterns do not tend to reflect the likely goals of distributive justice. In 2020, religious institutions were the largest recipient of indirect giving in the United States, totaling $131 billion and 28% of all giving. Giving to education was the next highest category, totaling $71 billion and 15% of all indirect support. Giving to arts and culture made up $19 billion or 4%, and support for the environment and animals totaled $16 billion or 3%.[1] Although religious institutions do engage in their own direct giving to those in need, much of the money donated to them is reserved for facilities maintenance, operating costs, and salaries. Similarly, giving to support education is often aimed at post-secondary institutions and schools with a connection to the donor rather than organizations emphasizing basic educational attainments among the people who most need them.[2] In India, giving is dominated by contributions to religious institutions.[3] Giving in the United Kingdom directs large amounts of support to animal welfare (26%) and medical research (25%).[4] And in Japan, individual giving often goes to religious groups (34.5%).[5] These all may be worthy causes to support in their own ways, but it is clear that giving in many places across the world is not aimed primarily at supporting the public's basic needs, including adequate nutrition, housing, and other social supports.

A variety of factors drive giving behavior in directions that are inconsistent with the goals of distributive justice and that decrease the positive impacts of donors' gifts. These include donors' tendency to spread smaller donations among a larger number of recipients to increase the positive feedback or "warm glow" received from making a donation and an aversion to risk that leads them to give to more conventional and less impactful initiatives. Donors are also reluctant to invest resources into gaining better information about the impacts of their donations, thus further undermining their ability to ensure the best outcomes of their gifts.[6]

For individual donors, personal identity matters greatly in determining which people and organizations they support. For example, they might support religious organizations matching their own religious beliefs; fund groups tied to the needs of their own family and friends, as when contributing to research on a specific form of cancer; or give to people and groups with similar personal experiences, such as immigrant support networks or groups to which they have ethnic ties. Moreover, donors often feel a duty of reciprocity to support organizations and causes that they have benefited from in the past.[7] Thus, one mechanism for explaining why giving by philanthropic institutions may privilege the needs and interests of older white men is that people from this demographic disproportionately make up the boards of nonprofit organizations and especially the longest-established and highest-revenue philanthropic groups.[8]

The gender of the donor can matter to who receives aid as well. For example, a study of donors found that women donate 63% more than men to fundraisers that involve children in need.[9] Women, and especially wealthy women, are also more likely than men to give to causes benefiting women and girls.[10] Among people giving large gifts of more than $1 million, women tend to give more than men to the arts, education, environmental causes, and health-related needs. Men, on the other hand, favor higher education and international causes.[11] Willer et al. ascribe gender differences in giving to a male tendency to favor giving where there is the potential for promoting their self-interest; thus, men may be more drawn to community-based giving where the impact of the gift is more visible to peers.[12] Women, on the other hand, are motivated by their children's futures, as when they give to environmental causes. These gender differences may be linked to empathy levels, with men exhibiting lower empathy than women and donating less in general to charitable causes. These differences in the targets of giving matter in part because women have been found to give more often and larger amounts than men overall.[13]

Importantly, some forms of bias in giving are more obviously pernicious than others. For example, a study of direct giving by Americans found that donors tended to view members of their own race as being more worthy of receiving aid than members of other races.[14] In a study of giving by all-white Christian church members, direct giving by these congregations decreased as the share of black residents in their communities increased.[15] Thus, racial bias and a preference toward members of one's own race, even if subconscious, can shape giving practices. Not surprisingly, support for philanthropic groups has been found to mirror systemic racism and other forms of bias in these organizations' communities as well. Philanthropies supporting racialized minorities and historically marginalized groups regularly face greater barriers to receiving support than other philanthropies. While these gaps may represent overt racism and other forms of bias in some instances, the causes of these inequities are often more subtle. They can include inequitable access to the social networks through which funding decisions are made, implicit biases that undermine relationship building, and grant application assessment approaches that disadvantage some communities.[16]

As race-based preferences in giving show, identity matters in giving. In this regard, philanthropies often engage in homophily—giving to groups and needs with similar characteristics to the philanthropic organization. This process includes directing giving through interpersonal networks that tend to favor groups and individuals with personal connections with the granting institution. In the international philanthropic sector, homophily can include favoring groups with organizational structures similar to those of philanthropies in high-income countries and organizations that employ highly educated local elites.[17] Focusing donations on meeting the needs of people in the lowest-income settings would arguably make the biggest impact, but, in practice, when giving by the wealthiest philanthropies is focused on the needs of low-income countries, spending is often directed at research that takes place in high-income countries and elite institutions within low-income countries.[18]

Philanthropies often also focus their attention and giving on the communities where they are based—for example, corporate philanthropies tend to give most in the communities where the corporation's headquarters are located.[19] Given that corporate headquarters are often clustered in urban and financial centers, this geographic bias in giving means that some areas are advantaged over others in terms of philanthropic support, and rural areas may be particularly disadvantaged.[20] In the United States, the assets of philanthropic foundations are highly focused in the Northeast and on the West Coast, meaning that people in these areas are more likely to receive attention from these foundations than those living in other regions.[21] One outcome of this clustering is that health-related giving by corporations during the COVID-19 pandemic tended to focus on areas with lower overall health-related needs in terms of access to care and insurance coverage.[22]

Homophily also disadvantages grassroots and more innovative recipients in favor of groups with more institutional connections and conventional outlooks.[23] For this reason, giving tends to be focused on institutions and individuals that follow professional norms similar to those of the philanthropic organization. In the context of corporate philanthropy, for example, groups lacking access to professional grant writers or overall capability to adhere to professional norms—factors that typically coincide with greater need—will be disadvantaged in receiving aid.[24] In effect, these homophilic grouping behaviors ensure that giving will not follow any plausible just distribution of help. Rather, giving can run counter to the goals of distributive justice if relatively privileged donors replicate their privilege when choosing which individuals and groups to support.

Who benefits from crowdfunding?

It's easy to imagine that giving via crowdfunding could address at least some of these tendencies toward inequality and distributive injustice within traditional giving practices. Of course, crowdfunding does not magically transform donors into unbiased justice seekers, unswayed by racism, parochialism, and suspect norms of deservingness. However, there is a potentially democratizing force in crowdfunding whereby decisions about who receives help are made by individuals and based on personal appeals rather than by large philanthropies that reflect the interests and attitudes of disproportionately white and male boards located in the wealthiest communities in the world. Moreover, whereas traditional giving by individuals is largely limited to their immediate community due to the geographic constraints of direct giving practices, the online nature of crowdfunding exposes donors to a larger community of need. Through crowdfunding, the donor is not limited to their immediate family and community, which may look very much like themselves in terms of socioeconomic status, race, ethnicity, and religion. Instead, there is more potential to give to any crowdfunding campaigner who can make the case that they are most in need of the donor's help. Thus, crowdfunding contains the potential to act as a form of less hierarchical form of mutual aid where funding decisions are driven by recipients and less-wealthy donors rather than the richest and most influential members of society.

Crowdfunding platforms do not typically hype themselves as vehicles specifically for rectifying social inequities. However, they do frequently describe themselves as helping to address basic needs, including the needs of the most disadvantaged in society. GoFundMe's leadership describes the platform as "a powerful engine for funding needs and dreams globally" and maintains that "While there is a lot of work to be done to tackle the world's socioeconomic disparities, we have started to address the inequalities we see in our own community."[25] Indian medical crowdfunding platform Milaap states that crowdfunding allows the public to address needs "more efficiently" and that increased "digital access" allows Indians to "mobilize greater support for urgent needs on time."[26] For the UK platform JustGiving, the claim to promote equity is built into the double meaning of its name.

In practice, however, crowdfunding does tend to replicate many of the inequities already found in the communities where these campaigns take place. There are wide differences in how well campaigns perform in terms of meeting their fundraising goals. While some crowdfunding campaigns meet or even greatly exceed their goals, this is the exception rather than the rule. In a survey of US-based medical crowdfunding campaigns, only 9.2% of campaigns met their fundraising goal; the mean amount raised was 41.75% of the goal—that is, substantially less than half of the amount sought.[27] A random selection of 200 medical campaigns on GoFundMe found that 90% of campaigns did not meet their stated goal and averaged just 40% of their targets, and 3.5% of these campaigns raised no money at all. These campaigns showed enormous variability in their success, raising from $0 to $20,000 from a mean of 36 donors to a high of 247 donors.[28] Similarly, within a selection of 100 medical crowdfunding campaigns on a Chinese crowdfunding platform, only 9% of campaigns met their stated fundraising goal. These campaigns performed similarly to the US examples, as they raised only 18% of their goals overall.[29] A review of 400 medical crowdfunding campaigns initiated by people in the United Kingdom on GoFundMe had higher success rates, with one-third reaching their fundraising goal.[30] Campaigns for COVID-19–related needs by US campaigners on GoFundMe performed particularly poorly. During the first half of 2020, an analysis of more than 164,000 of these campaigns showed that they raised a median of $65 out of $5,000 requested from two donors; 43.2% of these campaigns received no donations, and 90% did not reach their fundraising goal.[31] Despite these variations in success rates among studies of donation-based crowdfunding campaigns, it is clear that only a small subset of campaigns seeking help to meet essential needs are able to do so via crowdfunding. This observation raises the question of which campaigns fare better than others and why.

One factor influencing campaign success is the type of need being addressed through crowdfunding. Campaigns to support people who need organ transplants face significant challenges, given the high costs associated with these procedures and their aftercare. In one study, these campaigns fared very poorly, with 30.9% receiving no donations. The type of organ transplant in this study led to different success rates: heart and lung campaigns that received donations raised a mean of $5,985 and $5,189, respectively, compared with a mean of $3,501 for liver transplants.[32] Among Canadians seeking help related to organ transplantation, kidney transplantation campaigns received a mere 11.5% of their requested total, compared with 49.1% for liver transplantation campaigns.[33] Cancer-related crowdfunding campaigns are the most common type of medical crowdfunding campaign and show considerable variation as well. A study of 1,035 cancer-related campaigns on the GoFundMe platform detailed a median fundraising goal of $10,000 compared with a median raised of $2,125.[34] Among campaigners seeking help with medical expenses related to kidney cancer, the median fundraising goal was $10,000, but the median amount raised was only $1,450.[35] Another study of crowdfunding campaigns on GoFundMe seeking complementary and alternative cancer treatments found that these campaigners received nearly one-third of their requested amount.[36]

How needs are valued in a community may influence fundraising success. In a study on Canadians seeking help accessing addiction treatment services, only 1.6% of the amount requested had been pledged at the time of data collection.[37] Although it is hard to say with certainty in this case, the stigmatized nature of addiction may have contributed to the very low overall success of these campaigns. Similarly, campaigns discussing abortion on GoFundMe show considerable differences in their success rates. One study found that campaigns requesting support for a child the recipient birthed after considering abortion but choosing not to abort raised over twenty times as much money than campaigns seeking help to end a pregnancy. In this latter group, 75% of the campaigns received no donations at all.[38] A separate study of US-based campaigns for abortion services found similarly poor outcomes for these fundraisers. In this study, campaigns for abortion access had a median request of $610 but raised a median of $0.[39] By contrast, a study of 410 campaigns for medical care for transgender people demonstrated that these campaigners received on average 24% of the requested amount.[40] This success rate is more in line with averages for health-related campaigns despite the frequently stigmatized nature of care for transgender people.

Not surprisingly, given its influence on giving more generally, the race of the recipient also has an impact on crowdfunding success. A study of medical crowdfunding campaigns by US-based campaigners on the platform GiveForward between 2008 and 2012 showed that areas with a larger proportion of Asian and Native American or Hawaiian residents were less successful in fundraising than areas with a higher proportion of white residents.[41] In an analysis of US-based medical crowdfunding campaigns, being black was associated with receiving $22 less per donation, and people of color received fewer donations than white people.[42] Among Canadians crowdfunding for support for healthcare access and payments for education, racialized people are less likely to use crowdfunding than white Canadians, and they receive less financial support through crowdfunding than white Canadians.[43] In US medical crowdfunding campaigns, white people are greatly overrepresented as campaign recipients, making up 77.7% of the total compared with 8% black and 10% non-black people of color. This disparity means that insofar as crowdfunding is a means of addressing basic needs, it is white people—in the United States, at least—who disproportionately use this fundraising practice. During the COVID-19 pandemic, US-based campaigners seeking help had varied success based on the racial makeup of their home communities.[44] Campaigners residing in counties with proportionally higher populations of black residents received fewer donations than other counties. Rather than being a direct effect of racism or other forms of bias in giving, this differential giving may reflect racism indirectly insofar as the social networks of racialized minorities have fewer financial resources to support giving.[45] One exception to the trend of nonwhite crowdfunders having lower success rates was a study of medical crowdfunding campaigns for treatment for transgender people. This study found that people of color and white recipients raised similar percentages of their fundraising goals, and people of color raised slightly more overall per crowdfunding campaign.[46]

As with giving more generally, the gender of the recipient has an impact in crowdfunding success. There is evidence that women face some disadvantages compared with men in medical crowdfunding campaigns, with US-based women recipients receiving slightly fewer donations than men.[47] Among transgender people seeking medical care, recipients assigned male and female at birth received similar average campaign amounts, but campaigners assigned female at birth received 28% of their goal, compared with 16% for campaigners assigned male at birth.[48] There are significant inequities around who uses and takes on the labor of crowdfunding as well. Men and women in medical crowdfunding campaigns make up a similar proportion of recipients. However, women are greatly overrepresented among campaign organizers, including 80% of those campaigning on behalf of others in one study.[49] This suggests that the labor, including caregiving and emotional work, of running crowdfunding campaigns falls largely on the shoulders of women.

The age of the recipient impacts crowdfunding success as well. A study of US-based medical crowdfunding campaigns found that children receive substantially more funding overall than adults.[50] In crowdfunding campaigns by Canadians for their medical and educational needs, younger recipients were considerably more successful than older recipients in meeting their fundraising goals.[51] Similarly, crowdfunding campaigns related to organ transplantation were more successful for pediatric patients. Among these campaigns receiving donations, pediatric recipients received mean pledges of $5,161, compared with a mean of $3,479 for adults.[52] Similarly, among Canadians seeking funding for organ transplantation needs, adult campaigns for liver transplantation received 42.2% of their requests, compared with 60% for children. In this same study, kidney transplantation campaigns for adults received 10.6% of their requests, compared with 37.1% for children.[53]

Because crowdfunding relies on the ability to develop a compelling campaign narrative, the campaigner's education and ability to express themselves influence success. Medical crowdfunding campaigns in the United States have been found to be more successful in areas with proportionally higher levels of post-secondary education.[54] Similarly, campaigners seeking help with cancer-related expenses in Canada are disproportionately located in areas with above-average levels of post-secondary education.[55] In the United States, a study of crowdfunding campaigns hosted on GoFundMe found that these campaigns were more successful in counties with relatively more people working in information industries.[56] Crowdfunding campaigners consistently receive advice to write clear and detailed campaign narratives to convey the nature of their need and to explain what will be done with any donations. Educational attainment does not determine one's ability to engage in clear and compelling writing, but lack of training and experience in such writing likely creates barriers for some campaigners.

Crowdfunding relies on the campaigner and recipient's community to raise funding. Not surprisingly, then, the characteristics of those communities influence campaign success. The participation of the campaigner's and recipient's close friends and families is one source of influence, as crowdfunding campaigners do receive significantly more support from people closely related to them. In a study across the GoFundMe platform, donors with the same last name as the campaign recipient gave on average $29.27 more than other donors where the median donation was $50.[57] Medical crowdfunding recipients whose campaigns were organized by their friends and family members receive more donations than campaigners raising money for themselves.[58] In a poll of US crowdfunding donors, nearly a third reported that they had supported the campaigns of friends of a friend or acquaintances.[59] The wealth in these personal networks is likely to impact campaign success just as it provides other advantages to recipients. For example, people who have unstable housing often face steep barriers to succeeding with crowdfunding, as their closest contacts and potential donors lack stable housing themselves, thus making them poorly positioned to help one another financially.[60]

Professional networks also influence crowdfunding success. One crowdfunding campaigner describes reaching out to their professional network of video game industry members using Facebook and other contacts. Many of these contacts were well known and successful members of the industry, and they helped this campaigner raise over $40,000.[61] Similarly, the highest-earning campaigns in the United States during the COVID-19 pandemic included campaigns for employees of an expensive restaurant and out-of-work golf caddies. Other highly successful campaigns during this period were originated by well-known corporate entities or celebrities.[62]

Just as having privileged personal and professional networks favors crowdfunding success, being located in a wealthy community impacts campaign success as well. A study of US-based campaigns on the GoFundMe platform found that crowdfunding campaigns located in relatively wealthy counties are more successful than those in poorer counties, especially when these campaign are shared more widely on social media and gain exposure to relatively wealthy donors.[63] Among crowdfunding campaigns in the United States aiming to address needs related to the COVID-19 pandemic, campaigners in wealthy communities received much more support than fundraisers in lower-income areas. Campaigners in the highest-income quintile accounted for 32.4% of all donations and 38.9% of the total amount raised by these campaigns, compared with only 10% of donations and 8.8% of the total raised in the lowest-income quintile.[64] Crowdfunding campaigns are also more often created in relatively privileged areas. Among US-based campaigns for COVID-19–related needs, campaigns were more common in higher-income population quintiles, with the highest-income quintile accounting for 24.5% of campaigns, compared with 14.6% from the lowest-income quintile. This study also showed that areas with higher levels of postsecondary educational attainment were more likely to create crowdfunding campaigns.[65] In Canadian campaigns for cancer-related needs, these campaigns disproportionately took place in areas with higher incomes and rates of home ownership.[66]

Reaching beyond one's personal, professional, and online social networks can be important for viral success or reaching large fundraising goals. While US crowdfunding donors most commonly contribute to campaigns run by close friends and family, nearly 30% report giving to the campaigns of complete strangers.[67] Not surprisingly, then, in a sample of 200 US-based medical crowdfunding campaigns hosted on GoFundMe, the number of Facebook shares a campaign received was positively correlated with how much money it raised.[68] When trying to reach this wider audience, interviews with medical crowdfunding campaigners show that attracting traditional media coverage makes a huge difference toward getting support from strangers and people outside of the campaigner's social network.[69]

For its part, GoFundMe has increasingly criticized failures of the US government, in particular, to meet its citizens' basic needs and provide an effective social safety net. As a previous CEO of the company framed it, income inequality, coupled with chronic governmental inaction, "is a big driver of why we exist."[70] GoFundMe has acknowledged concerns with potential inequities and other problems in how the winners and losers of crowdfunding are chosen. In response, it has made efforts to promote campaigns targeting underserved needs, racialized minorities, and victims of discrimination through its philanthropic GoFundMe.org arm and its social media efforts. Promoting certain campaigns is itself a factor in crowdfunding success and can partially counter or reinforce inequities. For example, among US-based campaigns for needs stemming from the COVID-19 pandemic, four of the top-five-earning campaigns were initiated by or received support from GoFundMe.[71] Nonetheless, these efforts represent a tiny proportion of crowdfunding campaigns. As GoFundMe has acknowledged in response to criticisms of crowdfunding's inequities, "GoFundMe is an open platform and ultimately it is up to the GoFundMe community to decide which campaigns to donate to."[72] The more democratic nature of individual crowdfunding will only counteract inequities, then, if members of the public are willing to contribute in a more equitable manner. Extensive research on the practice of crowdfunding suggests they are not.

Mechanisms for the inequitable benefits of crowdfunding

The former CEO of GoFundMe, Rob Solomon, has described concerns that crowdfunding entrenches and exacerbates socioeconomic inequities as "hogwash."[73] Yet the evidence is clear that this giving practice at least emulates some of the forms of bias and inequality in traditional forms of giving. What is less clear, with the evidence available, is precisely how different forms of bias impact fundraising success, how the specific context of a fundraiser shapes these impacts, and which of these factors are most important in driving the distribution of crowdfunding donations. That said, the data on crowdfunding campaign success coupled with the larger history of inequality in giving allow some general observations.

First, the design of crowdfunding is in deep tension with the goals of justice. Again, putting aside the details of how we should understand the just and equitable distribution of basic goods, the values of prioritizing the worst-off locally or globally, using resources to raise well-being efficiently, rectifying past injustices, and creating equal opportunities to live a good life are all leading and plausible understandings of the goals of justice regarding the distribution of basic goods. Crowdfunding supports none of these values; instead, it distributes donations based on a mix of personal connections and, most problematically, based on who can make the most engaging appeal for help to the wider public.

In both cases, these distributive mechanisms are likely to maintain or exacerbate unjust outcomes. Donations by friends and family will predictably reaffirm existing inequities between communities. These can be inequities in the socioeconomic status of groups based on their location, race, immigration status, profession, and other factors. In practice, although most people using crowdfunding to appeal for support in meeting their basic needs are in a position of vulnerability and need, there will be large differences in their ability to use social networks to receive help. If their social networks are relatively disadvantaged because of racial discrimination, lack of economic opportunity, religious discrimination, or a myriad of other factors, then their donor network will likely be less able to help them. The wealth of the crowdfunder's social network does not determine how much they can raise through crowdfunding. Some communities may give a larger percentage of their wealth to others in need, and some crowdfunders will be able to mount campaigns that result in higher rates of giving. Nonetheless, insofar as one is receiving donations from existing social networks, the wealth of those networks and capacity for them to share resources creates an unlevel playing field in crowdfunding that will often reflect existing injustices.

Of course, the goal of many crowdfunding campaigns is not simply to receive donations from one's existing social network. Rather, campaigners hope also to broaden that network to include the connections of friends and family and perhaps even complete strangers. In these cases, socially constructed differences in the worthiness of the recipient will factor into how well the campaign performs with the general public, though of course these factors will influence giving from within the recipient's existing social network as well. As research on traditional giving and online crowdfunding has shown, these factors include the recipient's race, gender, and age; the nature of their need; and personal stories that demonstrate their worthiness to receive aid. Rather than distributing aid according to the recipient's need or doing the most good with one's donation, these factors tend to reinforce giving according to perceived worthiness and popularity as well as reinforce existing social biases.

Differences in people's ability to connect with an audience of strangers will also influence crowdfunding success. While living in a community with greater-than-average rates of post-secondary education may support crowdfunding campaigns through higher income, better-educated campaigners might also have an advantage in expressing themselves in their campaigns, absorbing and acting on advice on developing compelling crowdfunding campaigns, posting regular and informative updates, and producing appealing photos, videos, and other media. These less tangible forms of privilege may also extend to success in gaining media exposure through being able to effectively pitch a story to journalists or having connections with journalists and media influencers in one's social circles. And, just as community members are inevitably influenced by the social factors that shape giving, journalists are unlikely to be immune to these factors either.

When certain needs are stigmatized or seen as less worthy of support, these perceptions can greatly reduce one's ability to receive crowdfunding donations from both close connections and the wider community. Thus, crowdfunding campaigns to terminate a pregnancy seem to face significant barriers to success in North America, at least, which may be attributed in part to the common stigma against abortion there. That said, some needs that are stigmatized within one's larger community can still receive significant online support. Crowdfunding campaigns for trans people often fare relatively well despite the stigma they face in most parts of the world. This success may be due to particular factors in campaigns by trans people or strong support within the community of trans people and their allies, even if this support isn't found in the larger community. What this shows is that crowdfunding may not be inherently inequitable; when used by an existing community engaged in mutual aid activities, crowdfunding can be a tool to help coordinate and motivate giving. Crowdfunding did not create the solidarity and political consciousness found within some trans communities but it can facilitate rather than smother these forces.

Insofar as crowdfunding takes the form of a popularity contest, it is a varied and highly context-specific one. A variety of factors shape which campaigns are likely to reach outside of their immediate community and go viral within the larger world. For example, a 2021 crowdfunding campaign on GoFundMe sought support to help search for Gabby Petito, a young woman who was missing. This campaign raised nearly $90,000 in under two weeks before Petito was found dead.[74] The crowdfunding campaign for Petito was likely aided by a number of factors, including that she was a photogenic young white woman; her supporters produced a detailed and sympathetic campaign for her on her fundraising page and other social media platforms; she was a possible victim of violence by her boyfriend; and her case received extensive media coverage. Without denying her family's need for support or begrudging them their success, it's easy to think that these factors meant that her family likely received vastly more attention and support than other missing women, many of whom were racialized minorities, had fewer community supports, and were equally or more in need of help.

To its credit, GoFundMe responded to these concerns by promoting crowdfunding campaigns for missing people of color.[75] The highlighted campaigns all performed well, exceeding their goals in three of the four instances. Two of these campaigns seemingly benefited from this boosted visibility, receiving an influx of donations after GoFundMe's social media post. But this well-intentioned signal boosting of campaigns that might lack some of the advantages of Petito's campaign illustrates the wider problem. Giving in crowdfunding is not shaped by the demands of justice, nor is it even a random distribution of funding. Rather, it is shaped by the wider social forces of inequality and injustice that are repeated in campaigners' local communities of donors and magnified by the incentive to promote a campaign to a broader audience. These few otherwise neglected campaigns show us just that: they are lucky to be given extra attention, but the wider problem remains.

Conclusion

What Gabby Petito's campaign and those described at the beginning of this chapter show is that crowdfunding does not create a level playing field for people seeking help to support their basic needs. These inequities are not simply random but reflect and deepen many of those already seen in the campaigners' communities, including inequities along the lines of race, gender, income, education, location, and perceived deservingness for receiving help.

In one sense, there's nothing new here—this is one more chapter in the story of giving, whether by individuals or philanthropic institutions. Rather than being a passive part of this process, however, crowdfunding can amplify inequities in giving. This can occur because of the premium that crowd-funding puts on making oneself appealing to others through storytelling and visuals, consumed by the wider public through social media campaigns targeting strangers. Crowdfunding platforms can try to counter these effects, but even then they face questions of which campaigns should be picked as winners, which campaigns deserve public support, and to what degree it is up to individuals to decide which campaigns to donate to. These inequalities are most apparent when campaign recipients have very large unmet needs requiring the support not just of friends and family but the wider community of acquaintances, friends of friends, and complete strangers. In this way, the failure of communities to meet the basic needs of their residents, especially very large medical and housing needs, begets further injustices for those who need help.

5

Missing and masking injustice

> Mental health struggles and challenges don't disappear after one day, one post, or one fundraiser. If community care campaigns for severe mental illness are successful, the person in need survives another day which means the costs associated with survival continue. We shouldn't have to crowdfund to keep our friends alive by giving them their needed access to mental health treatment, yet the systems are still broken, so here we are.

News coverage of donation-based crowdfunding often laments that crowdfunding has become a common means of meeting people's basic needs. For example, an article praising the impact of crowdfunding on people's lives also notes that "GoFundMe shouldn't have to become one of the nation's biggest health insurers. If you can't afford food, there should be sufficient social safety nets to help you feed yourself and your family."[1] These criticisms also frequently note the role of crowdfunding in addressing the symptoms of social injustice while leaving the injustices themselves untouched. As one such article describes it, "The risk in giving medical aid on the basis of stories is that the theatre of change trumps actual systemic reform; the guy with resources helps an ailing friend, or donates to a stranger whose experiences resonate, and believes that he's done his part. Meanwhile, the causes of problems go untouched."[2] As these comments describe it, donation-based crowdfunding is not only a deeply flawed substitute for adequate public supports for basic needs, but it also undermines the goal of creating just social institutions that ensure that everyone's basic needs are met in the future.

Both direct and indirect giving certainly do have an important role to play in responding to social injustices. These injustices can include failures by the state to provide supports for the basic needs of its residents, the lack of opportunities due to systemic racism or other forms of bigotry and bias, and misuse of the state's power, as in cases of police brutality. Giving with

Appealing to the Crowd. Jeremy Snyder, Oxford University Press. © Oxford University Press 2024.
DOI: 10.1093/oso/9780197658130.003.0006

the aim of addressing the harms of social injustice can provide relief for the victims of injustice; however, there is justifiable uneasiness at the idea of relying on private giving in the long term when public institutions fail to address these basic needs. This discomfort arises particularly when injustice is chronic rather than the result of, for example, a delay in keeping up with rapid changes in economic conditions, technology, and social norms.

Thus, even if crowdfunding and other forms of giving can be a stopgap solution to inadequate social supports for basic needs and other injustices, they don't necessarily solve the root causes of these inadequacies. This is particularly concerning if, as discussed in the previous chapter, crowdfunding and other forms of giving provide relief in deeply inequitable ways. Even worse, giving might slow the demand for systemic reforms and reduce the visibility of these injustices, particularly for the relatively privileged recipients of giving. Crowdfunding can have a role to play in responding to systemic failures to provide the social conditions of justice. However, it does so in a context that make it hard to acknowledge, much less address, social injustice.

The place of giving in the face of injustice

Creating and maintaining institutions that support basic needs like nutrition, housing, medical care, physical security, and education through public and democratic means is reasonably viewed as the starting point for social justice.[3] Certainly, the sufficiency and stability of the public provision of just institutions is not always adequate. Economic shocks can change revenue from taxation and governments' ability and willingness to fund social supports. Changes in the political leadership of a community typically shift funding levels and priorities. Governments also reflect the biases of their constituents, limiting support to residents in need based on their race, ethnicity, gender, religion, or a myriad of other factors. That said, public supports for basic needs have the advantage of making these biases and inconsistencies relatively public as they are put into practice through public policy and legislation. Constitutional protections and other laws may prohibit discrimination in providing support, especially by public institutions. And changes in government support reflect political processes that can be relatively transparent and subject to political debate. These features are often lacking in private giving practices and therefore give reason to prefer public supports as a way of providing the social conditions of justice.[4]

Simultaneously, the advantages of public supports for just institutions give us reasons to be concerned about any potential for direct and indirect giving to erode these supports.

Of course, public provision and support of just institutions is often absent or insufficient. Moreover, there may be reasonable disagreement about the aims and structure of just social institutions. In these cases, giving by individuals can aim at least to address the symptoms of injustice and potentially encourage the creation of just institutions. However, as even many proponents of private giving will acknowledge, giving as a response to social injustice has significant flaws and limitations. As we've seen, giving directly to others can be unfocused and inconsistent. In these cases, giving practices are particularly ill-suited to rectifying social injustices as these are precisely the issues that require sustained political pressure and the organization of politically influential groups to address—tasks that are not easily supported by gifts directly to individuals in need.

A version of this critique has commonly been used against the effective altruism charitable movement on the grounds that effective altruism promotes direct aid to individuals rather than institutional change. Specifically, effective altruism, as practiced, is anti-political in the sense that it favors technical and economic solutions, including cash transfers, rather than political change. As a result, it can be seen as preferring Band-Aid solutions over addressing the root causes of need.[5] Supporters of effective altruism defend this approach to giving on the grounds that nothing in principle prevents effective altruists from advocating for political reforms if doing so is the most effective means of addressing needs over the long term. Moreover, the resources needed for institutional change and direct aid may be different, allowing for committed effective altruists to seek to aid others through both routes.[6] Nonetheless, these critics have pointed out that the sensibilities of effective altruists in practice have tended to give priority to highly individualistic projects that position themselves as rescuers and devalue the perspectives of those in need.[7] These forces tend to put effective altruism at odds with approaches like mutual aid that emphasize solidarity within communities engaged in giving with a focus on addressing the root causes of need through social movements.[8]

Indirect giving through philanthropic organizations can be seen as having greater potential to address social injustice than direct giving due to the organizations' potentially greater resources, focus, institutional expertise, and influence. However, they face their own limitations in bringing about systemic reforms. Because contributions to philanthropic organizations are commonly seen as voluntary, they may fluctuate more than public efforts, which are funded through taxation and provided through legislation, often as entitlements. Contributions to philanthropic organizations can dry up because of changes in economic conditions, the popularity of a specific philanthropy or cause, or the perceived value and desirability of donating. As with direct giving, however, in the face of public inaction or, worse, destruction of just institutions, philanthropic organizations have a role in addressing the symptoms of injustice and, potentially, supporting the creation and resilience of just institutions.

Giving, injustice, and democratic voice

Putting these broad limitations aside, a range of critics have argued that philanthropic organizations are very problematic vehicles for bringing about systemic reforms and social justice because of a lack of public accountability. This early concern against philanthropic foundations was expressed by the eighteenth-century liberal economist Anne-Robert-Jacques Turgot. What is distinctively problematic with indirect giving through philanthropic organizations, Turgot argues, is that these organizations may lumber on under their founders' instructions for far too long. In direct giving, an individual determines an aim for the act of giving and a means of carrying it out that takes into account the specific context of the donor and recipient. A philanthropic institution, however, may be less nimble because it represents its donors' wills at a moment in time and may not be able to adjust to changes in needs and the best means of addressing those needs, particularly after the donors' deaths.

> Society has not always the same needs; the nature and dispositions of properties, the divisions between different orders of the people, opinions, manners, the general occupations of the nation or of its different sections, the climate even, the maladies, and the other accidents of human life—all experience a continual variation. New needs arise, others cease to be felt. The proportion of those remaining declines from day to day, and along with them the utility of the foundations designed to relieve them diminishes or disappears.[9]

Turgot notes as an example of this issue the continued existence of leper hospitals in his time despite the general eradication of leprosy. The problem is that philanthropic foundations, especially as they employ supervisors and other administrators, take on a life of their own that becomes increasingly detached from the good intentions of their original supporters. This stands in contrast with both public policies that are ideally shaped by ongoing democratic accountability and direct giving, where donors can target their gifts in response to changes in needs and conditions. Particularly when aimed at those temporarily or unexpectedly unable to work or help themselves, direct giving can help by being highly responsive to immediate needs. Giving to philanthropies, on the other hand, may support an entity that is disconnected from its time, place, and original mission or may become so in the future.

While legal reforms have addressed some of Turgot's concerns, philanthropies still typically grant their extremely wealthy founders and supporters enormous control over domestic and international efforts to help those in need. Not surprisingly, this means that philanthropies reflect the biases and interests of their supporters and, in doing so, can actively undermine the aims of justice. In this vein, Anand Giridharadas argues that US philanthropies support the interests of their founders and actively work against more fundamental, systemic changes that would potentially reduce the wealth and power of their supporters. This phenomenon is exhibited by a failure to consider how these supporters' own businesses, wealth, and activities create and perpetuate injustice in preference of a belief that market mechanisms can create "win-win" solutions that benefit the poor while further enriching the wealthy. Giridharadas calls this worldview *MarketWorld*, where "social change should be pursued principally through the free market and voluntary action, not public life and the law and the reform of the systems that people share in common; that it should be supervised by the winners of capitalism and their allies, and not be antagonistic to their needs; and that the biggest beneficiaries of the status quo should play a leading role in the status quo's reform."[10] For example, Giridharadas writes, the organizer of a Silicon Valley philanthropy was told by its benefactors to drop usage of "social justice" in favor of "fairness" to avoid seeming to blame tech entrepreneurs for perpetuating an unjust division of resources. These entrepreneurs were happy to contribute to philanthropies so long as "no one questioned the entrepreneurs' fortunes and their personal status quo."[11]

Thus, giving through philanthropic organizations can be disconnected from the priorities and voices of those in need, particularly when this giving is dominated by philanthropic elites. Instead, it allows the rich and powerful to use philanthropic institutions to entrench and expand their influence, potentially deepening the social injustices that lead to vast global inequities. Even when it is not the intention of philanthropic founders and donors to shape institutions to their own benefit, by privileging their perspectives and values and empowering these philanthropies, rather than democratically accountable institutions, they ensure that any institutional reform that does come about is less likely to be in the interest of and reflect the values and priorities of those most in need.

The undemocratic nature of addressing basic needs through philanthropies is not easily solved by making giving to these organizations more accessible and representative of the general population. All adults in a community could be enabled to contribute to the philanthropy of their choice—for example, through a voucher to which all community members were entitled.[12] Seemingly, such a system would compel philanthropic organizations to be more responsive to the priorities of the mass of donors rather than a few elites. But even with more widespread participation in giving, some donors will give much more than others and thereby have a much more influential voice in the priorities set by these organizations, including in how they use their power to shape the public sector.

Even if mass participation in donating to philanthropic institutions meant that these institutions were responsive to the full range of their donors rather than the most prolific and influential ones, Emma Saunders-Hastings questions whether this development would be in line with democratic values. This mass of donors could choose to heavily favor specific religious institutions, for example, that would have outsized influence in providing public goods like healthcare and education and reinforce the privatization of these services.[13] For example, a private hospital run by a Catholic charity could reflect the priorities of that charity's donors and be shielded from democratic accountability.

An advantage of crowdfunding, then, is that it allows vast sums of money to be raised by a much larger and more representative cross-section of the public than in forms of giving dominated by the most powerful forces in a community. This money is then sent directly to those in need rather than being filtered through a potentially unaccountable or elite-captured organization. Rather than begging for help on the street or door to door, in crowdfunding the campaign recipient is typically allowed a much better-developed voice, including the space to describe themselves, their needs, and the processes that brought these needs about. While not all campaigners will take up these opportunities, crowdfunding is built to allow campaigners to tell highly personal stories about the recipient to encourage donors to support them. This feature allows campaigners to set the agenda in terms of identifying what their needs are and how donations can address these needs, making giving more egalitarian and democratic than in more elite-dominated and hierarchical practices. At the very least, then, donation-based crowdfunding can give voice to those who are unable to meet their basic needs; more optimistically, it can also be used to draw attention to the systemic failures that force some campaigners into crowdfunding.

But despite the potential of donation-based crowdfunding to give a wider range of donors and recipients a voice in addressing individual needs, it is very difficult to use this practice in a way that also promotes social justice. One key element in encouraging giving is to convince donors that their money will help the recipient and make a concrete difference in their lives. As GoFundMe presents it, "People are more likely to offer support when they believe they can help solve a specific problem," and so campaigners should communicate specific needs, what each need will cost to address, and how donations will improve their lives.[14] This kind of advice is applied to campaign updates as well, where campaigners are encouraged to communicate to potential donors that the money they have received is already making a difference. Thus, campaigners should first "recognize how your donors have helped so far," and updates for medical campaigns should tell readers how the recipient is doing and "how the funds are helping."[15,16] In short, campaigners may point out that a donation will not itself address the underlying social injustices creating the recipient's need; however, doing so runs counter to the advice given to campaigners and undermines the sense that the campaign would conclusively resolve the recipient's problems.

Another barrier to using crowdfunding campaigns to motivate institutional change is the tone that crowdfunding organizers are told to use. In particular, crowdfunding campaigners are regularly told to keep their campaigns personal rather than political and to present an optimistic outlook rather than focus on the negative elements in their lives. Campaigners are also told that they should keep their campaigns positive and demonstrate how their campaigns are succeeding in order to encourage additional donations. GoFundMe describes this approach in terms of encouraging "empathic joy" in potential donors, where the upbeat nature of the campaign and sense that it is succeeding for the recipient will translate to positive emotions in donors and a desire to be a continued part of this successful project.[17] This emphasis on positivity and sense that the campaign is succeeding necessarily runs counter to communicating to potential donors that there are much larger, systemic problems causing the recipients' needs that the campaign alone is not able to address.

In practice, crowdfunding campaigners do generally follow these cues and seek to present themselves and their campaigns in positive ways that tend to make it difficult to call attention to the systemic causes of their needs. For example, an interview study found that crowdfunding campaigners overwhelmingly choose images of the campaign recipients that show them smiling and happy. These campaigners tend not to represent the recipient as a person in need or as a victim of injustice or other harms. Rather, they seek to frame the recipients as hard-working and capable of recovery with a little help from those around them.[18] This approach is rewarded by donors. Among campaigns seeking support for health needs related to organ transplantation, campaigns with increased positive and optimistic language raised more money than campaigns with more negative language.[19] A separate study of health-related campaigns on GoFundMe found that when campaign text and images are both positive, campaigns see more success in meeting their goals.[20] Campaigners may feel the injustice of their situations deeply, as with one campaigner who noted that they "don't believe people should have to rely on other people to be able to afford living while undergoing cancer treatment." Nonetheless, this campaigner found an unreceptive audience among potential donors: their supporters became less interested in funding their treatment as it went on and expenses piled up, and the campaigner was eventually advised to stop asking people for money.[21]

Furthermore, the various approaches that crowdfunding campaigners take to establish the recipient's deservingness can make pushing for systemic changes difficult. As discussed, these approaches might include framing the person as hard-working and doing their best to meet their needs on their own; in this way, their current need is positioned as not due to some personal failing or fault but as a matter of external circumstances. These external factors could be explained in terms of social injustices that leave some people unable to meet their needs despite considerable effort, good intentions, and hard work; however, there's a tendency to describe these circumstances in terms of bad luck or misfortune—a cancer diagnosis rather than lack of affordable medical insurance or the closure of a factory rather than an austerity budget that eliminated unemployment supports. One reason for this tendency may be the feeling that blaming systemic failings can come across to donors as the campaigner making an excuse for their need or deflecting blame from themselves. If their need is the result of misfortune, however, this cause reflects a common vulnerability that could befall any person caught in the wrong place at the wrong time.

This theory is borne out as claims of recipients' worthiness in crowd-funding campaigns largely highlight their individual characteristics and contexts rather than systemic factors. Among Canadians seeking help with their health-related financial needs, their personal connections to potential donors, the depth of their need, and their history of giving to others were regularly cited as reasons for why they deserved help. But despite a publicly funded health system that is commonly seen as a source of pride and key to Canadian identity, the gaps in the health system and the injustice of these gaps did not factor into how Canadians justified their deservingness of support even for essential medical services.[22] In another study, Canadian campaigns for help related to organ transplantation could reasonably criticize the Canadian health system for failing to meet their health-related needs despite its claims to universal health insurance coverage. Nonetheless, only 8.9% of kidney- and 14.6% of liver-related campaigns even flagged the failure of the public insurance system to cover some costs related to transplantation.[23] Similarly, Chinese crowdfunders seeking help with health-related needs focus on individual rather than structural causes of deservingness, including the recipient's personal character, impacts on the recipient's family, losses due to illness, likely gains from receiving medical treatment, and depth of financial distress.[24]

Echoing Giridharadas's concerns with the priorities of philanthropic donors, crowdfunding as an alternative to systemic reforms is largely a market-based solution. Crowdfunding allows people to meet their needs through a competition for private donations mediated through largely for-profit, private crowdfunding platforms. Insofar as access to basic goods should be viewed as a human right or entitlement guaranteed for all, crowdfunding sends the message that, particularly where social institutions have failed to provide universal access to these goods, the private sector can reasonably step in. This message is particularly problematic because it places privately run platforms in control of how crowdfunding is shaped, which campaigns are supported and promoted, and how users' data are protected and commodified.[25] The online and viral aspects of crowdfunding may also be particularly suited to so-called *fast-food philanthropy*, where donors make small one-time donations and receive a warm-glow response without committing to supporting institutions and organizations over the long term.[26]

Finally, the ability of donation-based crowdfunding to give campaigners and recipients a larger and more democratically representative voice in setting giving priorities may be overstated. While these campaigns do largely represent the desires and priorities of those in need, we have already seen how the practice and incentives of crowdfunding shape and limit how these priorities are presented. Moreover, donors to campaigns can take on some of the role of philanthropic organizations in more hierarchical giving practices. Campaigners may feel beholden to the spoken and unspoken values of potential donors to convince them to give. When financial support has been promised, recipients may be pressured to follow through on their initial plans of how to use any funding raised or to respond to advice or demands from donors. This pressure is relevant, as a campaigner may wish to change a plan for medical treatment or repurpose the funding they raised for rent or to pursue a job-training opportunity instead. If campaigners are entitled to these funds, then they should have the freedom to choose how to use them. But if they are beholden to the wider mass of crowdfunding donors for continued support and to avoid accusations of misleading them, then campaigners are significantly constrained in how they present and act on their financial priorities.

Undermining justice

An even more damning criticism of some forms of giving is that they address the symptoms of social injustices in a way that makes systemic reforms more difficult and less likely to occur. That is, giving can not only fail to address systemic justice and represent democratic priorities but actually undermine progress toward just institutions. Turgot broaches this concern as well. Specifically, he worries that giving simply encourages and preserves the poverty that it professes to address.

> It is that precisely in those countries where gratuitous resources are most abundant, as in Spain and some parts of Italy, there misery is more common

and more widely spread than elsewhere. The reason is very simple, and a thousand travellers have observed it. To enable a large number of men to live gratuitously is to subsidize idleness and all the disorders which are its consequences; it is to render the condition of the ne'er-do-well preferable to that of the honest working-man.[27]

Here Turgot follows in a liberal tradition of identifying a class of indolent poor who could work but, if given the option, would choose not to do so in preference of receiving handouts from individuals, foundations, or the state. He does not argue that these individuals are undeserving of a greater portion of the wealth of their communities but rather that simply giving them this wealth in lieu of work will not achieve the aim of improving the lives of the poor. Turgot adds to this common critique of giving that it also undermines the economic health of the state by removing the potential productivity of those people who choose to receive aid rather than work for their living.

Oscar Wilde presents another form of this concern from a socialist perspective when he argues that the aim of the public should be to "reconstruct society on such a basis that poverty will be impossible" but that direct giving to the poor "prevented the carrying out of this aim." In this way he likens direct giving to the behavior of slave owners who were kind to their slaves "and so prevented the horror of the system being realized by those who suffered from it."[28] In Wilde's account, only a full realization of the true horrors of capitalism will bring about his preferred response of a socialist economic system. For Wilde, impoverished people who exhibit the so-called virtues of poverty by accepting their social position and expressing gratitude for giving participate in their own degradation. Only when the poor protest and are ungrateful for the meager gifts they receive can long-lasting reforms come about. For Wilde, and others presenting various forms of his argument, giving takes the edge off of the symptoms of social injustice. As a result, the victims of this injustice and their allies are less likely to take action to change or overthrow this unjust system.

Crowdfunding is not immune from this broad concern about the impacts of giving, and there is reason to think that it may also directly undermine campaigns for social justice. While donors to crowdfunding campaigns can have limited means, crowdfunding success is tied to having networks of relatively wealthy potential donors, the capacity to tell a compelling story of need, and technical know-how. As discussed in the previous chapter, these factors tend to favor a relatively privileged cohort of campaigners and make their interests and perspectives most visible. One problem with this tendency is that, insofar as crowdfunding is a means by which people can meet their basic needs, it makes structural solutions to these needs unnecessary.

As we have seen, crowdfunding is at best a deeply imperfect solution to meeting basic needs since the large majority of people do not meet their crowdfunding goals and the winners and losers in crowdfunding mirror existing social inequities. If relatively well connected, educated, technologically savvy, and otherwise privileged people are best positioned to succeed with crowdfunding, then these are the people most likely to treat it as an alternative to addressing social injustices or for whom the pressure to address gaps in social safety nets will be reduced. It is hard to quantify the effects of crowdfunding on movements to reform unjust and inadequate public supports for basic needs, and certainly the need to crowdfund is regularly used as evidence of systemic failures. That said, crowdfunding platforms and the winners among crowdfunders send a strong if not always explicit message that systemic reform is not necessary—or at least less pressing—as long as people can come together for one another via crowdfunding campaigns.

Crowdfunding platforms' descriptions of their aims make it clear that these larger, systemic reforms aren't alien to the practice of crowdfunding. But rather than encouraging these reforms, crowdfunding platforms unsurprisingly promote themselves as an alternative to institutional change. The stated aspirations of GoFundMe are very ambitious, including helping people to "raise money to make a lasting difference," "changing lives," and helping individuals "turn compassion into action" "because that is how change happens."[29] In its earliest days, GoFundMe noted structural problems facing people seeking access to medical care, including high "health insurance co-payments and deductibles" and "hospital stays, and medication costs, an unexpected injury or illness" that "can quickly plunge a family into huge medical debt." But crowdfunding, rather than systemic changes, is frequently presented as the solution to this problem. As the former CEO of GoFundMe Rob Solomon put it, "When you're sick and out of work, very often you have no income, and GoFundMe is a viable solution."[30]

Similarly, and not surprisingly, what is presented as a successful fundraiser is raising enough money to meet one's present needs, whether they are medical bills, rent, or food. While the underlying causes of these needs may make a brief appearance when discussing the history of these needs, addressing these causes is usually not part of the narrative. In this vein,

India's ImpactGuru describes itself as "a convenient and risk-free solution" to high medical costs.[31] This same platform notes that government-funded medical facilities provide care for free but are "almost always under-funded and overflowing, with substandard or dilapidated hospital equipment & infrastructure, and limited rural coverage." This description of public care is contrasted with stories of people who were able to access high-quality, private treatment via "alternative methods" like crowdfunding, marking this practice as a solution to the problem of underfunded public institutions.[32]

Thus, crowdfunding may distract from systemic change in the vein of Wilde rather than Turgot. Contrary to Turgot's general objection to giving, there is little reason to think that crowdfunding will serve as a viable alternative to work or self-support for a significant number of people given the low and inconsistent success rates seen in crowdfunding campaigns. However, crowdfunding can present itself as a market-based alternative to systemic change and satisfy the most influential segment of the public in need; if so, crowdfunding may reduce the demand for these changes. There are, of course, inconsistent messages about whether crowdfunding is an adequate solution to social injustice. When the US Congress delayed passing a COVID-19 relief package in early 2021, GoFundMe CEO Tim Cadogan wrote that "our platform was never meant to be a source of support for basic needs, and it can never be a replacement for robust federal COVID-19 relief that is generous and targeted to help the millions of Americans who are struggling."[33] But although crowdfunding is generally acknowledged as a flawed replacement for just social institutions and adequate public policy, in reality basic needs have always been at the heart of donation-based crowdfunding; in fact, GoFundMe included a medical category at its inception. Statements like Cadogan's are frequently coupled with stories of viral crowdfunding success, advice on the positive tone that campaigners should adopt, and emphasis on need as a result of bad luck rather than injustice. At the very least, these messages make it easier for people not inclined toward the cost and hard work of systemic reform to take the view that crowdfunding can come to the rescue. As a result, there is a strong reason to see crowdfunding as a *stopgap* to injustices in some cases, where it is better to rescue individuals from homelessness, lack of education, and limited access to healthcare rather than leave them in a state of need. But if crowdfunding is viewed as a viable *alternative* to systemic reforms or slows these reforms, then helping individuals can come at a cost to those left behind.

Context matters

Much of the messaging around crowdfunding and the factors favoring crowdfunding success push campaigners to ignore the underlying social injustices that create the needs they seek to relieve. That said, crowdfunding takes many diverse forms and addresses many different needs. In some cases, discussing these needs not only is acceptable but may even be the direct aim of the crowdfunding campaign. In other cases, crowdfunding is used to facilitate mutual aid where existing communities seek to support one another's needs and maintain social movements to address the root causes of these needs. The failure to address social injustice is a problem in the general practice of crowdfunding, then, but not something inherent to it.

Most directly, donation-based crowdfunding campaigns often select philanthropic organizations as recipients or are based around a more general cause. In some cases, crowdfunding platforms are built specifically to serve nonprofit organizations, as with the platforms Classy and Fundly. Other crowdfunding platforms include individual recipients who are raising money on behalf of a philanthropic organization or campaigns organized directly by nonprofit philanthropic organizations. As significant activity by individual donors has moved to crowdfunding platforms, nonprofits can pursue crowdfunding to support the activities they've already been undertaking—including promoting systemic reforms—and, ideally, expand their donor base in doing so. Importantly, though, while crowdfunding for philanthropic organizations can help address concerns that crowdfunding runs contrary to or fails to address systemic needs and social injustice, this form of giving would still be vulnerable to Saunders-Hastings's critique that philanthropies will tend to be driven by the priorities of their largest and most influential donors rather than the mass of donors through crowdfunding.[34]

In other cases, crowdfunding platforms pool individual campaigns into causes or otherwise try to raise funding for groups of people with a specific type of need. For example, the for-profit GoFundMe.com website is associated with a nonprofit version of its platform. GoFundMe.org, founded in 2019, highlights causes such as addressing hunger, helping the victims of specific disasters, or combatting hate crimes. The recipients of these causes can differ but include campaigns initiated on the for-profit.com version of the platform or traditional nonprofit organizations based in specific communities.

In practice, supporting philanthropic organizations and causes is not un-usual on crowdfunding platforms. In the United States, nearly half of people who supported crowdfunding campaigns in 2019 gave to charitable organ-izations, making up 22.1% of the total donations made to crowdfunding campaigns. Moreover, while 20% of US donors overall support social jus-tice causes, people who donate through crowdfunding are more likely (27%) than the general population of donors to do so. This greater propensity to support social justice causes among US crowdfunders may reflect that these donors are relatively younger and more diverse than those giving via tradi-tional means.[35]

As noted previously, crowdfunding platforms generally encourage positive messaging by campaigners, and this messaging is correlated with increased fundraising success. That said, there are potential cultural differences in the role of positive and negative emotions on crowdfunding success. A review of Chinese medical crowdfunding campaigns found that an increased number of negative emotions and phrases were correlated with success in reaching crowdfunding goals. The authors speculate that this may be due to Chinese donors being inclined to be moved by a "tragic narrative strategy."[36] Notably, however, in this case the success of negative sentiments came largely through casting the campaign recipient as the victim of a personal tragedy rather than through highlighting social injustice.

The example of Chinese crowdfunding aside, some communities are more prepared to point to the underlying causes of their needs in crowd-funding campaigns due to a history of calling attention to these causes and political engagement. These communities are often engaged in forms of mu-tual aid where the relationship between donors and recipients is relatively non-hierarchical and addressing individual needs is combined with creating and maintaining social movements to address the root causes of these needs. Canadians crowdfunding for treatment for substance use and addiction fre-quently called out what they saw as insufficient access to timely and effec-tive treatment options in the publicly funded health system. One campaigner described this inadequate support as "our government doesn't feel the need to assist with addiction treatment."[37] Similarly, crowdfunding campaigns by Canadians with Lyme disease often contain critical remarks about the lack of government support for the care that campaign recipients seek. This ire is motivated by the contested diagnosis of Lyme disease in Canada and else-where that pushes many people to seek diagnosis and treatment abroad or outside of the public health system in Canada.[38]

Campaigns for the health-related needs of members of the transgender community also often reflect the marginalization and political engagement of this community. In many cases these campaigners have been willing to forgo their privacy when campaigning for themselves to shift public perceptions about transgender people—for example, using these public-facing campaigns as a way to reject the common "trapped in the wrong body" narrative as motivating their desire for gender-affirming surgeries and to publicly affirm their gender identity. Receiving support through donations, including from strangers, friends, and family who had not previously explicitly supported their transgender identity, is seen as a way of shifting public values and normalizing trans bodies.[39] Importantly, campaigns for the health-related needs of transgender people do not typically take the form of calling for wider insurance coverage of gender-affirming medical care or other changes to the economic structures of medical care for trans people. That is, they typically frame gaps in insurance coverage as an individual rather than social issue.[40] That said, many actively take on some of the work of social justice in the form of widening community support for trans people.[41]

There is also a range of medical needs that are seen as receiving too little attention by and support from researchers and health systems. For example, people experiencing rare diseases, along with their loved ones, have long been advocates for greater research into these diseases and funding for treatments. In a guide for crowdfunding for treatments for people with rare diseases, campaigners are encouraged to "focus on the bigger picture" with the example of a campaign where the campaigners wanted to stress that they were not focused only on their own child's needs and "that all funding was going directly to our 501c3 nonprofit and to the research for a cure for all children. Our efforts are to help end a disease, and not to save just one child . . . but a whole lot of children."[42] In this way, connection to a larger community of people in need can help to develop norms of solidarity when crowdfunding.

Concerns about justice can also factor into which crowdfunding platform campaigners choose to use. For example, in interviews with trans men seeking top surgery, several campaigners mentioned choosing not to use the GoFundMe platform because GoFundMe had previously hosted a campaign to raise funds for white police officer Darren Wilson, who had shot and killed the unarmed black teenager Michael Brown in Ferguson, Missouri. As members of a marginalized group that has often been the target of violence and other hate crimes, these campaigners felt that their choice of crowd-funding platform should reflect their wider commitment to social justice.[43]

Moreover, some kinds of need are particularly well suited to supporting wider criticisms of social injustices. These include crowdfunding campaigns for legal representation, like those hosted on the crowdfunding platform CrowdJustice. For campaigners using this platform, references to perceived social injustices come naturally. For example, campaigners using this plat-form to fight for the protection of a seabed from dredging described their campaign as a response to "inadequacies" in governance and a means for donors to express a "lack of faith in the rigour of public administration."[44] The founder of this platform, Julia Salasky, has promoted it in terms of democratizing access to legal advice and so acting as a direct solution to structural barriers to legal access.[45]

But although these campaigns draw attention to the underlying injustices and systemic failings that create the need for crowdfunding, they also tend to present crowdfunding as at least a proximate solution to these failings. Rather than addressing the causes of these injustices, these campaigns again tend to present crowdfunding as an individualistic alternative to adequate social supports for the recipients' basic needs. This formulation doesn't typi-cally explicitly abandon support for systemic reforms; rather, these more po-litically active campaigns tend to draw attention to the systemic failing and then pivot to a request for support that is made necessary by this failing. In the case of CrowdJustice, for example, campaigners who sought to address social injustice through their campaigns found crowdfunding to be "passive" and ill-suited to promoting civic engagement while also shaped by luck and inequality in terms of which campaigns gain traction.[46] This outcome is not surprising, of course, given that the focus of crowdfunding campaigns is on obtaining resources for the recipient, and other interests are secondary.

Conclusion

Crowdfunding potentially gives those in need and less powerful donors a larger voice in setting giving priorities. However, the individualistic and market-driven structure of crowdfunding makes realizing the democratic ideal of crowdfunding challenging. Crowdfunding campaigns for individuals face significant pressure to ignore the structural causes of their needs in favor of taking an upbeat and optimistic approach to their fundraising appeal. For this reason, crowdfunding campaigns typically frame crowdfunding as a so-lution rather than a stopgap to systemic failures. Even when crowdfunding campaigns for individuals draw attention to the social injustices that make them necessary, the immediate focus of the campaign is on raising money to address the symptoms of these injustices. Crowdfunding campaigns to sup-port social causes and organizations are best prepared to use these resources to support systemic changes, helping those impacted by injustice while po-tentially addressing the underlying injustice as well. Crowdfunding has the appeal of being more democratic and supporting a wider range of voices than philanthropies supported by a few wealthy donors. However, even here, crowdfunding platforms serve as powerful mediators in crowdfunded phi-lanthropy, a point I return to in Chapter 9.

6

Crowdfrauding

I've tried loans but since I'm not working right now, on paper they won't help me until I'm able to show at least four paycheck stubs. When it comes to my family I come from my harder background so they don't have the means either. Soon as I start my new job and start getting paid I should be back on my feet again but for now I'm really going through a tough situation to keep my head above water. I don't know how to truly prove that my situation is real. All I can do is really hope that you trust that I'm serious about my situation.

In fall 2021, a series of prolonged rainstorms dumped vast amounts of water along the Fraser River Valley that runs eastward from my home in Vancouver, British Columbia. These storms caused massive flooding throughout the southwest of the province, washed out long stretches of highways, forced many people to evacuate their homes, and, in some cases, left these evacuees without homes to return to. The resulting loss of housing, personal property, and income was devastating to many and left them needing immediate help to pay for the costs of relocation and to begin to rebuild their lives.

In response, the federal government of Canada mobilized the military to help build dams, and the provincial government of British Columbia announced financial assistance for small businesses and individuals impacted by the floods. But even before these moves by the provincial and national governments, individual volunteers stepped in to help those in need. These independent initiatives included people in the flood zone helping to build barriers against rising water and rescuing people and their animals from danger. Some groups more removed from the immediate threat of rising flood waters airlifted meals to areas cut off from the rest of the province, while others sent cash donations to nonprofits and people organizing aid.

Appealing to the Crowd. Jeremy Snyder, Oxford University Press. © Oxford University Press 2024.
DOI: 10.1093/oso/9780197658130.003.0007

And, of course, crowdfunding campaigns to support those affected by these floods appeared almost immediately when the water began rising. As these campaigns for individuals and businesses increased in number, the news media took note. This media attention included a local news report that discussed these crowdfunding appeals and particularly flagged a hub for "verified" fundraisers on the GoFundMe platform that aimed to support people affected by the floods.[1] This hub went on to include nearly 200 campaigns, raising more than $1.5 million in donations that had been "verified" by the GoFundMe Trust and Safety team.[2]

This story of natural disaster and response by government, nonprofits, and individuals is not unusual. Increasingly, crowdfunding is a significant part of the public's response to the needs of those affected by natural disasters, high-profile tragedies, and other crises. And while the actions of crowdfunding campaigners and donors are largely an organic and unorganized response to sudden needs, crowdfunding platforms like GoFundMe can shape this response by identifying which campaigns are viewed as safe to support.

This move toward verifying crowdfunding campaigns after crises and other high-profile tragedies is motivated in large part by a history of fraudulent campaigns taking advantage of these incidents. While fraudulent campaigns are often identified quickly and shut down, some have been able to raise thousands or even hundreds of thousands of dollars. The outpouring of support that may follow a tragedy like the floods in British Columbia can make a huge and timely difference in the lives of the victims. But these crises also present an opportunity for fraudsters to create campaigns with falsified claims of need or even steal the identity of people genuinely in need.

Fraud in giving, understood as misrepresentation around key facts about the recipient and their needs, is hardly unique to crowdfunding. Giving to others creates a wide range of opportunities for fraudulent behavior, including deception about the way funds will be used, the recipient's needs, and the recipient's past conduct. Clear cases of fraud in giving certainly exist, but there is also a significant gray area concerning what kinds of conduct should count as fraud, particularly where the recipient is in a situation of genuine need or undergoing significant discrimination in accessing opportunities to meet their needs. Crowdfunding takes place in this already contested arena and raises distinctive ethical concerns around fraud, including how donors can be deceived and how crowdfunding platforms respond to the perceived danger of fraud.

Fraud in giving and receiving

Before examining fraud in the context of crowdfunding, it is useful to understand how fraud takes place more generally in giving practices and what responses this potential for fraud has generated. Recipients of donations can misrepresent the nature of their need in a variety of ways. Most directly, recipients can lie about or fake a need, potentially defrauding donors. While the incidence of these misrepresentations is often exaggerated, giving creates an incentive for people to fabricate or exaggerate needs for their own benefit. Thus, there is a long history of individual donors and institutions questioning—sometimes but not always with justification—whether potential recipients of their aid are legitimately ill, unable to work, or otherwise unable to meet their own needs.[3]

These misrepresentations can take various forms and stem from different motivations, including cases where people are in genuine need but do not meet the criteria for receiving help. For example, members of the "undeserving poor" who are able to work but unable to find employment or have histories of substance use, mental illness, participation in sex work, or other stigmatized pasts and sources of need might disguise these facts in order to receive help. Similarly, recipients might misrepresent their degree of need or incapacitation in order to qualify for or motivate giving by others, particularly where social supports are inadequate.

In some instances, would-be recipients engage in what is much more clearly fraud. The archetype for this form of fraud is a case where the recipient is not in a position of need but claims need for self-enrichment. In other cases, recipients might steal the identity of a real person with genuine needs, especially when giving does not involve an in-person transfer between people familiar to one another. Close connection to the recipient can counter identity theft, but these connections may be more tenuous, given modern telecommunications and the ease of transferring funds online.

Misrepresenting needs, ranging from outright fraud to exaggeration, has a long history and was a common concern, for example, in charitable efforts in Victorian England. As I discussed in more detail in Chapter 3, one manifestation of the scrutiny of those in need was the Charity Organisation Society and scientific charity efforts aimed at differentiating genuine and "deserving" poverty from those who "chose" to be poor or fell into a life of dependence.[4] During this period in particular, there was common skepticism about how genuine professed need was. As one commentator from that time put it, charitable donors face a horde of fraudsters, from "the pretended broken-down lady or gentleman to the female street beggar with borrowed children."[5] Personal connections with the recipient are commonly seen as insulating against these forms of fraud as they make misrepresentation of the recipient's needs harder to sustain. As a result, home visits and other potentially invasive means of policing giving were often preferred to donations to people soliciting help in public or responding to "begging letters" where the veracity of the recipient's claims was less clear.[6] Thus, the specter of fraud, whether or not the perceived scope of this problem is accurate, goes hand in hand with invasive means of determining the legitimacy of the recipient's need and their deservingness for aid.

Other forms of fraud among recipients take place in terms of how donated resources are used. Recipients may have genuine needs but use donations in ways that the donor did not agree to or expect. Less perniciously, they might apply aid to genuine needs but not those that had been the gift's target. This kind of reallocation can happen, for example, when the recipient develops new, more pressing needs or prioritizes their needs differently than does the donor. This repurposing of gifts raises questions of who should have the final word on how aid is used, particularly if the recipient redirects the funding to address needs to which they are arguably entitled to have supported, like housing, healthcare, and education. Returning to Victorian England, surveillance of the poor was often conducted with the aim of ensuring that philanthropic aid was used efficiently and had the intended effect of ending dependence on giving.[7] In other cases, the concern about donation misuse is that the recipient may have genuine needs but does not address these genuine needs at all with the donated resources. This kind of concern is common in the policing of welfare supports, as when welfare recipients are accused of using food stamps for highly processed foods, cigarettes, or alcohol.[8]

Whether a need is legitimate and donated resources are used appropriately can be contested and include problematic attitudes toward socioeconomically disadvantaged and vulnerable people. Attitudes about which people are most likely to fake or exaggerate their needs match existing racial, socioeconomic, gender, and other types of biases within societies, just as notions of which people in need are "deserving" of help are often discriminatory.[9] Moreover, who gets investigated for potential fraud when receiving help from individuals and institutions typically traces attitudes about which people are most deserving of aid and worthy of trust. As I explored in Chapter 3, these determinations often reflect discriminatory social attitudes. Similarly, what kinds of behaviors are viewed as fraudulent, including how resources are used and what information is disclosed to donors, will be viewed through these lenses of deservingness and trustworthiness.

While most attention around fraud in giving practices focuses on recipients of giving, donors can engage in fraud as well. There is typically a presumption of trust, especially around philanthropic organizations, given their stated missions of promoting social good without personal interest or profit. While past misconduct among donor organizations makes it clear that this trust is not always warranted, philanthropic organizations benefit from their avowedly non–self-interested structure in a way that for-profit organizations and other self-interested groups do not typically receive. This presumption of trust extends to the common use of volunteer workers that both deepens the appearance of selfless motivation and, in some cases, populates organizations with nonexperts that can make it easier for people within these organizations to engage in fraud.[10]

Philanthropic organizations are typically themselves recipients of donations and may employ a large number of people to raise, administer, and distribute these funds. Through these activities, philanthropies can engage in fraud in a variety of ways. Most centrally, fraud in these organizations takes the form of misappropriating funding, where people within the organization keep some of the money raised for their own use. Such misappropriation can be undertaken by a range of actors, including employees or volunteers within the philanthropic organization, contractors undertaking work on behalf of the organization, and trustees of the organization. Most directly, this misuse of funds is clear and intentional, as in cases where resources are embezzled for personal use.

In other cases, misuse of funds within donor institutions involves a more subtle intermixing of private interests with the purported mission of the philanthropy. Typically, these actions take the form of self-dealing, nepotism, and cronyism in administering the philanthropic institution and using fees and other benefits for trustees, employees, and others connected to the organization. Administrators of philanthropic institutions may intermix their personal lives and needs with those of the institution, taking advantage of a lack of oversight to obtain indefensibly high salaries and benefits, hire family members despite a lack of qualifications, and use contracts to benefit businesses in which the administrator has a personal interest.[11]

Philanthropies and donors may also engage in fraud in giving to take advantage of tax benefits or reputational advantages of giving. Tax relief is often attached to charitable giving, which, as noted in Chapter 1, raises ethical concerns even when giving is well-intentioned, transparent, and efficient. But in other cases, donors may misrepresent the value of their donations to receive undeserved tax benefits or gain public recognition for their alleged generosity.[12] Similarly, donations may be structured to directly or indirectly benefit the donor in ways that run afoul of tax regulations governing charitable donations or misrepresent the nature and intention of the donation to the public. In some cases, corporate leaders may take advantage of insider knowledge about imminent drops in the value of the stock they hold, donating these holdings to charity to maximize the tax value of these contributions.[13] Outside of tax benefits, donations to individuals or philanthropic organizations can be used to improve the image of the donor, especially when the donor's wealth has been made by ethically problematic means. For example, cryptocurrency entrepreneur Sam Bankman-Fried heavily supported the effective altruism movement before being accused of fraud.[14]

In other cases, a philanthropy may misrepresent its aims or how it will use donations or other resources entrusted to it. This misuse of funds can include misappropriation of resources for the personal gain of those connected to the philanthropy, as with other cases of misappropriation. It can also include well-intentioned expenditures that are distinct from those communicated to donors. Misinformation of this kind can undermine trust and the consent of donors. These actions are especially concerning if donors would not have contributed their support otherwise or if their aim was to support a specific need that the philanthropy promised to address.

Philanthropies are subject to laws about how the funding they raise should be distributed, how they manage conflicts of interest, and how any tax benefits they claim can be justified. Individuals and organizations running afoul of these regulations are regularly identified, prosecuted, and punished. However, the difference in power between donors and recipients may make identifying fraud less likely among well-off donors. Socially marginalized and relatively powerless recipients can find it difficult to voice concerns with the conduct of a philanthropy due to fear of losing access to aid. These recipients may also question whether they will be heard and believed if they do voice concerns. Moreover, there is frequently an expectation that distributing aid to populations in great need is extremely challenging and that success in these endeavors may be uneven or difficult to quantify. In these cases, misuse of resources can more easily be written off as an artifact of the recipient population's characteristics rather than a failure by the donor organization.[15]

Crowdfrauding

Fraud in donation-based crowdfunding centers almost entirely on crowdfunding campaigners and campaign recipients. Donations by individuals to charitable crowdfunding campaigns are not significant sources of fraud in that they are generally simply transfers of funds without the expectation of repayment, don't create opportunities for self-dealing, and are often not tax deductible. Donation-based crowdfunding platforms could, in theory, siphon off funds donated through their systems or otherwise manipulate the donation process to capture donations and other resources. However, there have been no reports of such events. Rather, criticism of the financial conduct of charitable crowdfunding platforms is usually restricted to the fees that some platforms charge as part of the fundraising process.

GoFundMe gives a broad definition of how funding might be misused by campaigners and recipients. This misuse can include cases where the "organizer does not deliver funds to the intended beneficiary," "the fundraiser's content is inaccurate with respect to a material fact about the organizer, beneficiary, or purpose, which GoFundMe determines is the principal reason upon which a reasonable donor would rely in making a contribution," or "other deceptive conduct by the organizer or beneficiary."[16] Understood in this way, it is hard to determine how common fraud is among crowdfunding campaigners and recipients. From April 2016 to September 2018, the now defunct website GoFraudMe reported on hundreds of presumptive cases of fraud on charitable crowdfunding websites.[17] These reports were drawn from news coverage of crowdfunding fraud; as such, they would capture only the subset of fraud that was reported to law enforcement agencies and received news coverage.

The GoFundMe crowdfunding platform claims that only 0.1% of the campaigns it hosts are fraudulent.[18] Of the 250,000 health-related campaigns that GoFundMe claims to host yearly, for example, this would amount to only 250 fraudulent medical crowdfunding campaigns per year. India's Milaap claims that less than 0.05% of the 240,000 campaigns initiated on its platform every year are fraudulent, amounting to roughly 120 campaigns yearly. At the other extreme, India's Ketto rejects about 23% of campaigns seeking to use its platform because of deficiencies in the documentation used to establish the legitimacy of these campaigns.[19] Not all of these campaigns are fraudulent, of course, but this figure does demonstrate that many campaigners in India, at least, might struggle to meet stringent requirements to document the legitimacy of the campaign recipient's needs.

The very low numbers of fraudulent campaigns reported by GoFundMe and Milaap are certainly an undercount of how many arguably fraudulent campaigns they host as these numbers reflect only campaigns they have positively identified as fraudulent. Moreover, these platforms have an incentive to underplay the potential for fraud on their platforms in order to foster trust among potential donors. By rejecting very large numbers of campaigns as not clearly legitimate, Ketto is an outlier. That said, if the real number of fraudulent campaigns is near to the numbers reported by GoFundMe, Milaap, and GoFraudMe, this is a very small number of fraudulent campaigns when compared with the hundreds of thousands of campaigns initiated yearly on these and other platforms.

Numbers aside, a review of media reports of fraud in medical crowdfunding campaigns identified four types of fraud.[20] The most commonly reported type involves cases of faking or exaggerating one's own illness. This kind of fraud can be generalized beyond medical crowdfunding to include any cases of falsifying or exaggerating one's own needs. These instances of fraud often focus on fabricated cancer diagnoses, where the money raised for treatment will not actually be used for medical care. In many of these cases, campaigners go to significant lengths to feign the authenticity of their needs, including shaving their heads for photos on their campaign page to give the impression that they are undergoing chemotherapy. This form of fraud may be exposed when friends and family members of the recipient come forward to disclose that the crowdfunder was not in fact ill as described in the campaign. In one typical case, neighbors exposed a fraudulent campaign where the recipient claimed to have a neurological condition that required extensive and expensive medical support or else they would die. This campaign raised more than $100,000 and was exposed when neighbors saw the campaigner walking in public despite claims that she was dying and housebound.[21]

Similarly, campaigners can fake or exaggerate need on behalf of another person. These cases have considerable overlap with instances of misrepresenting one's own basic needs. However, this type of fraud often includes asymmetries in power between the intended recipient of the campaign and the person engaging in fraud. In the medical context, these cases can take the form of a relatively healthy adult misrepresenting the needs of someone in their care, including a child or older parent. While not always present, this power asymmetry is often found in these cases where the intended recipient is not aware of the fraud or not in a position to easily deny the campaigner's claims about them and their needs.[22]

One of the most well-known cases of crowdfunding fraud fits into this category. In late 2017, Kate McClure organized a crowdfunding campaign on behalf of Johnny Bobbitt Jr., a veteran experiencing homelessness. McClure wrote that Bobbitt had spent his last $20 to help her to buy gas for her car after it stopped in a dangerous position near interstate traffic. Out of a sense of gratitude, McClure and her boyfriend, Mark D'Amico, sought to raise $10,000 to help Bobbitt find housing. The campaign went viral and received extensive news coverage that helped it to raise more than $400,000 from more than 14,000 donors. But in reality, McClure and D'Amico had known Bobbitt before their claimed first contact. Although Bobbitt was in fact a veteran experiencing homelessness, the road rescue story was completely fabricated. Bobbitt was aware of and participated in the deception, but the campaign was administered by McClure and D'Amico, and they spent the vast majority of the donations on themselves, with relatively little going to Bobbitt. When this fraud was revealed, GoFundMe agreed to refund all donations that the campaign had received.[23]

A third type of fraud in crowdfunding campaigns involves the campaigner taking on a false identity. In these cases, the campaigner claims to raise funds for a real person with genuine needs; however, they have no connection with the person and pocket those funds for themselves. This fraud is typically enabled by the campaigner using news coverage or other publicity around a person or group of people who need help. This impersonation can take the form of the fraudster pretending to be the actual person needing help. In other cases, the campaigner claims to be in contact with the person in need as a neighbor, friend, family member, or other contact, and they falsely state that the money raised will be directed to the person in genuine need. Campaigners may copy information, images, video, and other details from social media and news reports to create the fake account and the impression that the campaigner is the person in genuine need or has a close connection to them. In other instances, campaigners simply copy elements of legitimate crowdfunding campaigns to create a fraudulent campaign.

This kind of fraud regularly accompanies high-profile disasters and tragedies, as with the collapse of an apartment building in Florida in 2021.

After this disaster, with many members of the public wanting to help its victims, at least 23 suspicious campaigns were identified on the GoFundMe platform and removed. The wide incidence of fraud following this event led Florida's chief financial officer to complain that GoFundMe needs to be "held accountable" as they "have done nothing to ensure the transparency of the dollars that are donated by good-hearted people actually get to those that truly need it."[24] While GoFundMe indicated that these fundraisers were identified quickly and did not raise any money, in other cases they can take money and attention away from legitimate efforts to help those in need. For example, one fraudulent campaign purported to raise money for the family of a bus driver killed in a crash. Not only did this campaign receive donations that might have gone to a legitimate campaign running concurrently, but the victim's family was forced to take time away from mourning to warn potential donors about the fraud.[25]

Finally, crowdfunding campaigns can engage in fraud when they raise resources for someone with a genuine need but then fail to use these resources to address that need. In some relatively clear cases of this form of fraud, a person intentionally uses their genuine need to raise funds for themselves but doesn't use those funds toward that need. In other cases, campaigners raising money on behalf of another person or group fail to transfer all of the money raised to the advertised recipient. This type of fraud also includes less clear instances of miscommunication with donors. For example, campaigners may fail to clearly communicate the full extent of their intended expenditures or fail to describe intended uses for the funding that donors may not have supported. In one case, a person seeking donations to support treatment for a genuine medical need didn't mention needing help paying their rent and buying food because of lost income during their illness. When they spent campaign resources on these genuine needs as well, donors became concerned that they had been misled.[26]

One complication around determining what constitutes fraud or misuse of donations is that needs and the best means of addressing these needs can change over the course of a campaign. This is particularly true of medical crowdfunding campaigns where optimal treatment types and locations can easily change as new information is learned, especially when recipients are seeking experimental or unproven medical treatments. In one example, a crowdfunding campaigner learned that their husband's cancer treatment was no longer effective and sought explicit permission from donors to redirect their contributions to an alternative treatment. For the campaigner, this change created the worry that donors would withdraw their funds and thereby add to the campaigner's hardship.[27] Thus, although crowdfunding is intended in these cases to help relieve the campaigner's and recipient's difficulties, the need to maintain trustworthiness over the course of medical treatment can create a new source of emotional distress. More generally, people in dynamic situations of need may have shifting priorities as they respond to a natural disaster in real time or deal with a loss of income and rapid pileup of bills.

De-frauding crowdfunding

Potential donors to crowdfunding campaigns receive a range of advice on how to avoid contributing to fraudulent campaigns. The most common—and likely most effective—advice is to give only to campaign organizers or recipients with whom the donor is already familiar and has a relationship of trust. In these cases, the campaign may simply be a means for easily collecting donations from people already knowledgeable about the recipient's need and for updating their community on the progress of the campaign and any changes in the recipient's needs. If donors have any questions or concerns about the campaign's legitimacy in these cases, they will have the further option of directly contacting the campaigner, recipient, or both to rule out fraud or misinformation.[28] This focused giving will be highly effective in combating cases of identity theft and many instances of faking an illness or other need, unless the recipient has successfully misled close family and friends as well. It would, however, rule out giving to viral campaigns or helping people affected by natural disasters or other emergencies that often capture the attention of crowdfunding donors.

Another piece of advice for avoiding fraudulent campaigns is to examine the campaign text for details about the recipient's need and what they will do with the funding they receive. Potential donors are told that legitimate campaigners "have no incentive not to give information" and that campaigners "that are trying to scam you try to avoid giving too much information because they don't want things that you could check."[29] Similarly, people considering donating to these campaigns are advised to independently check any claims disclosed in the campaign and contact the campaign organizer for additional details about the campaign.[30] News coverage of a campaign can also be used to verify that campaign details are truthful.[31]

GoFundMe directs potential donors to make sure that every campaign they support has a range of information in the campaign text, including the relationship between the campaigner and recipient, how funds raised will be used, and how the recipient will access funds received. These details, which can then be verified by donors, are meant to encourage trust in the campaign.[32]

Examining images and videos is also seen as a way to help ensure that a crowdfunding campaign is legitimate. This vigilance includes being skeptical of campaigns that do not include images and videos. When images are part of the campaign, they can be closely examined to ensure that they are recent and not stock images. *Money* magazine goes so far as to suggest that potential donors reverse image search campaign pictures to ensure that they have not been copied from other sites and investigate the recipient's social media profiles to match images from the campaign to a real person with an online presence.[33] People considering donating to a campaign can specifically investigate the campaigner's social media profiles like Facebook to "get a sense of whether or not it's a legitimate account" including by checking to see if the page has recent activity like new photos of the campaigner or recipient.[34] GoFundMe explicitly encourages campaigners to link their campaigns to their Facebook accounts so that potential donors can be reassured that the campaigner is "trustworthy" and so that the campaign can be listed in GoFundMe's public directory.[35]

Crowdfunding platforms have developed increasingly sophisticated responses to fraud, given high-profile crowdfunding scams like the aforementioned Philadelphia couple raising money to benefit a veteran experiencing homelessness. In many cases, these responses are automated processes aimed at weeding out copycat campaigns where all or part of an existing, legitimate campaign is cloned. These processes can scan images and text in new campaigns against a database of existing and completed campaigns to ensure that duplication is not taking place. GoFundMe also indicates that it has added new processes to determine how funds will be paid out to named beneficiaries so that the Philadelphia fraud would not succeed today.[36] It's not clear whether this claim is true, however—in that case the named recipient, Johnny Bobbitt Jr., was aware of and participated in the fraud. However, verifying the payout of funds with named recipients in at least high-profile campaigns could eliminate some instances of fraud.

Other platforms boast less clear antifraud procedures, including JustGiving's claim that they "run ID checks on every Page owner" and "hold" their names and addresses, and Milaap's preference to transfer funds to hospitals or other service providers.[37] In contrast, India's Ketto has an extensive vetting process where a "campaigner needs to submit legal identification proof, documents supporting the cause, a cost estimation letter, etc. Once the documents are uploaded, a dedicated team authenticates the campaign based on the submitted legal identity proofs."[38] Crowdfunding platforms also typically allow users to flag suspicious campaigns, which triggers a review process. There has been a push for standardization of industry responses to fraud through the development of best practices for the sector. GoFundMe has partnered with entrepreneurial crowdfunding platform Indiegogo to form the Crowdfunding Trust Alliance to develop and implement industry standards and identify fraudulent campaigns. At this time, however, it is not clear what these standards will entail. Only these two platforms have signed on, and GoFundMe is the only donation-based crowdfunding platform involved.[39]

Additional protections can be used to verify the legitimacy of high-profile, viral campaigns or campaigns that emerge when an emergency event attracts news coverage. This is the approach that GoFundMe has taken with high-profile events, where it creates hubs of "verified" campaigns, as with the flooding-related campaigns I discussed at the beginning of this chapter. According to GoFundMe, its verification process includes reviews of campaigns to ensure the accuracy of personal information in the campaign, confirm the identity of campaign recipients, and "make sure that all funds raised on GoFundMe are going to the right place." GoFundMe further describes this verification process as "on par with the financial industry" and requiring "government-issued identification, address details, and other forms of ID." In the end, being verified means that GoFundMe knows "the identity of the organizer, who they are raising funds for, the organizer's relationship to the recipient of the funds, and how the funds will be used."[40] This verification process is initiated by GoFundMe and does not apply to all campaigns.

The costs of combatting fraud

Fraud in donation-based crowdfunding campaigns does happen. It's hard to know how common it is and how much fraud goes unidentified by crowdfunding platforms, law-enforcement agencies, and the press. That said, outside of high-profile and successful campaigns like the McClure and D'Amico fraud in Philadelphia, there's little evidence that donors being misled and their resources being squandered are a common occurrence. Rather, antifraud efforts like the Crowdfunding Trust Alliance are motivated to a significant degree by the desire to build trust among potential donors whose contributions support the operations and profitability of crowdfunding platforms. Speaking on the creation of the Crowdfunding Trust Alliance, an Indiegogo vice-president acknowledged this point: "A high-profile failure reflects on the whole industry. It's in all of our best interests that platforms are reputable."[41] Thus, above and beyond rooting out any actual instances of fraud in crowdfunding, these platforms have a strong incentive to convince the public that the campaigns they host are legitimate and to co-opt campaigners into supporting this aim.

Campaigners are told by these crowdfunding platforms that they must open up their lives to assure potential donors that they are real people with real needs. As noted above, this practice commonly involves providing their real name and identity to the public and detailing the nature of their needs, including hospital bills, unemployment notices, rent invoices, and other bills. These campaigners are further encouraged to post images and videos of the recipient, seek out news coverage, and link the campaign to their social media accounts with the aim of demonstrating that the recipient is a real person with real needs who will receive any money that is donated to the campaign.

Research on donation-based crowdfunding shows that following these invasive recommendations does have an impact on reducing concerns about fraud and spurring donations. Kim et al. detail a range of factors that help establish the credibility of medical crowdfunding campaigns.[42] These include providing extensive details of any external financial support, such as insurance coverage; independent verification of the details of the illness or need; verification of the identity of the crowdfunding campaigner and recipient; regular updates on the recipient's medical condition and treatment; and emotional descriptions of the recipients' situation and need. Campaigners are aware that potential donors may be wary of fraudulent campaigns and often see providing copious details about their needs and regular updates as part of a compact with donors that establishes credibility and accountability and demonstrates how their donations will be used.

Crucially, though, reassuring potential donors of the legitimacy of crowdfunding campaigns comes at a significant cost to the campaigner's and recipient's privacy. As discussed in Chapters 2 and 3, crowdfunding already creates enormous pressures on campaigners and recipients to provide details about their personal lives, emotional states, and needs in order to demonstrate that they are worthy of help from others. But providing these details, although helping to establish the authenticity of the recipient and their need, undermines their privacy. Campaigners wishing to protect the anonymity of the recipient face a substantial challenge to their ability to raise money for their needs. Thus, it is reasonable to think that providing extensive details around the recipient's financial situation, needs, and emotional states, among other things, is a necessity rather than an option when proving their authenticity to people outside of their immediate social circle.

Moreover, efforts to demonstrate the legitimacy of campaigns can widen inequities in crowdfunding success, like those discussed in Chapter 4. Where specific racialized groups are popularly associated with fraud or other criminal activity, as is the case with welfare fraud, members of these groups are also likely to receive increased scrutiny in crowdfunding campaigns. More generally, following the advice given to campaigners about establishing the legitimacy of their campaign often requires the kinds of resources and training that are more likely to be found among more privileged communities, such as providing regular, detailed updates; independent verification of medical needs and treatment options; and video and other multimedia content help to establish the credibility of campaigns. Paradoxically, the ability to provide this information also reflects access to resources, including the time to produce these outputs, prior access to medical professionals, facility with online technologies, and the ability to clearly communicate with others. Research on crowdfunding campaigns also shows that concerns around campaign legitimacy will tend to amplify other inequities in crowdfunding success. Kim et al. show that potential donors tie credibility to campaign success, finding less successful campaigns less credible.[43] Similarly, the presence of personal comments on campaign pages helps to establish credibility but also demonstrates that the prior existence of donor networks helps to produce donations from strangers, further benefiting these campaigns. Thus, campaigners already facing inequities in the ability to succeed in crowdfunding may be found less trustworthy as a result of this more limited success.

An additional cost of combatting fraud in crowdfunding campaigns is that campaigners will necessarily cede some control over how crowdfunding funds are used. Campaigners are told that they must be extremely clear about how all funds received will be spent. Campaign updates should be used to notify donors of any changes in their needs, and, if these lead to changes in how funds will be used, campaigners should seek permission from donors to make these changes. If donors feel they were misled about how their donations will be used, they can report the campaign to the crowdfunding platform and potentially have their donations withheld. These safeguards are all reasonable in preventing clear cases of fraud, where the recipient seeks to put funds to uses completely disconnected from the campaign and where donors would not otherwise have supported the campaign. However, this heightened concern with fraud also gives donors de facto control over, for example, the recipient's medical decisions and erodes a significant degree of the recipient's autonomy over how they will meet their basic needs. This is problematic in its own right and even more so when the recipient is responding to changes in their needs and priorities. As mentioned in the previous chapter, this response to concerns around fraud shifts power over the fundraiser to donors, thus undermining the power of recipients to voice their needs and priorities and reducing the democratizing potential of crowdfunding.

Targeted interventions like GoFundMe's verified fundraiser hubs can help combat spikes in fraudulent activity that seek to take advantage of public interest in a newsworthy event. But these interventions also demonstrate the costs of antifraud activities. According to GoFundMe, the goal of these interventions is in large part to assure donors that "your funds will make it to those in need." It actively promotes the hubs it develops of verified campaigns to news media so that these campaigns are vastly more likely to receive news coverage and public attention than unverified campaigns.[44]

GoFundMe is clear that not being verified does not mean that a campaign is fraudulent but that the platform has "yet to confirm" the identity of the organizer and recipient and how they will use any funds raised.[45] But there is a large cost to not being verified. In the case of the British Columbia floods, the median amount requested by verified campaigns was $10,000, and they raised a median of $4,858 from 44 donors. By comparison, unverified campaigns also had a median goal of $10,000 but raised only a median of $220 from 4 donors. Of course, some of the unverified campaigns may have been fraudulent or lacked the clarity, emotional resonance, and appeal found in verified campaigns. But in other cases, campaigners had situations that made verification more challenging. For example, in one unverified campaign, the recipient was a single mother with a child with autism spectrum disorder whose name was omitted because "she is embarrassed and hates getting any help," leaving the campaigner to worry that "because her name isn't listed that this may get bypassed." Other unverified campaigns had no clear signs of fraud but may have experienced barriers to verification like limited internet access, difficulties accessing bank and other personal records while evacuating their homes, and a lack of friends or family members in a position to act as campaigners on their behalf. And even verified campaigns can struggle with the requirements these interventions impose. One verified campaign in the British Columbia floods hub on GoFundMe complained that the more than $20,000 it had raised was frozen by the platform for lack of sufficient details on how the funding would be used. The campaigner flagged repeated emails from GoFundMe "asking the same questions again and again." Responding to these questions was challenging given changing conditions in a disaster zone where "every minute and every dollar of help counts."

Conclusion

Online donation-based crowdfunding continues a long tradition of fraud in giving. It also creates new opportunities for fraud, given the online nature of this type of giving. The virality of some online crowdfunding campaigns gives fraudsters the opportunity to take advantage of a much larger segment of the general public, as with the Philadelphia couple pretending to help a veteran experiencing homelessness. The relative anonymity of online crowdfunding also benefits fraudsters who take on the identity of genuine people in need—something much more difficult to do when giving happens in person. In these ways, crowdfunding uses and builds on other fraudulent behaviors, and a lack of in-person contact and the ease of electronic transfers of funds make it easier to take advantage of others' generosity.

But much of the response to these real instances of fraud are deeply problematic in their own right and difficult to justify. Rather than solving a problem where crowdfunding donors are regularly being defrauded, these responses are seemingly motivated by the desire to protect the brands of specific crowdfunding platforms and this form of giving more generally. Just as home visits by groups like the Victorian Charity Organisation Society were highly invasive, crowdfunding platforms now increasingly demand that campaigners turn over a trove of personal and financial details. These platforms, like home visitors, can at least keep these personal details private from the general public while giving their stamp of approval on campaigns as verified or legitimate. But campaigners also face enormous pressure to disclose personal details on their public-facing campaigns in order to convince potential donors that their needs are genuine and that they are who they say they are. In this way, crowdfunding campaigners are compelled to police themselves for public consumption without any hope for privacy or equitable treatment.

7

Misinformation and hate

My dad had to die knowing that the Mexicans and Hispanics were coming into our country illegally, by the thousands, with no end in sight; and bringing drugs to our children, guns to their gangs, and murdering innocent American citizens. My dad had to die thinking that at any time our guns could be taken away from us by the government, and we would no longer be able to protect ourselves against anyone. My dad had to die knowing that homosexuals were able to perform the sacred act of marriage—even though the Bible clearly states that marriage is only meant to be between man and woman. My dad had to die knowing that homosexuals were also able to adopt innocent children, only to force them into that sick and perverted lifestyle. . . . To honor my father and continue his legacy, I started Healthy Husbands and Happy Fathers (HH && HH), a large multi-family camp site on our property that is dedicated to preserving the Proud and True American family.

In the previous chapter, I discussed how fraudulent crowdfunding campaigns are harmful when they mislead donors and misuse resources that might otherwise have benefited someone in genuine need. In one case, the hundreds of thousands of dollars raised by a Philadelphia couple to help a man experiencing homelessness find housing and restart his life were instead largely spent on gifts for themselves, including cars, vacations, and other luxuries. Donors were not just misled in this case, but other crowdfunding campaigners may have missed out on the opportunity to have their legitimate needs supported by these donors.

But even when crowdfunding campaigners are transparent and honest about their intended use of any gifts they receive, these campaigns may be harmful to others. This harm can happen in a variety of ways, but here I focus specifically on crowdfunding campaigns for causes that undermine

Appealing to the Crowd. Jeremy Snyder, Oxford University Press. © Oxford University Press 2024.
DOI: 10.1093/oso/9780197658130.003.0008

science and the public's health and promote discrimination and intolerance of others—in short, campaigns that spread misinformation and hate. As in other tech sectors, crowdfunding companies have had to confront people who seek to use their services to spread misinformation, denigrate other groups, and advocate for violence, among other harmful activities. This has been a learning process for these companies, with many platforms becoming more active in screening how their services are used and intervening to prohibit some activities. At the same time, crowdfunding platforms are different from other social media platforms in that they facilitate financial transfers to others. As a result, the free speech debates that are also embroiling other tech platforms are further complicated by the fact that money, rather than simply speech, is intrinsic to crowdfunding.

Giving for the lesser good

It should not be surprising that giving practices have often been coupled with horrific racist, sexist, and classist aims that reflect the many forms of discrimination and hatred directed at various groups—some of which have been detailed in previous chapters. To take one of the innumerable examples, residential schools for Indigenous children in Canada were funded in part by gifts from individuals and religious institutions (especially the Catholic Church). These schools in many cases had the explicit aim of cultural genocide against Indigenous peoples, which was also coupled with physical and sexual assault, poor living conditions, and overall neglect. Yet those funding these schools typically viewed themselves as engaged in positive, beneficent acts that would help these children.[1]

Of course, giving in support of hate, misinformation, and other direct harms is not just a historical artifact. A look at the groups that have been given tax-exempt status in the United States as philanthropic organizations demonstrates this point clearly. Specifically, a number of hate groups—understood as groups whose aim is to promote hostility to those belonging to another race, ethnicity, religion, nationality, sexual orientation, or group defined by other characteristics—have been awarded charitable status in the United States. These groups include the New Century Foundation, a group whose position is that nonwhite people are inferior to whites, nonwhites are harming the United States, and increasing racial diversity in the United States is undesirable.[2] Another white supremacist group, Richard Spencer's

National Policy Institute, enjoys charitable nonprofit status as an educational organization. This tax status was briefly removed but only because of a failure to submit necessary tax return information and not because of its harmful messaging.

Hate groups harm others by promoting hostility toward specific groups. In other cases, philanthropic organizations promote a genuinely held belief about what is in others' best interest but, in doing so, harm these people and spread misinformation. For example, the Family Research Council has been given tax-exempt status as an educational organization in the United States. This group regularly promotes hateful and false claims about lesbian, gay, bisexual, and transgender people, including that the gay rights movement is linked to pedophilia and the "recruitment" of youth into a homosexual lifestyle, marriages among same sex couples are unstable and undermine the family unit, and gay teens are inherently unhappier than straight teens.[3]

It is notable that these groups have been given tax-exempt status in the United States as nonprofit organizations. As discussed in Chapter 1, in many jurisdictions, donations to philanthropic organizations that have official nonprofit status are tax deductible. These organizations and the corresponding state support for them can be criticized as not representing the priorities of the majority within a community even if these organizations are promoting ends that the majority find desirable.[4] But, as these examples show, nonprofit organizations can also support causes that promote hate and spread misinformation that make the lives of marginalized community members worse. Giving tax-exempt status to hate groups and other organizations that harm others has several negative effects, including diverting tax revenue from projects that could help people or have other positive impacts, subsidizing the activities of groups that harm others, and sending the message that the government supports or condones harmful activities and messages.[5]

The success of philanthropic organizations that engage in harmful actions and misinformation depends in part on how socially acceptable their messaging and missions are or can be made to be. This, in turn, depends in part on larger social trends in their communities. Thus, while white supremacist and other hate groups have managed to retain charitable status in the United States and support for racial hatred has a long history in the United States and elsewhere, the social acceptability of this mission—at least when it is overt—has generally declined. In other cases, these groups can take advantage of new public concerns and events to greatly expand their operations and finances. During the COVID-19 pandemic, anti-vaccine groups that operated before the pandemic have seen donations to their cause increase significantly. For example, Robert F. Kennedy Jr.'s Children's Health Defense anti-vaccine nonprofit organization doubled its revenue from donations in 2020, raising $6.8 million. This support, in turn, allowed this group to reach a much wider print and online audience.[6]

Philanthropic organizations that are engaged in work benefiting others may also have their messaging hijacked by groups with more problematic agendas. For example, the philanthropic organization Save the Children has long raised legitimate concerns about child trafficking and worked worldwide to address this problem. In recent years, the QAnon conspiracy movement has used research, fundraisers, and messaging from this organization to support false claims that Hollywood elites, leaders of the Democratic party in the United States, and others have engaged in and covered up child trafficking. By adopting the motto "Save the Children" QAnon has been able to confuse donors and participants about its relationship with the legitimate philanthropy Save the Children. Using this name also complicates crackdowns by social media platforms that may be uncertain which discussions and accounts are associated with the legitimate organization as opposed to the conspiracy movement. Moreover, co-opting the language of Save the Children has been useful in recruiting new members, and this loose association with the legitimate philanthropy helps remove some initial reluctance to engage with the conspiracy movement's more extreme claims.[7] Legitimate philanthropies are not responsible for the harms perpetrated by groups that co-opt their names and messages, of course, but this example does highlight the need for legitimate groups to monitor and, to the extent they can, control how their names and messages are used.

Groups whose activities harm others and spread harmful misinformation can also take advantage of direct and indirect giving structures and regulations to downplay or hide their more controversial activities while still receiving support. Designation of a group as a charitable organization is often taken to imply state support or approval by the local government or other regulators. This status, coupled with innocuous-sounding names and descriptions of their activities, can lead some donors, philanthropies, and grant-making institutions to support these groups where they would not have done so if they were aware of the full range of their activities and positions.[8]

Oversight of how donations are distributed—and potentially used to support hate and misinformation—can be particularly challenging for large philanthropic organizations that seek to donate to many smaller nonprofits. For example, the AmazonSmile program is a private philanthropic foundation that enables customers using the Amazon website to donate 0.5% of the price of their purchases to the philanthropy of their choice. In the past, this program has been used to support organizations that threaten the rights of lesbian, gay, bisexual, and transgender people—groups such as the National Organization for Marriage Education Fund and Focus on the Family.[9] More recently, this program has been modified to exclude organizations labeled as hate groups by the Southern Poverty Law Center and groups suspected of supporting terrorism. While this program now also prohibits support for groups engaged in illegal, deceptive, and misleading activities, AmazonSmile continues to actively support other harmful organizations, such as anti-vaccine nonprofits. These include organizations that regularly make false claims about COVID-19 vaccines, encourage distrust about the safety of these vaccines, and support lawsuits against vaccine mandates. Despite banning terrorism and hate-related nonprofits, Amazon has defended allowing anti-vaccine groups to use its program because "We respect that our customers have a wide variety of viewpoints on this matter, which is why the charities in question continue to be included in the list of organizations customers can choose from as part of AmazonSmile."[10] However, this decision shows clearly how supporting other organizations puts philanthropies in the position of having to draw lines on what groups they will support directly or allow their customers and donors to support.

Crowdfunding hate and harm

As with more traditional forms of giving, donation-based crowdfunding campaigns that support hate groups, hateful messaging against others, and other harmful groups and causes are easy to find. Similar to crowdfunding in general, campaigns that promote harmful actors and causes often attract few donors, raise little money, and fall short of their fundraising goals. This was the case, for example, with a campaign by the owner of a deli in New Jersey that lost business after posting a sign in his business celebrating "white heritage" and "white history month" immediately following Black History Month in the United States. This store owner was told by his black and Jewish neighbors that they found the sign offensive and felt it mocked Black History Month; however, the owner only removed the sign after a significant loss of business. In response, the store owner initiated a crowdfunding campaign to make up for this lost income and keep his business solvent. He was able to raise a few hundred dollars through this crowdfunding campaign, but not enough to keep his business open.[11]

But, in some cases, campaigns supporting hateful messaging can be much more successful and benefit from the viral potential of online fundraising. The GoFundMe campaign to build a border wall between the United States and Mexico is a notable example. After the US Congress failed to fund construction of a border wall despite President Donald Trump's pledge to do so, the We Build the Wall crowdfunding campaign sought to build the wall using private funds. This campaign was able to raise more than $25 million in donations and begin the construction of sections of border wall on private land. While reasonable people can disagree over the requirements of border security, priorities of immigration policy, and appropriate treatment of undocumented migrants, it is clear that this particular project was fueled and supported in significant part by hateful attitudes toward Latino immigrants to the United States. At an event showing off a portion of the wall built by these funds and hosted by campaign organizers Brian Kolfage and Steve Bannon, speakers denounced immigration as an "invasion" and "infection," where immigrants "are coming here to do damage. They're coming here to steal *your* money. It's gotta stop. You people, the American patriots, are the ones that are leading this charge. This is the firing of the first shot."[12]

This campaign did hit significant roadblocks along the way, including having to refund more than $10 million in pledges after the campaign's aim was changed from building the wall on public land through the US government to building it without government involvement on private land. Eventually, both Kolfage and Bannon would also be charged with fraud for pocketing some of these donations.[13] While the We Build the Wall campaign fell dramatically short of its goal of completing a border wall between the United States and Mexico and it became mired in a criminal prosecution, it demonstrates that the most successful crowdfunding campaigns, like well-financed philanthropic organizations, are able to shape news coverage, political discussion and priorities, and popular perceptions. Money is in a significant way convertible to power, and crowdfunding can serve as a platform for people with hateful and harmful messages to gain and project that power.

Crowdfunding campaigns have also been used to pay for the legal defense of people who have been accused of hate crimes, murder, political violence, and other harmful activities. These include legal defense funds for police officers who have shot and killed racialized minorities, such as the GoFundMe fundraiser that brought in more than $200,000 for the white police officer who shot and killed the unarmed black teenager Michael Brown.[14] Crowdfunding campaigns have also been active in supporting the legal costs of people who participated in the January 6, 2021, insurrection in the US Capitol, raising hundreds of thousands of dollars in campaigns describing these defendants as "political prisoners" and "patriots."[15] This is not to say that people accused of crimes, no matter how serious, should not be entitled to a legal defense. However, the quality of one's defense is often connected to the amount of money one has to spend on lawyers, expert witnesses, and other resources, meaning that these campaigns make it more likely that these defendants will be found not guilty, reach a favorable plea bargain, or receive lighter punishments than people with fewer financial resources. In these cases, one can reasonably question the aims of donors in favoring these defendants versus the many others in need of legal representation in the United States and elsewhere. In fact, these donations are typically made not in the interest of universal access to high-quality legal representation but in support of the hateful and harmful messages and actions of specific defendants.

Crowdfunding campaigns may themselves contain hateful messages or attitudes as well. Fundraisers for so-called conversion therapy meant to change recipients' sexual orientation or gender identity typically include bigoted language about gay, lesbian, and bisexual people—language that is often highly personalized and directed at the campaign recipient by close family.[16] To take another example, a crowdfunding campaign on the Indian platform Milaap sought to aid victims of a riot that took place in Delhi. This campaign was organized by Kapil Mishra, the Delhi-based leader of the Hindu nationalist Bharatiya Janata Party (BJP)—who was also accused of having instigated these riots. While aiding riot victims is laudatory, Mishra chose to explicitly allow only Hindus to benefit from the campaign and propagate a message of Hindu superiority over Muslims.[17]

Crowdfunding can make campaigners a target for hateful attacks as well. Because crowdfunding campaigns are normally conducted in public and benefit from widespread attention, campaigns for stigmatized needs can attract undesired social media attention, abusive comments, and personal threats. These forms of hate speech can take place directly on the crowdfunding campaign page, as these pages typically include options to leave comments.

When this abuse happens, crowdfunding platforms become responsible for moderating and removing these comments—a task they may perform with differing levels of energy and competence. In other cases, campaigns are linked to through other social media platforms, with invitations to attack the campaigner. This kind of abuse has happened, for example, to some crowdfunders in India seeking help with gender-affirming surgery.[18] These attacks are much more difficult for crowdfunding platforms to police or stop as they are coordinated through other social media platforms. That said, the social and public dimensions of crowdfunding enable these attacks and make it difficult for crowdfunding campaigners to make their appeals in private.

Because crowdfunding is more direct and less institutionally mediated than some other mechanisms for giving, it may be particularly attractive to fringe movements and groups that have not received mainstream support or are locked out of institutional support because of their beliefs or messages. A study of crowdfunding campaigns for political causes in Canada on the GoFundMe platform found that these campaigns tended to support extreme right-wing causes and frequently used aggressive, misleading, and hateful rhetoric. This language included unsubstantiated charges that the prime minister of Canada was receiving bribes and engaged in other criminal conduct. Anti-Muslim political campaigns were also common and spread hateful messaging about that religion. Left-wing and progressive political campaigns were also identified in this study, but they were less common and more closely associated with mainstream movements, including protecting the environment and ensuring justice for Indigenous groups. While political groups across the spectrum of causes and interests may use crowdfunding, then, it may be particularly appealing for those groups that struggle to raise funding by other means and may see little support for their views and voices in more institutionally mediated venues, including social media platforms.[19]

While campaigns that support hate groups and include hateful messaging are clearly problematic, they are not the only harmful groups and causes supported through crowdfunding platforms. Medical clinics selling unproven and potentially dangerous medical interventions are common beneficiaries of crowdfunding campaigns. These interventions include stem cell treatments that are not proved to be effective and have caused significant harm, homeopathic treatments that are completely ineffective, and other potentially dangerous interventions such as hyperbaric oxygen treatments for people with brain injuries.[20-22] Crowdfunding campaigns typically do not provide a direct benefit to these clinics. Rather, they fund treatments for the campaign recipients and in doing so supply these clinics with paying customers. These treatments can be directly harmful to the patient, as when stem cell treatments cause significant side effects or even death.[23] In other instances, the treatments are ineffective, in which case customers have wasted their own money and that of their donors. This financial loss may also be coupled with negative health impacts if the crowdfunding recipient chooses to forgo proven effective treatment in favor of unproven and ineffective treatments made available through crowdfunding. In other cases, seeking these ineffective treatments can mean less time spent with friends and family or coming to terms with a medical diagnosis.

These crowdfunding campaigns have raised substantial amounts of money that is then sent to clinics selling unproven medical treatments. One analysis of just over 1,000 campaigns for unproven stem cell treatments for neurological treatments documented more than $5 million in donations.[24] A set of 1,636 campaigns for homeopathic cancer treatments, hyperbaric oxygen therapy for brain injury, stem cell treatments for brain injury, and long-term antibiotics for Lyme disease raised nearly $6.8 million.[25] Nearly 1,400 campaigns for complementary and alternative cancer treatments brought in over $12.7 million.[26] The success of individual campaigns, like all crowdfunding campaigns, is variable, and many fall well short of their goals. Others, like a viral campaign for an unproven treatment for Charlie Gard, a British infant, raised £1,352,060.[27] Crowdfunding is a significant source of revenue for these businesses because private and public insurance typically does not pay for interventions that haven't received regulatory approval or that are not proved to be effective. In some cases, clinics have even expressly referred would-be patients to crowdfunding platforms to pay for their services.[28] Thus, these crowdfunding campaigns not only allow campaigners to access these treatments but also support the ability of these clinics to remain open for other paying customers.

Viral misinformation

Crowdfunding campaigns are much like other forms of giving. In all of these forms, donations can support groups, individuals, and causes that directly harm others and spread hateful attitudes toward marginalized groups. They can also promote harmful misinformation, including false claims of medical cures, climate change denialism, and lies about voting results. These effects are not unique to crowdfunding as giving has historically supported hateful and harmful causes and spread misinformation to the wider public.

What is particularly distinctive about crowdfunding's role in promoting hate, misinformation, and other harms through giving is found in its online and social dimensions. As a form of social media, crowdfunding campaigns are designed to be shared and engaged with by as large an array of potential donors as possible. Campaign pages typically have options to share the campaign on other social media platforms like Twitter and Facebook to encourage other people to view and potentially contribute to the campaign. It is also common for donors to be able to leave comments on the campaign page that they can then share with their online contacts. Even when people choose not to contribute to a campaign or feel they are not financially able to support it, they are often encouraged to share it on social media or through email so that others might support the campaign financially.

The online and social nature of crowdfunding means that the impact of these campaigns is not limited to generating financial support for the campaign recipient. In addition, misinformation and hateful messaging can be spread to donors and even people who simply view the campaign. This concern is supported by research on misinformation in crowdfunding campaigns that demonstrates the considerable reach of campaigns beyond their immediate donor base. The number of times these campaigns are shared on social media far outstrips the number of donations. For example, in one study, 1,396 campaigns seeking complementary and alternative cancer treatments received 122,701 donations and 577,351—or well over four times as many—shares on Facebook alone.[29] Similarly, a group of 1,030 campaigns for unproven stem cell treatments for neurological diseases included 38,713 donations and 199,490 Facebook shares.[30] These numbers do not include sharing on other social media platforms or directly through email as these activities are not tracked on the GoFundMe website where these studies were conducted. Thus, these numbers understate the wider impact of these campaigns in spreading misinformation online.

In the context of medical misinformation, campaigners have a strong incentive to misinform potential donors about the effectiveness of unproven medical treatments and other interventions because donors are less likely to support a medical intervention or other campaign where whether it will help the recipient is highly uncertain. Campaigners are likely to expect donors to want to know that they will get their money's worth in the sense that their donation will have a positive impact on the recipient's life. For this reason, it is reasonable to expect campaigners to exaggerate the likelihood of positive outcomes and underestimate or simply ignore any risks to the recipient. This is not necessarily intentional on the part of the campaigner, and they themselves may be misinformed about the safety and efficacy of the intervention. In other cases, they may be aware of the genuine uncertainty around an unproven intervention but feel compelled to put its efficacy in the best light possible in the interest of reaching their fundraising goal, even if this means not being fully honest in their campaigns.

Systematic exaggeration of the safety and efficacy of unproven treatments in crowdfunding campaigns not only follows the logic of crowdfunding as a competition for donations but is also borne out in the research on these campaigns. Among crowdfunding campaigns for homeopathic cancer treatments, for example, 29% made unsubstantiated positive claims about the efficacy of these treatments, compared with 1% that noted uncertainty about their efficacy.[31] A majority of campaigns seeking funding to use cannabidiol to treat cancer stated without evidence that this intervention was definitely effective in treating their cancer and extending their lives.[32] And, despite evidence that stem cell interventions include risks including infection, crowdfunding campaigns for unproven stem cell interventions rarely mentioned the risks of these treatments and, when they did so, exclusively claimed that stem cell interventions entailed no risk and were safer than conventional treatments.[33]

Medical campaigns are also highly effective in terms of spreading misinformation as they often take the form of patient testimonials. Clinics selling directly to consumers often use patient testimonials on their websites and social media pages because this form of advertising is highly effective. Crowdfunding campaigns extend this practice, often including testimonials from people known to and trusted by those viewing and donating to these campaigns and sharing them online. Notably, for-profit clinics and other businesses selling unproven medical treatments or other allegedly life-saving interventions may hedge their statements around efficacy and safety to avoid running afoul of local regulations or to avoid the potential for lawsuits. These fears do not similarly limit the claims of crowdfunding campaigners, however, as these claims reflect campaigners' own experiences and expectations. Thus, where patient testimonials and other claims by these businesses betray some concern for legal liability, crowdfunding allows these claims to be amplified and further exaggerated without supporting evidence.[34]

These campaigns also muddy the ground between legitimate medical institutions and for-profit clinics selling unproven treatments directly to consumers. Crowdfunding campaigns for unproven medical interventions frequently use the language of medical research to communicate the perceived scientific legitimacy of these interventions. References to studies and research are often used by for-profit clinics on their websites and sales materials which are then picked up in the language of crowdfunding campaigners. Campaigners may link to media coverage of the clinics where they wish to purchase treatment, YouTube testimonials, and the clinic's website. In some cases, for-profit clinics sell products still being researched elsewhere. These legitimate research activities then become deliberately confused with the product being sold directly to consumers ahead of clear evidence of efficacy and safety. This language, and the muddiness between the for-profit clinics and ongoing research activities, is then reproduced on crowdfunding campaign pages and shared extensively and effectively online.[35]

Most research on how crowdfunding amplifies campaign narratives online has focused on medical misinformation. But the same logic of sharing applies to other forms of harmful messaging as well, including hateful speech. Where these messages are included in crowdfunding campaigns, they are likely to be shared via other social media and have an impact far beyond the financial resources they receive. As with campaigns including medical misinformation, these messages are shared among personal contacts and can be particularly persuasive. Campaigners for hateful ends and unproven medical treatments all have an incentive to exaggerate the facts motivating the need for financial support and the likely success of their projects. Thus, in the We Build the Wall fundraiser, for example, the campaigners made false claims about the danger undocumented migration poses to the American way of life in exaggerated terms meant to motivate giving and provoke responses of hatred and fear. These claims were then reproduced widely on other social media platforms, even among people who did not support the campaign financially.

Gatekeeping crowdfunding

Crowdfunding campaigns, like other forms of giving, can support organizations, businesses, and individuals that perpetuate hate, discrimination, misinformation, and other harmful beliefs and outcomes. Moreover, these

campaigns are highly effective at spreading these messages and misinformation to donors and a much wider web of people viewing these campaigns.
These problems put crowdfunding platforms in a position of having to decide which campaigns they will host and how they will enforce prohibitions
on certain types of campaigns.

A look at the terms of service of the largest donation-based crowdfunding
platforms shows that they have the ability to ban campaigns supporting activities that encourage hate, intolerance, and discrimination. For example,
GoFundMe prohibits campaign content "that reflects or promotes behavior
that we deem, in our sole discretion, to be an abuse of power or in support
of hate, violence, harassment, bullying, discrimination, terrorism, or intolerance of any kind relating to race, ethnicity, national origin, religious
affiliation, sexual orientation, sex, gender, gender identity, gender expression, serious disabilities or diseases." Language prohibiting discriminatory
campaigns was first added when GoFundMe was criticized for hosting a
campaign to pay for the legal defense of a bakery that refused to fill an order
for a lesbian couple.[36] This platform also includes more general prohibitions
on "offensive, graphic, perverse or sensitive content" and "any other activity
that GoFundMe may deem, in its sole discretion, to be unacceptable."[37]
Similarly, Milaap includes a prohibition against "the promotion of hate, violence, harassment, discrimination or terrorism, or racial, ethnic, or gender
intolerance of any kind," and Ketto restricts "racism, bigotry, hatred or physical harm of any kind against any group or individual."[38,39] In New Zealand,
the crowdfunding platform Givealittle has a general prohibition on content
that "promotes or provides inflammatory or demeaning opinions of an individual or group."[40] These variations aside, prohibitions on hateful and
discriminatory content are standard in the donation-based crowdfunding
sector.

These prohibitions are also shaped by the particular cultural context of the
crowdfunding platform's location and primary clientele. For example, while
GoFundMe explicitly prohibits content that expresses intolerance on the
basis of sexual orientation, gender identity, and gender expression, India's
Milaap and Ketto do not have these restrictions. At the same time, Milaap
forbids campaigns that would "end the life of an animal" and limits campaigns
related to religious activities, including "utilisation for activities that propa-
gate/preach a religion including but not limited to construction and/or con-
secration of religious symbols, institutions, events, evangelism, organizing
sermons, or any other activity that could be interpreted as a religious activity

by potential donors or authorities."[41] In the same vein, India's Ketto prohibits "blasphemous" content.[42]

A platform's specific history can also shape its terms of service. The backlash GoFundMe received for hosting legal support campaigns for people accused of violence, hate crimes, and other forms of harmful conduct further shaped the kinds of campaigns the platform now prohibits. As a result, it does not allow campaigns to pay for "legal defense of alleged crimes associated with hate, violence, harassment, bullying, discrimination, terrorism, or intolerance of any kind relating to race, ethnicity, national origin, religious affiliation, sexual orientation, sex, gender, gender identity, gender expression, serious disabilities or diseases, financial crimes or crimes of deception."[43] As these changes demonstrate, the terms of service of crowdfunding sites are frequently reactive and are regularly refined in response to current events.

Tracking community norms about what kinds of fundraising are acceptable can be complicated, and taking an overly restrictive interpretation of these norms can backfire for crowdfunding platforms. For example, in 2014, GoFundMe removed a campaign seeking financial help to pay to terminate the campaigner's pregnancy. It followed this decision with a blanket prohibition against campaigns to pay for abortion services along with "sorcery" and activities related to the "adult industry." The rationale given for this decision was to "ensure a positive experience for all visitors," and this goal seemingly took the form of removing campaigns for any activities that donors or other viewers might find objectionable.[44] Flagging abortion-related campaigns for special treatment is not unique to GoFundMe, as Milaap specifically references a prohibition on fundraising for abortion services "unless in accordance with applicable laws."[45] GoFundMe's ban on abortion-related services (and sorcery for that matter) was later reversed, and campaigns to support abortion-related services for individuals and for abortion providers are now hosted on this platform. This experience demonstrates how crowdfunding platforms are often used to fund needs touching on culturally, religiously, and politically divisive issues. For this reason, attempts to remain neutral about what conduct counts as hateful and discriminatory are unlikely to succeed.

Misinformation, especially around medical treatments, can be restricted on these websites as well. GoFundMe has a direct prohibition on fundraising for medical interventions that do not have regulatory approval, including "pharmaceuticals or similar products or therapies that are either illegal, prohibited, or enjoined by an applicable regulatory body."[46] This restriction could be used to prohibit fundraisers for clinics that skirt local regulations on selling unproven medical treatments, though in practice these clinics generally operate in jurisdictions that allow the sale of unproven stem cell interventions and other treatments that haven't been approved in the campaigner's home country. Previously, GoFundMe had more restrictive language prohibiting "products that make health claims that have not been approved or verified" by local regulators. This more restrictive language was used to justify GoFundMe shutting down fundraisers for treatment at Germany's Hallwang Clinic, a facility that offers unproven and disproven cancer treatments.[47]

GoFundMe has acted to restrict other forms of medical misinformation on its platform, responding in part to public concern that it was hosting and facilitating this misinformation. After it was demonstrated that anti-vaccine groups had raised at least $170,000 on GoFundMe to support their activities, GoFundMe explicitly banned fundraisers for these groups. As with the ban on fundraisers for treatment at the Hallwang Clinic, this action against anti-vaccine groups was based on an earlier version of GoFundMe's terms of service that prohibited fundraisers for medical products and services that made claims that had not been verified. Later versions of its terms of service would only restrict campaigns for products that have not been approved by regulators.[48] These examples show that bans on funding unapproved medical interventions and misinformation are inconsistent and reactive, with only the Hallwang Clinic specifically banned by GoFundMe and only vaccine misinformation prohibited. Other clinics selling unproven treatments and other forms of medical misinformation remain common on GoFundMe and other crowdfunding platforms.

Even when crowdfunding platforms are determined to strictly monitor what kinds of campaigns use their websites, crafting enforceable terms of service is challenging. When terms of service prohibit specific activities, groups can find ways to raise money in support of individuals and events associated with hate-based content that circumvent these restrictions. For example, various college Republican groups used GoFundMe to fundraise to bring Milo Yiannopoulos to their campus to speak. Yiannopoulos is associated with the alt-right movement in the United States, has engaged in targeted racist harassment and anti-Muslim hate speech, and has been banned from other social media platforms like Twitter. However, these fundraisers were able to circumvent GoFundMe's prohibitions of activities in support of hate and discrimination by limiting their appeal to paying for security costs and the venue for the speech but not for Yiannopoulos's direct fees.[49] GoFundMe and other crowdfunding platforms can take advantage of more general permissions to close campaigns they find objectionable, but doing so opens them to accusations of taking sides in culture war debates and censoring specific political views.

When some social media platforms ban users for hateful or misleading statements, they can often find a home on other platforms. This was the case for Brian Kolfage, one of the organizers of the hugely successful We Build the Wall crowdfunding campaign. After Facebook took down several pages he organized that were filled with hateful and misleading language and images, he initiated a crowdfunding campaign to challenge this ban in court. This campaign, which raised nearly $75,000, likely served as a proof of concept of an alternative way to monetize and proliferate Kolfage's messaging around immigration.[50] After GoFundMe removed the wall campaign from its platform, Kolfage announced that his group would move it to FundRazr, a donation-based crowdfunding platform with headquarters in Canada.[51]

Kolfage's migration from fundraising platform to fundraising platform in search of a supportive home traces a larger trend on social media websites. As platforms like Twitter, YouTube, and Facebook have become more active in prohibiting hateful and abusive language and misinformation, people banned from these platforms have been forced to seek an audience elsewhere. In some cases, they move from one mainstream platform to another when one is banned from, for example, YouTube but still allowed to maintain a presence on Facebook. But, in other cases, whether because they have been banned from all mainstream platforms or because of a sense of persecution by platforms that restrict hateful speech and misinformation, less-restrictive alternative platforms have emerged. Thus, Gab, Gettr, and other websites advertise themselves as right-wing or more permissive alternatives to Twitter, Rumble has taken a position as an alternative to YouTube, and MeWe substitutes for Facebook.[52]

Restrictions on content and recipients on crowdfunding platforms have also inspired less-restrictive alternatives. In the United States, the most prominent of these is GiveSendGo, the self-described "#1 free Christian crowdfunding site" and "the leader in freedom fundraising."[53] This platform includes categories that highlight its Christian orientation, including fundraising for religious missions, churches, and evangelism. Its terms of use are similar to those on other, secular crowdfunding platforms and include prohibitions on fundraisers for "illegal activities" and specifically activities violating "any law, statute, ordinance or regulation" regarding "items that promote hate, violence, racial intolerance."[54]

But while GiveSendGo hosts fundraisers related to a wide range of activities found on other crowdfunding platforms, its particular claim to fame has been in hosting campaigns that GoFundMe refuses to host or has removed. These fundraisers have included campaigns for anti-gay conversion therapy, hate groups like the Proud Boys, and vaccine conspiracy theorists. Following GoFundMe's decision not to allow fundraising for the legal defense of people accused of violent crimes, GiveSendGo has become an enthusiastic host of campaigns featuring people accused of taking part in the January 6, 2021, insurrection in the United States, police officers accused of assault and murder, and Kyle Rittenhouse.

Rittenhouse was indicted for (and later acquitted of) murder after shooting three people at a Black Lives Matter protest in Wisconsin, which led to the death of two of them. After GoFundMe removed fundraisers for Rittenhouse's legal defense, GiveSendGo not only allowed these fundraisers to be hosted on its platform but issued enthusiastic press releases, including the argument that "everyone should be afforded the right to be innocent until proven guilty no matter what our personal beliefs are."[55] By comparison, GoFundMe defended its decision to bar these fundraisers as they "care deeply about human rights and have written terms to address this—we do not allow fundraisers that support hate, violence, harassment, bullying, discrimination; or involves weaponry."[56] As a result, the campaign for Rittenhouse was still able to find a home and was very successful in raising money for his highly effective legal defense.

Conclusion

Reasonable people can disagree about whether crowdfunding platforms should prohibit fundraisers for people accused of violent crimes or take a more inclusive approach to hosting campaigns regardless of their content. GiveSendGo has taken the latter position to an extreme, with their CEO Jacob Wells declaring that "If the KKK or any other group of people, if what they're doing is within the law, I would consider it an honor to have them use the platform and share the hope of Jesus with them."[57] To some extent, this is a difference in branding. GiveSendGo has staked out a position in the crowdfunding landscape as both a Christian enterprise and embracer of "freedom," understood as limiting very few fundraisers based on their content. GoFundMe, by comparison, brands itself around being a trusted force for positive change, highlighting the campaigns of so-called GoFundMe Heroes and causes championed by historically marginalized groups.

But regardless of their brand, crowdfunding platforms are put in a position of gatekeeping access to their websites. As a general rule, these platforms at the very least won't host fundraisers for illegal activities or fraudulent purposes. And, despite its focus on allowing people to crowdfund for any legal purpose, even GiveSendGo prohibits fundraisers for abortion services.[58] These red lines put them in a position of deciding what fundraising activities are acceptable and which are not, effectively shaping access to this practice and how money will flow to a range of causes. As we have seen, in some cases these causes include campaigns that harm others through hate, misinformation, and other means. This in itself is not new in the context of giving practices. However, crowdfunding has the potential to spread these messages more widely than in other giving practices, given its status as a form of social media, its integration into other social media platforms, and the incentives it creates for campaigners to exaggerate and expand on misinformation.

8

Crowdfunding during a pandemic

I'm sorry to have to ask for help but I've been struggling since I had Covid back in October and now I have it again plus the flu. My two oldest kids are here for the summer and we definitely didn't plan on me getting sick. I literally just paid my rent and utilities this week and will be way behind on my car payment and groceries and meds. I am praying that none of the kids get sick. I'm a waitress and I make a living day to day by having tips. I won't be able to wait tables again until Monday unless one of the kids gets sick too, then it's more days off from work. Tips aren't so great these days anyway in this small town as business is a little slow. And at $2.50 an hour with only working 3 or 4 days a week, my check is usually between $20 and $30 every week. If the two older kids get sick, I will have to pay co-pays for insurance and meds. I can send proof of car payment if needed. Anything helps, even if it's just prayers. Thank you in advance. I promise if there is any money left over, I will pay it forward. I have people that can vouch for me paying it forward last time I had Covid.

During the COVID-19 pandemic, use of donation-based crowdfunding expanded greatly in reaction to the illness, economic impacts, and social disruptions caused directly and indirectly by the pandemic. This expanded use of crowdfunding demonstrated both the positive and negative aspects of crowdfunding as it gained wider visibility and took a more central and influential position among the mechanisms used to meet people's basic needs. Crowdfunding platforms in some instances also took a more expansive role in shaping giving practices during the pandemic in ways that will have impacts after the pandemic's end.

Appealing to the Crowd. Jeremy Snyder, Oxford University Press. © Oxford University Press 2024.
DOI: 10.1093/oso/9780197658130.003.0009

Crowdfunding to the rescue

While the visibility of and participation in donation-based crowdfunding has been steadily increasing over the past decade, the COVID-19 pandemic instigated a marked acceleration in this trend. For example, in 2017, major disasters, including wildfires, hurricanes, an earthquake in Mexico, and a mass shooting in Las Vegas, accounted for 61,469 campaigns on the GoFundMe crowdfunding platform. During 2020, however, this platform hosted over 300,000 COVID-19–related campaigns.[1] This increase in activity took place in part because the pandemic created massive new pressures on health systems by increasing demand, straining medical supplies, and stressing health workers through illness and overwork. Both wealthy regions with well-functioning and financed public insurance and health systems and areas with fewer resources struggled to cope with these demands. In Venezuela, long-standing economic problems and the decay of the public health system meant that many people sought help from friends and family abroad through crowdfunding campaigns.[2] A similar story played out in India, where inadequate insurance and a spike in need left many with medical debt and led to an increased use of crowdfunding.[3] One Indian news analysis described the effect of the pandemic in India as causing massive strain on already fragile social support systems, leading to a "seismic shift" in giving where it was "crowdfunding to the rescue."[4]

As illness and restrictions on businesses and social gatherings spread during the first wave of coronavirus infections in early 2020, GoFundMe saw a rapid rise in campaign activity. It quickly set up a hub for COVID-19–related fundraisers and sought to increase the visibility of these campaigns. By March 20, 2020, COVID-19–related fundraisers on GoFundMe had raised $40 million from 22,000 campaigns.[5] Between March 20 and 24, 13,000 additional COVID-19–related campaigns were created, amounting to a 60% increase.[6] March 25 saw the highest number of campaigns created during the first pandemic wave, and March 26 was the most active day for donations, with over $7.9 million raised on that day alone. According to GoFundMe's own numbers, by August 31, 2020, crowdfunding on the platform had increased to $625 million, pledged from 9 million donations, for 150,000 COVID-19–related fundraisers.[7] A separate analysis identified 175,000 campaigns for COVID-19–related needs on GoFundMe initiated between January 1 and July 31, 2020, which raised more than $416 million from 4.75 million donors.[8] Yet another study found that 51,763 US-based

COVID-19–related campaigns initiated from January 1 to May 10, 2020, raised over $237 million.[9] On GoFundMe, COVID-19–related campaigns during 2020 focused on the United States. The largest of these fundraisers in the United States brought in $136 million in donations, compared with nearly $18 million for fundraisers with recipients in Italy and $1.3 million for recipients in Spain.[10]

A similar flurry of crowdfunding activity took place on India-based crowdfunding platforms. Milaap reported hosting nearly 68,000 COVID-19–related campaigns that raised $62.7 million from over 1.5 million donations. This platform highlighted select campaigns in a COVID-19 campaign hub, including campaigns for healthcare workers, people with medical needs, and people out of work due to the global economic downturn exacerbated by public health measures. To promote these campaigns, Milaap announced that it was treating the pandemic as akin to a natural disaster and waiving its fees for hosting these campaigns.[11] Elsewhere in India, by the end of May 2021, Ketto reported raising $48.6 million from 213,000 donors for 4,420 COVID-related campaigns. As with Milaap, all platform fees were waived for these campaigns. Ketto highlighted campaigns to address oxygen shortages in Indian hospitals, address shortages of medical equipment and personal protective equipment, and help feed people in need during the pandemic.[12] A third major Indian crowdfunding platform, ImpactGuru, recorded $11.3 million donated by 57,580 people to campaigns related to COVID-19, highlighting the needs of people ill from the virus and healthcare workers.[13]

One advantage of crowdfunding over more institutionalized philanthropic and public support is that it can be very nimble in responding to emerging and emergency needs. This agility was demonstrated as crowdfunding platforms, campaigners, and donors quickly responded to the rapidly changing landscape during the early days of the COVID-19 pandemic. Early in this crisis, many campaigns focused on supporting people in China, where the COVID-19 outbreak was initially centered, and helping migrants and visitors seeking to get home as travel restrictions were put into place. As cases of the virus were discovered elsewhere in the world, the focus of crowdfunding campaigns expanded to include aid to frontline health workers combatting the virus and help for small business owners and employees who lost out on income due to pandemic mitigation measures.

A closer look at data from GoFundMe shows these shifts in crowdfunding aims in the early days of the pandemic and the ways regional differences shaped these aims. In one study of US-based campaigns from January 1 to

May 10, 2020, most campaigns were initiated after March 11 and peaked in mid-March, with significant declines in April of that year. This trend followed peaks in infections during the first wave of the pandemic in the United States and easing of mitigation measures in many areas.[14] In the US, COVID-related campaigns largely sought help with living expenses and lost wages (88%), followed by help purchasing medical supplies and relief for health workers. Notably, in Italy, which experienced much more severe early impacts from the COVID-19 outbreak compared with the United States, most campaigns focused on the needs of health workers (54.6%), with the second-most-common goal being raising funds for medical expenses (26.9%).[15] During the first months of the COVID-19 pandemic, campaigns with Canadian organizers most commonly focused on raising money for local and global philanthropic organizations and for the purchase of personal protective equipment. By comparison, very few (6%) of these campaigns sought help for businesses during this period, despite the financial impacts of local and national lockdowns and other preventive measures.[16] UK crowd-funding site JustGiving noted that with the pandemic "we're in this together" and highlighted campaigns for people who had medical needs, faced home-lessness, or were dealing with social isolation and loneliness, and campaigns for animals and pets.[17] Crowdfunding platforms in France showed a signif-icant upsurge in activity in April 2020, initially focusing on responding to needs related to infection with COVID-19 and efforts to reduce its spread. These campaigns made up the majority of all crowdfunding activity on the French platforms Leetchi, Ulule, and KissKissBankBank during that time. As the pandemic went on, other campaigns aimed to raise money to thank medical staff struggling under the demand created by the first wave of the pandemic, provide personal protective and other medical equipment, and help populations made vulnerable by systemic injustice, including battered women, refugees, and people experiencing homelessness.[18]

Later on in the pandemic, regionalized impacts of COVID-19 and gov-ernment responses continued to influence crowdfunding campaigns. While much of the world experienced waves of COVID-19 outbreaks with different variants shaping the spread of the virus, New Zealand initially and success-fully pursued a zero-COVID policy that sought to prevent the virus from entering the country, especially before vaccines were widely accessible. As a result, crowdfunding campaigns by New Zealand residents during the first year of the pandemic tended to focus on navigating the impacts of its highly restrictive lockdown measures. These included delays and cancellations in accessing healthcare both domestically and abroad, loss of employment and income, increased mental health burdens from social isolation and worry, difficulty accessing education for children with disabilities, and isolation in unsafe living conditions.[19] By comparison, in Canada, growth in campaigns related to COVID-19 closely followed key events in that country, including the first identified domestic cases, introduction of lockdown measures, and eventual easing of lockdowns and other restrictions after the first wave of infections.[20]

Broad economic rather than medical needs dominated crowdfunding activity on GoFundMe. Fundraisers addressing the needs of small businesses and people experiencing unemployment made up nearly 60% of campaigns, and campaigns for food and financial support represented 6.9% of campaigns initiated between March 1 and August 31, 2020. By comparison, campaigns for personal protective equipment and other supports for frontline medical workers came in at 9.0%, medical needs constituted 3.2%, and memorials and funeral costs 2.0%.[21] In response to this focus on needs outside of the medical category, GoFundMe created a new fundraising category for rent, food, and monthly bills in October 2020.[22] While crowdfunding campaigners worldwide sought help with paying medical bills, making up for lost income, sustaining a business, and supplying medical workers with equipment, some communities struggled to survive at all. In India, one platform highlighted a specific campaign for a migrant laborer impacted by that country's lockdown. For this person, due to pandemic mitigation measures, "death due to COVID-19 was a distant possibility but death due to starvation a very real, very close reality."[23] For others, school closures meant that people already struggling to afford school fees would need to find alternative online education and pay for internet access. As a result, their children may be "deprived of basic education."[24]

As social isolation mandates impacted income, businesses, and employment, GoFundMe took a more activist position in calling on government action to complement crowdfunding by individuals. In early 2021, as the US government debated a COVID-19 relief package, GoFundMe CEO Tim Cadogan published an opinion article in *USA Today* arguing that federal assistance was needed and that crowdfunding should not be used to replace public supports. As part of this call for public action, Cadogan noted that COVID-19–related crowdfunding had persisted through the pandemic and that the new category for rent and basic living expenses already made up 13% of all campaigns. In January 2021, moreover, fundraisers for food-related expenses were up 45% from one year earlier. Cadogan noted specific examples of the impact of crowdfunding, including that it had saved some small businesses from having to fire employees or close altogether.[25]

One problem for crowdfunding platforms during the pandemic was the optics of benefiting from others' suffering—an issue that may have factored into Cadogan's criticism of the US Congress. The rapid increase in crowd-funding activity benefited these platforms in that they would receive greater revenues as a result, either through set percentages of the totals donated to these campaigns or through voluntary tips from donors. As noted above, several Indian crowdfunding platforms responded by waiving their set fees for COVID-related campaigns. GoFundMe, which did not have a set fee, announced during the first wave of the pandemic that it would be donating $1.5 million to support communities that had been affected by the pandemic and frontline workers and organizations acting to combat these effects.[26] This donation should be put in context, however. Given that GoFundMe announced that COVID-19–related campaigns had received $40 million in donations during this period, that platform potentially took in $2 million in tips if these were made at a rate of 5% (in line with its previous manda-tory fee).

Privacy, consent, and a case of "information extortion"

The benefits of crowdfunding during the COVID-19 pandemic were gen-uine and spread across much of the world; however, they came with signifi-cant costs. People seeking help from the public due to the direct impacts of COVID-19 and the indirect impacts of mitigation measures had to expose normally private and personal details to the public. The financial impacts of these mitigation measures were widespread, and people who were now out of work or in danger of losing their businesses were compelled to publicly discuss their savings, income, and access to other sources of help like public relief and private insurance. For people with COVID-19–related health needs, this information disclosure included both the medical and financial impacts of the virus—how it had harmed their health and why they were un-able to afford medical care for themselves or others. People suffering from long COVID symptoms without clear diagnoses or protocols for treatment faced experiences similar to those of other people with contested diseases and diagnoses. In these cases, campaigners were forced to offer unusually extensive details and justifications to convince others that their needs were genuine and their desired treatments were potentially effective. Perhaps most distressingly, crowdfunding campaigns during the pandemic commonly raised money for funeral costs for loved ones who died from COVID-19, requiring them to explain their needs and experiences to the public during an extremely difficult moment in their lives.[27]

Whereas these costs to privacy were similar to those before the pandemic, other privacy-related issues were more specific to crowdfunding in response to COVID-19. Among the common COVID-19 mitigation measures put in place during the first wave of the virus were limitations to in-person dining in restaurants. These policies created enormous financial pressures for restaurants and bars. Although some of these businesses were able to pivot to takeout dining and others later benefited from government supports, many businesses were forced to lay off workers over the short term and faced the potential of permanent closure as the pandemic dragged on. This specific aspect of the pandemic motivated a partnership between GoFundMe and Yelp, a website that publishes crowdsourced reviews of restaurants and other businesses. Intending to help businesses struggling with physical distancing mandates, these two companies announced that they would cooperate to use the restaurant profiles hosted on Yelp to create fundraising pages on GoFundMe that would help these businesses and their employees to manage the impacts of pandemic restrictions.[28]

While the specific intention of this plan was to help businesses in need, both GoFundMe and Yelp were also motivated by self-interest. Yelp profits from a healthy restaurant sector both indirectly through advertising revenue and more directly through a business it owns that diners can use to secure reservations. GoFundMe receives tips for the campaigns it hosts and would benefit from having its platform hosting these fundraisers. Both businesses received a public relations boost from this move as well, something particularly valuable to GoFundMe, given that its business model involves benefiting from (while also relieving some of) the harm and suffering created by the pandemic. That said, these companies also pledged to give $500 to campaigns that raised at least $500 through these crowdfunding campaigns, up to $1 million.[29]

This program was arguably well intentioned, but its implementation introduced substantial concerns about privacy and the consent of these businesses to participate in this fundraising initiative. Crucially, tens of thousands of restaurants listed on Yelp were automatically given crowdfunding pages on GoFundMe without their consent or knowledge. In some cases, restaurant owners were surprised to discover these pages and learned about them from customers and colleagues who saw them linked to their Yelp profiles. Several of these businesses objected, noting that it was not consensual, "causes harm to our reputation," and creates additional work and stress during a period of crisis.[30] These automatically generated campaigns could send a message of need that owners did not wish to send to the public or interfere with more targeted campaigns for their employees or to benefit health workers and others impacted by the pandemic.[31] Others worried that these fundraisers could negatively impact their ability to claim losses via private insurance or participate in public relief opportunities.[32]

Furthermore, the process for removing these campaigns was onerous and required private information from business owners. Specifically, these owners initially had to claim a crowdfunding page in order to remove it, a process that required them to submit an identity card like a driver's license and their employer identification number used in tax reporting. As one owner expressed to GoFundMe, they were "not comfortable giving you a scan" of this information, particularly as they had never agreed to create the crowdfunding page in the first place.[33] Another objected more strongly, saying "I can't believe that I have to deal with this right now! Forcing people to Opt-In so that they can Opt-Out?! A copy of my drivers license? My business EIN? Information Extortion. I'm done."[34] Following sustained criticism of the rollout of this crowdfunding initiative, the companies changed it to an opt-in system where interested businesses would agree to have crowdfunding pages created for them.

Supporting healthcare heroes and other deserving recipients

Crowdfunding campaigners are compelled to establish why they deserve help from others, particularly when they seek contributions from outside of their immediate social networks. This was true before the pandemic, and the scale of need resulting from COVID-19 meant that many people sought aid from donors they did not know personally. For some campaigners, establishing their deservingness for receiving help meant being highly transparent about how they would use donated funds. This process could include clearly detailing medical needs and medical decision-making to establish that the campaign recipient was a responsible person and would put donations to good use. Given the disruptions created by pandemic mitigation measures and heightened demand for medical services, this information could include how the recipient was navigating these disruptions and how they shaped their needs.[35]

In many instances, campaigns evoked past contributions by the recipients to their communities, particularly in the case of campaigns for businesses or people facing unemployment. In the typical form of these campaigns, the business or individual stated that they had offered employment to others, given service to the community, and been a positive economic and personal force for those around them. In a representative example from these fundraisers, one person initiated a crowdfunding campaign to support their favorite restaurant so that "we can work together to help them through this unprecedented period, as they have helped us all in the last 25 years."[36] As this campaigner expressed, through no fault of their own—in fact, by doing their part to stem the spread of the pandemic—this business was no longer able to bring in its normal income. Campaigns such as this one appealed to a sense of reciprocity, portraying people suffering economically from COVID-19 mitigation strategies as particularly deserving of support because of their past contributions to their community and because they bore the brunt of the costs of physical distancing measures.

Crowdfunding campaigners in New Zealand found ways to express their deservingness for receiving help that included performing acts of kindness for potential donors. These acts focused on the shared experience of the extreme lockdown measures taken in New Zealand, expressions hoping for the safety and well-being of those reading the campaign page, and reminders to check in on loved ones, older adults, and other vulnerable people. In some cases, these expressions of kindness mirrored those made by political leaders during the pandemic. Other campaigners expressed gratitude and shared their wisdom with potential donors as a form of reciprocal labor. This shared wisdom was often highly practical and turned on the shared experience of lockdown measures in pursuit of a zero-COVID policy in New Zealand. For example, chronically ill people and those with long-term experiences of social isolation and limited mobility could share their coping strategies and lived experiences with donors who might be new to these experiences.[37]

Sympathy for people impacted directly and indirectly by the pandemic and the global reach of the outbreak meant COVID-related campaigns at first received more interest and support than other campaigns. During the initial period of crowdfunding for COVID-19–related needs, campaigns in the United States raised more money per campaign (median $930) and donors (median 14) than non-COVID-19–related campaigns (median $625, 11 donors), though the goals of the COVID-19–related campaigns were also higher (median $5,000) than the others (median $4,000). COVID-19–related campaigns also received much more traction on social media during this period, receiving a median 23 Facebook shares compared with a median of 0 shares for other campaigns. While the large majority of both groups had the campaign beneficiary also listed as the campaigner, COVID-19–related campaigns were about twice as likely (7.1% compared with 3.8%) to list a philanthropic organization as the beneficiary.[38] Arguably, the public saw COVID-related campaigns as particularly deserving of their support during the early stages of the pandemic.

Within COVID-related campaigns, inequities suggest that some needs were seen as more deserving of help than others. On the GoFundMe platform, COVID-19–related campaigns from the first half of 2020 received the highest mean number of donations in the Funerals and Memorials; Medical, Illness, and Healing; and Volunteer and Faith categories. By comparison, campaigns in the Dreams, Hopes, and Wishes; Education and Learning; and Babies, Kids, and Families categories performed less well. When looking at keywords within these campaigns, those referencing medical and business needs performed relatively well, especially campaigns indicating severe medical needs. By comparison, campaigns with keywords discussing rent, eviction, and job loss performed much less well.[39] Although it can be hard to tell, this difference in success by category may align with a greater sense of deservingness among those whose health was severely impacted by the pandemic, at least within this specific dataset. If that interpretation is correct, then people whose primary loss was individual (rather than business) income were seen as less deserving of help, or at least their needs motivated less financial help by donors.

Many indicators of deservingness during the pandemic, such as being hard-working, contributing to the community, and being responsible with money, are common to non-pandemic campaigns as well. Other language of deservingness was more specific to the context of COVID-19. Many early and highly successful fundraisers focused on the needs of small businesses that lost customers or were forced to close in response to pandemic mitigation measures. These businesses were extolled as "the heart of our communities" and positive contributors to employment and the overall economy. Mitigation measures were for the good of us all, but these businesses were framed as having taken on a disproportionate burden of the communal effort to stem the spread of the coronavirus and were therefore deserving of help in return.[40]

Healthcare workers were also singled out for their deservingness. In the first months of the pandemic, crowdfunding campaigns often mirrored tropes of healthcare workers being heroic in their efforts to treat people infected with COVID-19 and prevent the spread of the virus, putting their own lives at risk in doing so. Fundraisers for these heroes often focused on providing personal protective equipment when sourcing these supplies was difficult and on offering food, massages, and other benefits as a public thank you for their efforts. The largest single COVID-related fundraiser on the GoFundMe platform was the Frontline Responders Fund, which was initiated in March 2020 and raised nearly $8.3 million from 30,000 donations. Among these supporters was Arnold Schwarzenegger, who contributed $1 million and expressed that "Our doctors, nurses and hospital staff are the real action heroes of this crisis."[41] Indian platform Ketto encouraged potential donors to support campaigns for "frontline COVID-19 warriors" like healthcare workers, police officers, and municipality workers as a "token of respect."[42] And, in the United Kingdom, a large fundraiser for "extra support" for hospital staff described these workers as "our front-line heroes."[43] As the pandemic wore on, this messaging about the special deservingness of healthcare workers for crowdfunded donations continued. In some respects, these workers' needs changed, relying less on public support for personal protective equipment. But funding for food and other benefits persisted on the logic that continued waves of infection and hospitalization meant that healthcare workers "deserve to be uplifted and appreciated more than ever."[44]

Crowdfunding for caddies and the NHS

While many people benefited greatly from the massive increase in crowdfunding activity during the pandemic, these benefits were not distributed equitably. On GoFundMe, the top 1% of campaigns (in terms of money raised) pulled in 23.1% of all donations and 23.6% of all funding pledged during the initial period of the pandemic. Moreover, just forty-eight of the highest-grossing campaigns accounted for 8% of overall donations. As was the case before the pandemic, crowdfunding campaigns related to the

COVID-19 pandemic tended to be created in wealthier—and presumably less needy—areas. Among GoFundMe campaigns, fundraisers were created more often in the highest-income quintiles. Campaigns in the highest-income quintile received by far the largest number of donations, accounting for nearly a third overall, and a whopping 38.9% of the total money donated to COVID-19–related campaigns. This compared with only 10% of the overall number of donors in the lowest-income quintile and 8.8% of the total money contributed. These findings are particularly striking because, during this time, the fewest COVID-19 infections took place in the highest-income quintile, while most occurred in the lowest-income quartile.[45]

As seen in past analyses of crowdfunding, educational attainment influenced crowdfunding campaigns during the pandemic. Higher educational attainment was positively correlated with COVID-19–related campaign creation in the United States.[46] COVID-19–related campaigns in the United States also had longer campaign narratives than non-COVID-19–related campaigns, and this longer text was coupled with a median 25% more success reaching their campaign goals.[47] This outcome matches previous research showing a similar positive correlation and suggests that higher income, facility with online technologies, and the ability to express oneself in written narratives all favor willingness to create crowdfunding campaigns and success raising funds with these campaigns.

Race has been associated with crowdfunding success in past studies, and this dynamic appears in COVID-19–related campaigns as well. Among GoFundMe campaigns for US-based campaigners, fundraisers based in areas with relatively higher numbers of black residents fared worse on average than other campaigns in terms of the number of donations received. Campaigns in areas with higher numbers of Hispanic residents did better on average by this same measure, but this finding may be connected to high-income white residents in these communities.[48]

Crowdfunding platforms also directly contribute to an uneven playing field for campaigners. They actively highlight certain campaigns and, in doing so, make it more likely that these fundraisers will be supported. For example, GoFundMe actively promoted campaigns for small businesses through its Small Business Relief Initiative and partnerships with other companies such as Yelp. Not coincidentally, fundraisers for small businesses and unemployment made up nearly 60% of campaigns created between March 1 and August 31, 2020. By comparison, campaigns for direct medical needs made up only 3.2% of campaigns.[49] GoFundMe's involvement also tipped the balance in favor of certain campaigns in the early days of the pandemic, as nine of the fifty most successful campaigns were initiated by GoFundMe, received donations from the platform, or otherwise had money directed to them by GoFundMe.[50]

In addition to support from GoFundMe, celebrity support helped shape which campaigns had the greatest success. One campaign to send supplies to medical professionals raised over $3.3 million after it was shared online by Pharrell Williams and Kim Kardashian, among others.[51] Among the most successful campaigns in the early days of the pandemic were those connected to a high-end restaurant, a golf club with wealthy and famous clientele, and two high-priced social clubs. Twenty of the fifty highest-earning campaigns were initiated by or benefited companies rather than individuals.[52] Among restaurant owners seeking funding to save their businesses and replace income reduced due to COVID-19 mitigation measures, campaigns for restaurants located in urban centers in New York and California received a mean of $9,651, compared with a mean of $7,380 outside of these areas.[53]

The viral campaigns that caught celebrity and public attention ranged from seemingly high-priority needs like personal protective equipment for frontline health workers to worthwhile but perhaps less pressing needs like supporting out-of-work golf caddies at high-end golf resorts. Even when high-profile campaigns focused on the needs of relatively marginalized people with fewer resources, the biases of those supporting them helped shape who would get the most support. For example, during the first wave of the pandemic in the United States, journalist Yashar Ali started a GoFundMe campaign for hourly workers put out of work by the pandemic. This campaign quickly raised half of its $1 million goal after it was shared by high-profile actors, singers, and other performers with large online followings. However, this fundraiser was targeted at nonprofit groups in New York City and San Francisco, reflecting Ali's personal connections.[54] This bias shouldn't reflect poorly on the intentions of this campaigner or its supporters but does demonstrate that, even among relatively powerless people in need, urban tech and media centers are likely to be given more attention than other areas. GoFundMe's own data show this trend as well, with coastal states like New York, Washington, Oregon, and California in the top five of fundraisers per capita (with Colorado as the exception).[55]

Even if the funding raised by crowdfunding were distributed more equitably, it is not a sufficient replacement for well-funded and -administered public social supports for basic needs. This was no different during the

COVID-19 pandemic. As in the past, crowdfunding campaigns for COVID-19–related needs typically did not achieve their fundraising goals. In an analysis of over 160,000 campaigns initiated on GoFundMe during the first half of 2020, the median campaign had a goal of $5,000 but raised $65 from two donors. Falling short of their campaign goal was typical in this dataset, as 90% of campaigns missed their mark. Even limited success was elusive for many campaigns, as 43.2% of them received no donations whatsoever.[56] By comparison, an analysis of US-based campaigns on GoFundMe from March 11 to May 10, 2020, found a median goal of $5,000 and median raised of $930.[57] Similarly, a smaller analysis of COVID-19–related campaigns on GoFundMe from March 3 to March 20, 2020, found a median fundraising goal of $10,000 and median amount raised of $1,642.[58] The relatively greater success of these early campaigns may be due to the novelty of the pandemic at that time and less concentrated need, though even these campaigns fell well short of their goals. For many crowdfunders, the sheer growth in crowdfunding activity throughout the pandemic displayed the inadequacy of this means of addressing need. Given that so many individuals and businesses were suddenly suffering in similar ways from the effects of illness and physical distancing measures, it was very difficult for many of these campaigns to stand out from one another and reach their fundraising goals.

To a significant extent, crowdfunding is a response to failures to provide sufficient and timely public supports for people in need. In some cases, crowdfunding platforms highlight this inadequacy, as when India's Ketto put the need for crowdfunding in the lap of governments who did not learn the lesson of SARS and Ebola outbreaks and "failed miserably to handle the COVID-19 pandemic."[59] In the United Kingdom, one of the largest COVID-19–related fundraisers aimed to "provide extra support to NHS [National Health Service] staff and patients" given the "extraordinary demands of fighting the virus," thus drawing attention to the failures of the NHS. This campaign raised over £2 million from 3,214 donations.[60] Crowdfunding platforms like Ketto are sometimes presented as stepping into this gap: "Where governments are failing to reach every needy person, people are coming forward through social media platforms. A rapid increase in the fundraisers and donors came as a ray of hope during these dark times."[61] But, as the inequities and inadequacies of crowdfunding show, it was a deeply flawed solution to these failures and was driven by elite priorities before, during, and as the pandemic has continued.

Finally, crowdfunding during the pandemic created new burdens on people who were already struggling to manage the financial and personal costs of pandemic mitigation measures. For example, Colt Taylor used crowdfunding to try to support his restaurant's employees after his business was forced to shut down during the first wave of the pandemic. As he put it, "It is a hard road with GoFundMe. It is up to the organizer to market it and get it out there. The struggle I have is that I'm so understaffed and going through all of my own difficulties, I don't really have time to do that."[62] While filling out paperwork for government supports is also burdensome, the emotional work of creating a crowdfunding campaign, establishing one's deservingness and legitimacy, and providing updates on one's needs is particularly demanding.

Fraud, hate, misinformation, and a convoy

Any upsurge in public interest in crowdfunding creates opportunities to defraud donors. The sheer number of campaigns started, especially during the first wave of the COVID-19 pandemic, meant that oversight of these campaigns would be difficult and fraud harder to detect. In France, the increase in crowdfunding activity during the first wave of the COVID-19 pandemic led to warnings from the government to beware of the potential for fraudulent crowdfunding campaigns.[63] GoFundMe noted this issue as well and, as CEO Tim Cadogan cautioned, "In terms of what they do with the funds, there are some limits to our ability to validate that. There is an element of trust in this—we can't validate everything."[64] This position is not unreasonable given that even the best oversight created by these platforms would struggle to accommodate the massive surge in campaign creation. Moreover, requiring strict validation would likely slow down the flow of financial resources to those desperately in need and undermine their privacy. Nonetheless, it illustrates that a global emergency like the COVID-19 pandemic creates a spike in need that cannot be easily accommodated under existing antifraud measures aimed at more isolated natural disasters and emergencies.

The development of a vaccine against COVID-19 was initially seen as the most promising means of ending the pandemic. It also drew the interest of people who wished to spread misinformation about vaccines and COVID-19 treatments via crowdfunding campaigns. In 2019, GoFundMe enacted a policy banning fundraisers for groups that promoted misinformation about vaccine safety and efficacy. This policy led to hundreds of campaigns being removed from its platform before and during the COVID-19 pandemic. As vaccines became available for COVID-19, GoFundMe began applying resource labels to some campaigns related to vaccines. These labels directed potential donors to the US Centers for Disease Control (CDC) and the World Health Organization (WHO) websites for fact-based information on vaccine safety. At the same time, this policy still allowed for fundraisers for legal fees to challenge vaccine mandates and dispute or pay fines for people who have violated these mandates.[65] But even fundraisers restricted to legal costs regularly spread misinformation about vaccines for COVID-19. Many campaigns discussing "medical freedom" and "informed consent" around vaccines made false claims that these vaccines are dangerous, alter human DNA, and are ineffective. These and other campaigns also regularly made false claims about unproven or disproven COVID treatments, including hydroxychloroquine and ivermectin. By focusing on fundraisers for legal fees, these groups have raised hundreds of thousands of dollars on GoFundMe and other crowdfunding platforms and are actively spreading medical misinformation.[66]

While GoFundMe has instituted some limits on fundraising for anti-vaccine groups, GiveSendGo has stayed true to its brand as an all-things-go crowdfunding platform and GoFundMe alternative. GiveSendGo has hosted a broad range of anti-vaccine fundraisers during the pandemic, including a campaign for a reporter who alleges that she was prevented from reporting negative stories about COVID-19 vaccines and from promoting hydroxychloroquine as a COVID treatment; a former Facebook employee who objected to that platform's decision to remove some content with vaccine misinformation; and a documentary on the alleged dangers of vaccinating children.[67] Other campaigns mix vaccine misinformation with objections to mask mandates and tout ivermectin and vitamins as effective treatments for COVID-19.[68] Some of these campaigns have been highly successful, raising hundreds of thousands of dollars, while others have fallen well short of their goals or failed to raise any money.

Campaigns that engage in fraud and spread misinformation have taken place throughout the COVID-19 pandemic. But one event early in the third year of the COVID-19 outbreak illustrated the power of crowdfunding to mix potentially fraudulent activities with hate and misinformation. In mid-January 2022, a series of fundraisers began appearing on GoFundMe to support Canadian truck drivers who were organizing a protest to take place in

Ottawa, Canada's capital city. Initially, this protest was focused narrowly on the Canadian government's decision to end an exemption that allowed truck drivers crossing the US–Canada border to be unvaccinated. As it went on, this protest and many of the fundraisers supporting it objected to all vaccine mandates within Canada and all pandemic restrictions more generally, including mask mandates and limits on social gatherings.[69]

While a number of crowdfunding campaigns were organized to support truckers wishing to travel to Ottawa for the protest, by far the most visible and successful campaign was initiated by Tamara Lich (and later joined by Benjamin Dichter) on January 15, on the GoFundMe platform. Lich, who had previously worked for right-wing political parties in Canada, initially set the campaign's goal at $100,000 to help truckers force the federal government to "cease all mandates against its people" and specifically "help with the costs of fuel, food and lodgings to help ease the pressures of this arduous task."[70] Support for this fundraiser rapidly grew. It met its initial goal the day after it was started and had brought in over $250,000 within its first three days. As each fundraising goal was reached, the organizers increased the total being sought, aiming for and surpassing $1 million within a week of the campaign's start.

As the trucker campaign gained more donations and public attention, concerns with how this money would be used started appearing. The campaign was amended to include a note that the money raised would be "dispersed to our Truckers to aid them with the cost of the journey" and that "funds will be spent to help cover the cost of fuel for our Truckers first and foremost, will be used to assist with food if needed and contribute to shelter if needed."[71] These clarifications were likely required by GoFundMe as the fundraiser continued to bring in massive support. On January 25, news broke that the funds had not yet been released by GoFundMe to the campaign organizers. Specifically, GoFundMe communicated that it would be withholding the nearly $5 million that had been raised to that point as "We require that fundraisers be transparent about the flow of funds and have a clear plan for how those funds will be spent. In this case, we are in touch with the organizer to verify that information."[72] Two days later, GoFundMe released $1 million of the now $6.2 million that had been raised to pay for fuel costs.[73] The campaigners updated the campaign to indicate that funds would go "directly to our bulk fuel supplier" and "need not flow through anyone else" and that any leftover money would "be donated to a credible Veterans organization which will be chosen by the donors."[74]

While initial concerns with this fundraiser focused on clarity around how the money would be used and the potential for fraud, other concerns quickly arose based on those organizing and promoting the fundraiser and the protest itself. Observers noted that the campaign leaders had ties to far-right political parties and organizations within Canada.[75] The majority of comments left by contributors to the campaign evoked freedom and expressed support for the truck convoy. Others, however, spread vaccine misinformation, anti-Semitism, threats of violence toward Canadian Prime Minister Justin Trudeau, and QAnon conspiracy theories. When the convoy reached Ottawa at the end of January, some protesters flew Nazi and Confederate flags and deployed banners on a statue of Canadian hero Terry Fox.[76] While the broader protest involved parades of honking trucks in other Canadian cities, in Ottawa a fleet of large trucks and other vehicles settled into place around Parliament, honking horns, disrupting access to the downtown area, and promising to stay until all COVID-related mandates were lifted.

Given this situation, it was reasonable to think that GoFundMe should close campaigns associated with the protest. In addition to questions about how the money would be used, these funds were now clearly supporting ongoing vaccine misinformation as well as hateful conduct and ongoing violations of the law through the unlawful occupation of sections of Ottawa.[77] The primary campaign in support of the trucker convoy continued to receive exposure and donations, eventually topping $10 million pledged from nearly 125,000 donations and becoming the second-largest Canadian crowdfunding campaign of all time. Finally, on February 2, 2022, GoFundMe froze the campaign and closed it completely two days later. Its reason for doing so was that "the previously peaceful demonstration has become an occupation, with police reports of violence and other unlawful activity" and thus the campaign was in violation of its terms of service. After initially indicating that the donated money would be redirected to "credible and established charities chosen by the Freedom Convoy 2022 organizers and verified by GoFundMe," GoFundMe quickly began refunding all donations other than the money that had already been disbursed to the campaigners.[78]

As is now tradition, GiveSendGo rapidly moved in to take GoFundMe's place. The platform had already been lobbying for the organizers to move to its platform and hosted some smaller convoy-related campaigns. Lich and Dichter joined with an existing GiveSendGo campaign and encouraged previous donors to support their new fundraiser.[79] These—and many other—donors did give to the new campaign, and it eventually surpassed the amount raised by the GoFundMe fundraiser. While GiveSendGo also has terms of service that prohibit fundraising in support of illegal activities, it took the view that the campaign was in support of civil disobedience and enthusiastically promoted the campaign, even after orders by local, provincial, and federal agencies for the protesters to end the blockade and occupation.[80] Canadian Prime Minister Trudeau would eventually invoke the Emergencies Act, which, in addition to making it easier to remove the protesters from Ottawa, allowed the government to freeze some bank accounts associated with the protest, including those connected to the GiveSendGo crowdfunding campaign.[81]

Despite the cancellation of the GoFundMe campaign and eventual freezing of accounts linked to the GiveSendGo fundraiser, crowdfunding had an important role in creating and sustaining the trucker convoy protests. The rapid success of the GoFundMe campaign raised the visibility of the convoy protest as it proceeded toward Ottawa and gave the impression that the protest was an organic movement with widespread support in Canada.[82] This impression was not entirely accurate, as the majority of funding received for the GiveSendGo campaign came from US donors, and the campaign was promoted across US right-wing media; however, this point was only fully clear well after the convoy had settled into place in Ottawa.[83] Moreover, the money that flowed to the supporters via crowdfunding helped sustain these protests. While GoFundMe only released $1 million of the money raised through its platform, and it is not clear how much of the funds raised via GiveSendGo made it to the protesters, this amount of money is still substantial and paid for fuel, lodging, and legal fees that allowed the protesters to continue occupying Ottawa with little personal cost or risk. Moreover, the GiveSendGo campaign was expanded to include funding for "Permanent infrastructure for continuing advocacy in whatever form that takes," meaning that this fundraiser could have an impact beyond the specific protest in Ottawa.[84]

Conclusion

In many respects, donation-based crowdfunding during the global COVID-19 pandemic confirmed the prior understanding of the benefits of and problems with this practice. Use of crowdfunding expanded greatly during this period, reflecting a sharp growth in need. This interest in crowdfunding also demonstrated shortcomings in health and social systems supporting those directly affected by the virus and indirectly by physical distancing measures. While public institutions and philanthropic organizations responded to these needs as well, crowdfunding allowed targeted and timely help for many. But, as always, this help came at a cost to personal privacy, raised problematic questions about who is most deserving of support, distributed help inequitably, failed to address underlying gaps in social supports, and projected misinformation and other problematic messaging to the public. In these ways, crowdfunding during the pandemic is what it always was—just more so.

But, at the same time, new facets of crowdfunding emerged during the pandemic that raise questions about the future directions of this practice. In particular, GoFundMe's partnership with Yelp to auto-generate campaigns undermined consent and privacy but also demonstrated a desire by this platform (and potentially others) to take a more formal role as a safety net during times of crisis. Similarly, the use of crowdfunding by anti-vaccine mandate protesters and dueling decisions by GoFundMe and GiveSendGo to host these fundraisers demonstrated that crowdfunding companies are having a more consequential role in shaping political and policy debates, deciding whose voices can be heard, and funneling money to political movements at home and abroad. These and other actions by crowdfunding platforms demonstrate an increasingly formalized role in giving, not simply as a conduit for individual donors but as an institutional force that shapes giving practices.

9

Crowdfunding as a mediated practice

Direct giving takes place between individuals, whereas indirect giving includes various kinds of organizations that act as intermediaries to receive and then redirect financial resources. This distinction is important because these different modes of giving generate different practical, political, and ethical issues. In indirect giving, institutions—including community organizations, small nonprofit groups, and large and richly endowed foundations—often have a more lasting presence in addressing local, national, and global needs. Philanthropic intermediaries between donors and recipients have the advantage of institutional memory and expertise in managing laws and local bureaucracy. As a result, they may be particularly proficient in using donations effectively, including through addressing the root causes of need. However, as we saw in Chapter 1, philanthropic institutions have been criticized for distributing funds inequitably, prioritizing the values and concerns of their wealthiest and most influential donors, and undermining democratic values in determining what needs and responses are prioritized in a society.

By comparison, donations directly to those in need have the potential to better represent the priorities and values of the wider public, particularly when these donors represent a more diverse and less wealthy cross-section of their communities. As I have discussed in the preceding chapters, however, direct giving carries its own downsides. The closer contact between donor and recipient can undermine the recipient's privacy and dignity, individual donors may lack the expertise and knowledge to make donations highly effective, and direct giving carries its own concerns about equity in terms of who receives these gifts. As a result, neither of these broad modes of giving is inherently superior to the other, and there is good reason to consider both of their relative strengths and weaknesses when seeking to promote effective, fair, and dignified giving practices—something I will turn to in the concluding chapter of this book.

But before doing that, I want to complicate the distinction between direct and indirect giving as I have presented it—and particularly crowdfunding's

Appealing to the Crowd. Jeremy Snyder, Oxford University Press. © Oxford University Press 2024.
DOI: 10.1093/oso/9780197658130.003.0010

place within these forms of giving. Donation-based crowdfunding is typically presented as a direct giving practice in that it allows peer-to-peer giving without the need for philanthropic intermediaries to hold and direct gifts. This is how I've generally discussed crowdfunding up to this point and how most donation-based crowdfunding takes place. But placing crowdfunding fully under the umbrella of direct giving misses some important ways it can be an indirect and highly mediated practice as well. First, philanthropic organizations, ranging from small community projects to larger nonprofits and foundations, use crowdfunding to raise funds. Thus, while crowdfunding particularly empowers peer-to-peer giving, it is not closed off to participation by philanthropic organizations—in fact, these organizations are increasingly fundraising through crowdfunding platforms and mechanisms. Second, and more importantly, crowdfunding platforms are increasingly taking on philanthropy-like characteristics. To some extent, these platforms have always shaped giving practices and do not simply act as frictionless go-betweens to facilitate peer-to-peer giving. But, as I will demonstrate, the role of crowdfunding platforms in shaping giving is increasing as crowdfunding undergoes consolidation and expansion, amounting to a turn toward a mediated and less direct giving practice.

Crowdfunding for nonprofits and institutions

The development and increased usage of online technologies has transformed giving practices. For example, giving by low- and middle-income Americans to philanthropic organizations and other entities with tax-exempt status is often portrayed as being in decline over the past decade. This change in giving has been influenced in part by economic events including the Great Recession, growing income inequality, and changes in the US tax code. But part of the issue is also a shift to online giving and peer-to-peer giving that often bypasses philanthropic intermediaries. These new giving practices may not be tracked in reports on giving, leading to a false impression that overall giving is declining in low- and middle-income groups.[1]

Because of these shifts in giving behaviors worldwide, many philanthropic organizations have moved to enable and encourage online donations. Online fundraising creates a number of advantages for traditional philanthropies. It creates new ways for philanthropies to reach out to potential donors, keep donors informed about their activities and impact, and creates detailed databases of donor behaviors and preferences that enable highly tailored fundraising appeals and donor retention efforts. Like crowdfunding campaigners, traditional philanthropies have embraced social media and social networking platforms to increase their visibility and connect with new and existing donors.[2] Mobile phones have also enabled philanthropies to reach out to often younger donors to encourage frictionless giving in reaction to current events. Mobile technology has been key for philanthropies in less economically developed areas, where potential donors may not have access to other online technologies.[3]

The embrace of online giving by philanthropies extends to using online crowdfunding platforms as well. Interestingly, this trend is a return to the roots for some crowdfunding platforms. As discussed in Chapter 1, several of the largest donation-based crowdfunding platforms were created with a focus on facilitating crowdfunding by philanthropic organizations rather than individuals. For example, GoFundMe's previous incarnation, CreateAFund, initially focused on trying to enroll charities to use their platform in exchange for a subscription-based fee—crowdfunding by individuals was an afterthought that was only later developed into their central business.[4] In India, the crowdfunding platform Milaap started as a microlending platform for rural entrepreneurial projects and then began partnerships with hospitals to fundraise for their patients' medical bills before turning largely to personal fundraisers.[5] These origins reflect the role of philanthropic organizations in shaping the initial ways crowdfunding platforms sought to make themselves profitable.

As the donation-based crowdfunding sector matures and consolidates, GoFundMe is returning to emphasizing hosting philanthropic organizations as a means to continue its rapid growth. In particular, it has moved to develop infrastructure to allow philanthropic organizations to fundraise from the public via their own websites and to host institutions on versions of the GoFundMe platform. This infrastructure includes software for tracking financial transactions by donors, gathering data, and reporting on donors and technical support for nonprofits and other philanthropic organizations. This capacity has been developed through GoFundMe's purchase of the donation-based crowdfunding platform CrowdRise, which had previously focused on hosting campaigns for philanthropic organizations. Philanthropies using these services pay a subscription fee, and donors have the option to provide a tip to GoFundMe, as with its campaigns for individuals. In its announcement for this service, GoFundMe notes that this option allows successful fundraisers on GoFundMe.com to evolve into ongoing philanthropic projects using these services, further blurring the distinction between crowdfunding for individuals and organizations.[6] In early 2022, GoFundMe built on its investment in philanthropic infrastructure by acquiring Classy, a company that provides software and technical support for philanthropic organizations. The logic for this acquisition was that the "philanthropic market is about $500 billion annually in the U.S. alone and right now, online giving is a small fraction of that."[7] This growth strategy makes it clear that expanding support for online giving to philanthropic organizations is an enormous financial opportunity for for-profit platforms.

These acquisitions allow GoFundMe and other platforms to apply their expertise with online crowdfunding for individuals to the larger philanthropic giving marketplace. This is achieved by using their software and payment-processing infrastructure and marketing expertise to allow philanthropic organizations to fundraise from the public under their own banners and websites. In other cases, philanthropic organizations act similarly to individual campaigners, organizing crowdfunding campaigns hosted on crowdfunding platforms. Large nonprofit organizations have partnered with GoFundMe on the nonprofit.org version of its website, and smaller organizations, many without tax-exempt status, often appear on the for-profit version of the website as well. The participation of philanthropic organizations on crowdfunding platforms is not simply a US-based phenomenon. On the Chinese crowdfunding platform Tencent Gong Yi, public and private foundations, private nonprofit organizations, and social institutions regularly participate in crowdfunding campaigns. Campaigns for philanthropic organizations range from 22.6% of health-related fundraisers to 72.3% of fundraisers for environmental causes.[8]

In other cases, crowdfunding platforms have focused on fundraising for institutions and causes rather than individuals throughout their histories. Australia-based Chuffed allows fundraisers for individuals but has historically focused on nonprofits, social enterprises, and other philanthropic organizations. Fundraisers on this platform must be for social, political, or community causes, and the organizations receiving funding are often small, grassroots groups that have a small donor base and are looking to expand their operations or take on specific projects.[9] Crowdfunding platforms can use hybrid models as well, as is the case with the US-based Watsi platform. This organization partners with medical providers, largely in low-income settings across the world. These medical providers give patients the option of crowdfunding for their medical care and then submitting their names and needs to Watsi to host a fundraising campaign. These campaigns mimic traditional fundraising appeals that ask donors to "adopt" a hungry child in need or attempt to personalize donations for systemic needs like inadequate medical insurance. Donors to Watsi are provided with updates about the status of the patient they are supporting, much as with traditional crowd-funding campaigns for individuals. Patients who do not wish to be featured in this way can be supported through donations to a general fund that Watsi manages. Watsi is itself a nonprofit organization and receives financial sup-port from other philanthropic groups.[10] Elsewhere, India's ImpactGuru, while largely hosting campaigns for individuals, has also developed a monthly donation option where the platform selects campaigns to support from these donations.[11] In all of these cases, donated funds to these platforms can be tax deductible.

In short, crowdfunding has always allowed for campaigns by philan-thropic organizations alongside individuals. Increasingly, these platforms are providing the infrastructure to support crowdfunding by philanthropic organizations, including among platforms that have traditionally focused on giving to individuals. The motivation for for-profit crowdfunding platforms to enable and encourage participation by philanthropic organizations is clear. These platforms can collect tips on individual donations and subscrip-tion fees for the use of their software and payment-processing infrastructure. But there are several reasons why traditional philanthropic organizations would want to become involved in online crowdfunding to receive donations independent of the interests of host platforms.

Most obviously, expanding into online crowdfunding campaigning allows philanthropies to take advantage of the social aspects of online crowd-funding that can make crowdfunding campaigns massively successful. These include sharing via other online social networks, incorporating images and video into the campaign, and posting regular updates on the progress of the fundraiser and impact of the funds raised. The audience for online crowd-funding campaigns may be different from the philanthropy's existing donor base as well, particularly if donations are currently raised via more tradi-tional mail or telephone fundraising appeals. As a result, crowdfunding may allow the philanthropy to diversify its donor base, including adding more variation in terms of the age, income, geography, political values, and eth-nicity of donors. A further advantage of this more diverse donor base, espe-cially if the philanthropy's existing donor base is smaller, wealthier, and more homogenous, is that the philanthropy's stakeholders may become more representative of the public at large and push the philanthropy toward activities that are more democratically responsive. A corollary to this benefit is that philanthropies can learn what motivates giving to their causes from a wider donor base and tailor their fundraising activities based on this data.[12]

Curating causes

In addition to hosting philanthropic organizations and providing them with crowdfunding know-how, crowdfunding platforms themselves take on philanthropy-like activities. While crowdfunding platforms often present themselves as removing intermediaries from between donors and recipients, they do not function simply as a neutral medium for transferring financial resources online. Each platform makes design choices that are then foisted onto campaigners, including allowing and promoting images and video, integrating widgets to easily share campaigns on other social media platforms, allowing updates on the campaign, prominently displaying statistics on money raised and shares received, and posting comments from donors and non-donors alike. These and other design choices shape the experience of crowdfunding for campaigners and donors, including exacerbating or mitigating many of the ethical and political concerns discussed in the previous chapters. Moreover, they create a structure for campaigns that helps determine which fundraisers will be most successful. These structures, in turn, create pressures on campaigners to hew to the most rewarding modes of crowdfunding, incentivizing choices around content and voice in campaigns.

A further design choice by crowdfunding platforms shapes which campaigns are more likely to be noticed by potential donors who are not already familiar with the recipient's campaign. Specifically, crowdfunding platforms make choices around their search and display algorithms that determine which campaigns appear first when searching their websites and which campaigns appear on their landing pages. These are typically not random or chronological results but often include an element of promotion of campaigns that have performed well on the platform recently. Other search functions such as GoFundMe's "Discover" option and ImpactGuru's "Browse" button display a list of high-profile or well-performing campaigns to viewers. These modes of viewing campaigns and the algorithms that select campaigns to display through these and similar search options curate a list of high-performing campaigns that are then more likely to receive support from the public. Campaigns that are likely to be supported through these means are generally not those that focus on donations from close friends and family but are those seeking and receiving viral support from the larger public. Through this mechanism, highlighted campaigns create a false impression about the success and visibility of typical crowdfunding campaigns and their likelihood of receiving viral support.

Crowdfunding platforms are well aware of critiques of these design choices as well as concerns around how crowdfunding operates in practice, particularly the concern that crowdfunding disadvantages racialized minorities and other groups and exacerbates existing social inequities. Partially in response to these concerns, GoFundMe has become more active in publicly criticizing failures by the US government to address social needs and in promoting campaigns for Black Lives Matter, groups addressing anti-Asian hate, and LGBTQ support groups, among other marginalized communities. In the case of GoFundMe, this platform has increasingly staked out a public identity tied to social and political causes. During the COVID-19 pandemic, this advocacy included chiding the US Congress for failing to quickly pass a pandemic relief bill and bemoaning that this inaction obligated Americans to resort to crowdfunding to meet their basic needs.[13] As discussed in the previous two chapters, social and political neutrality among US-based crowdfunding platforms in particular has been further challenged by decisions by GoFundMe and GiveSendGo over whether to host campaigns relating to political violence, medical misinformation, and hateful and discriminatory causes.

GoFundMe has also become more active in creating campaigns and amalgamating others into larger causes. As discussed in the previous chapter, GoFundMe partnered with the online business-rating service Yelp to proactively create crowdfunding campaigns for restaurants that may have been impacted by pandemic mitigation measures. Other platforms regularly partner with celebrities or other influencers to create and promote fundraisers for causes they have long supported or the cause of the day. These collaborations can serve as marketing messages for crowdfunding platforms, associating them with popular projects and people. To take one recent example, GoFundMe has actively promoted a fundraiser by Ukrainian-born actress Mila Kunis to support refugees from the Russian invasion of Ukraine.[14] While often praiseworthy, these partnerships demonstrate that crowdfunding platforms are not politically and socially neutral and can take on the role of powerful intermediaries that shape the behaviors of donors and campaigners and help choose winners in the competition for online donations.[15]

Most strikingly, GoFundMe has begun developing a nonprofit arm that benefits philanthropies and fundraisers initiated by individual campaigners. Whereas GoFundMe.com hosts fundraisers largely for individuals, its.org cousin hosts what it refers to as "causes." These causes include long-running categories such as Basic Necessities, America's Food Fund, and Justice and Equality, as well as timely and temporary causes, such as a COVID-19 General Relief Fund and the Ukraine Humanitarian Fund. In some cases, these causes take the form of partnerships with nonprofit organizations such as The Asian American Foundation (TAFF) in its effort to help the victims of hate crimes against Asian Americans. Other causes, such as the Basic Necessities Cause, distribute donations both to nonprofit organizations and to crowdfunding campaigns initiated through GoFundMe's for-profit.com branch.

As with crowdfunding campaigns for individuals, these causes have wildly different levels of success. TAFF's cause aiding Asian American victims of hate crimes raised $500,436 of its $1 million goal in six months. However, $500,000 of that funding was a seed donation from TAFF itself, and only six other donors contributed during that six-month period. By comparison, the Basic Necessities Cause raised over $525,000 of its $600,000 goal from 8,300 donors over a year-and-a-half period. Other, timely causes have the opportunity to have a viral effect akin to traditional crowdfunding campaigns. This was the case for the Ukrainian Humanitarian Fund, which raised nearly $2.5 million from 21,800 donors in a little over two months.

As the amalgamation of GoFundMe.com campaigns for individuals into GoFundMe.org causes shows, there is some blurring between these two entities. The .org version is sold as being particularly appealing for potential donors who are driven by wanting to address specific kinds of needs or respond to events rather than aid specific individuals. Beyond these benefits, giving to a cause via GoFundMe.org rather than an individual via GoFundMe.com allows many donors to receive tax benefits. As GoFundMe. org's CEO Yoshi Inoue described it on the launch of the new platform, "Together with GoFundMe, we are expanding the benefits of social fundraising and continuing to support some of the most impactful needs within our community with tax-deductible donations."[16] To maintain this status, donations are made directly to GoFundMe.org rather than individual recipients. GoFundMe.org is then entrusted to distribute these funds on behalf of donors. This tax-exempt status applies specifically to US donors, but the organization is also "working to expand our tax exempt status to other countries."[17]

Other platforms working directly with nonprofit organizations and other eligible parties are able to take advantage of tax regulations as well. For example, Watsi.org sends all donors a tax-deductible receipt for use in the United States for all donations.[18] India's Ketto also touts tax advantages to donating via its platform.[19] Ketto's competitor Milaap goes so far as to highlight the tax benefits of eligible campaigns by adding the tag "Receive tax benefits by donating to this campaign" at the bottom of their search results. Thus, by becoming a more active intermediary between donors and recipients, these and other crowdfunding platforms are able to extend the advantage of tax deductions to their donors, operating more like traditional philanthropic institutions in the process.

Crowdfunding and big tech

The ongoing process of acquisition and merger in the crowdfunding sector highlights concerns about the role of crowdfunding platforms in giving. In part, these concerns mirror worries that have been raised as part of a critique of "big tech" companies. This critique traditionally focuses on a few of the largest Western technology companies—Apple, Amazon, Microsoft, Google (renamed Alphabet), and Facebook (rechristened Meta). The concern directed at these companies is that they have become enormously powerful collectively and in their given fields, approaching monopolistic power in some marketplaces. This power includes control over online search and advertising (Alphabet), specific platforms and software ecosystems (Apple, Microsoft), and online shopping (Amazon). This control gives these companies the ability to massively influence pricing and supplier behavior, limit and shape consumer choice, and undermine the privacy of users.[20]

Concerns with near-monopolistic power among big tech firms applies to social media platforms as well. Platforms like Facebook and Twitter face public, corporate, internal, and regulatory pressures to create and enforce policies around hate speech, misinformation, harassment, and foreign interference in domestic politics. They also accumulate vast insights into user behaviors, interests, and relationships that potentially have commercial value to advertisers and others. These platforms have taken action in the recent past to shape and limit speech on their websites, including around vaccines and the COVID-19 pandemic, the rights and status of trans people, racial and religious bias and bigotry, and calls for harm against specific people. Individuals and groups who have been banned by these platforms or had their posts restricted or removed as a result of these policies have frequently responded with charges of censorship and rights violations.[21] Alternative social media platforms have developed in response to the restrictions of the most dominant platforms, but their success has been limited by the need for a critical mass of participants to make a social media platform appealing to use. If the large majority of your friends, public officials, celebrities, and other influential people are not regular participants on an alternative platform, then it will struggle to draw regular users even among those who object to the restrictions placed on participation on the dominant platforms. Thus, Facebook and Twitter are able to maintain a dominant position as social media platforms in the West because of their status as pioneers in this area that have been able to sustain a critical mass of active participants.[22] As the case of Twitter shows, however, when a dominant social media platform chooses to significantly change its moderation policies or alienates a large and influential part of its user base, the potential for successful competitors to emerge does increase.

In some respects, GoFundMe's position in crowdfunding—at least in North America—reflects that of big tech actors. It has purchased many of its competitors and folded them and their users into its own platform. Its name has achieved a strong public connection with crowdfunding activity so that it is not uncommon to hear people say they've "started a GoFundMe" as a generic term for crowdfunding. As with the dominant social media platforms, it has also faced pressure to restrict what forms of speech and what activities it will host. In response, it has restricted fundraisers that spread misinformation about vaccines and support violence or the legal defense of those accused of violence,[23] including the campaign supporting the anti–COVID-19-mandate convoy and occupation of Ottawa, as discussed in the previous chapter, resulting in a backlash among US and Canadian politicians and threats to use legislation and lawsuits to restrict GoFundMe's power as a big tech player in the crowdfunding sector.

Despite these strong similarities between GoFundMe and big tech actors, particularly in social media, there is an important disanalogy between these two contexts. Whereas the critical mass of participants on a social media platform makes it more difficult for alternative and more per-missive platforms to catch on, the same might not apply to crowdfunding. When GoFundMe froze the funds raised by the trucker protesters and even-tually removed their campaign, these organizers were able to quickly shift to the more permissive GiveSendGo platform and then reach and surpass the millions raised on GoFundMe.[24] As crowdfunding participation is more intermittent than participation on social media platforms, it is easy for campaigners and mobilized donors to quickly shift platforms and then proceed with what matters in the context of crowdfunding—donating and receiving funds, encouraging others to donate, and providing participants with updates about the specific activity these funds are being used for. The dominance of a platform like GoFundMe means that campaigners on alter-native platforms like GiveSendGo may struggle to attract casual donors with no connection to the campaigner and no political motivation to seek out a campaign restricted on GoFundMe. But if there is a donor base for restricted fundraisers, alternative crowdfunding platforms can provide them a space to be highly successful in raising funds from their proponents.

But in other respects, the big tech critique is appropriate to actors like GoFundMe and demonstrates how the promise of crowdfunding as a form of democratized and disintermediated giving is not all it is sold to be. Each crowdfunding platform imposes a structure on the campaigns that are hosted on them. Even if alternatives to the largest mainstream platforms exist, these are still not a neutral, disintermediated space in which donors and recipients make financial transactions.[25] To take the example of GiveSendGo as a GoFundMe alternative, GiveSendGo follows the standard structure of crowdfunding platforms, where campaigners are allowed and encouraged to post details about their needs, photos, and updates. Donors are allowed to leave messages and share the campaign via other social media platforms. Given its aggressively religious identity as "the #1 free Christian crowd-funding site," GiveSendGo also gives campaign viewers the option to "pray" for the campaigner in the form of sending them an "encouraging message or prayer."[26] And, just as GoFundMe limits some campaign types and messages, GiveSendGo's religious identity results in some limitations of its own, in-cluding prohibiting campaigns for abortion-related services.[27]

Furthermore, the religious and highly permissive identity of GiveSendGo as a "free speech" crowdfunding platform makes it more akin to conserv-ative social media alternatives and, as such, demonstrates the centrality of mainstream platforms like GoFundMe. Many campaigns on GiveSendGo are enormously successful, particularly those promoting prominent right-wing causes. However, its embrace of campaigns supporting Kyle Rittenhouse, vaccine conspiracy theorists, and January 6 rioters make it unlikely that mainstream philanthropic foundations would be willing to partner with it. Moreover, GiveSendGo's religious identity will likely appeal to only a subset of donors and campaigners. GoFundMe's decision to shape and limit campaigns in line with what is acceptable to potential mainstream corporate and philanthropic partners ensures that alternatives like GiveSendGo are unlikely to challenge its move to greater involvement as a conduit for philanthropic fundraising and status as a major philanthropic intermediary itself.

Finally, GoFundMe's move to expand into the online infrastructure of philanthropic fundraising is not likely to be challenged by niche alternatives. It remains to be seen how dominant GoFundMe will become in terms of hosting philanthropic and cause-based campaigns through its .org version and providing the online infrastructure for philanthropic organizations engaging in online crowdfunding. GoFundMe's centrality in donation-based crowdfunding may be limited to North America or become more widespread in the West and globally. Regardless, the development of one or more dominant players in the online crowdfunding sector is increasingly leading to re-intermediation between donors and campaigners if, in fact, these intermediaries were ever truly lacking. As with other dominant actors in big tech and elsewhere, this accumulation of market share will give intermediaries like GoFundMe substantial say over what kinds of campaigns can be hosted on the most visible platforms, what kinds of information these campaigns must share to succeed, and what causes will be given the privilege of elevated visibility among the wider public.

The worst of both worlds?

As I noted as the start of this chapter, both direct and indirect giving practices have strengths and weaknesses. Very broadly, philanthropic intermediaries can contribute expertise and long-term vision that can make giving more effective, including by addressing the root causes of need. However, in some cases they better reflect the priorities and values of their wealthiest and most powerful contributors and advisors and can act to undercut democratic voices in addressing basic needs. By contrast, direct giving can better reflect the values and priorities of the broader public. But even in peer-to-peer giving, the voices of the wealthiest are more powerful than those with less to give. At the same time, the intimate nature of direct giving creates additional costs for recipients.

There is good reason to try to direct both forms of giving in ways that complement one another and promote their relative strengths. Crowdfunding should be part of this conversation, particularly given its recent turn toward becoming a more institutionally mediated practice. Unfortunately, there is good reason to worry that this turn will recreate some of the historical concerns with indirect giving while also failing to address the many ethical shortcomings of crowdfunding for individuals.

The increased participation of traditional philanthropic organizations in online fundraising generally and crowdfunding specifically has numerous benefits. Beyond the obvious benefit of increased funding for these organizations, they can also help smaller donors steer the priorities of philanthropic organizations and in turn help these organizations better understand the priorities and values of smaller donors while expanding and diversifying their donor base. However, embracing crowdfunding exposes these organizations to the dangers of this giving practice. Crowdfunding campaigns by philanthropic organizations can follow trends in crowdfunding and focus on specific individuals and projects rather than developing long-term infrastructure and expertise and maintaining already successful programs.[28] These dangers also include creating pressure for these organizations to chase trends and shorter-term projects with the aim of competing with other organizations and individuals for donations.

Obviously, institutional competition for donors has always been a facet of indirect giving. Moreover, these organizations have used personal contacts, mail appeals, phone calls, and door-to-door fundraising to bring in donors in the past, raising issues akin to those created by online crowdfunding appeals. But what is specific about the entry into online crowdfunding is the creation of a broad marketplace for competition among philanthropic organizations and individuals, potentially at the cost of the advantages of these organizations as mission-oriented and guided by expertise. Consider, for example, that the philanthropic crowdfunding platform GlobalGiving gives organizations advice for crowdfunding that closely emulates advice given to individual crowdfunding campaigners. This advice includes focusing on storytelling about individuals told in the first person, using the social networks of close connections, making extensive use of photos and videos, and thanking donors for their contributions.[29] In this same vein, Australia's Chuffed suggests that philanthropic organizations use videos and images that include faces, act "ridiculously enthusiastic," create "great content" for influencers, and use "narrative storytelling over facts" because "people share stories not facts."[30] While a philanthropic organization may resist the kinds of messaging that are likely to lead to crowdfunding success, the same logic of conformity for individuals applies to organizations: if you want to be successful in the popularity contest that crowdfunding encourages, some formats and messages are more likely to lead to success than others, and this success is decoupled from other values such as efficacy and equity. Even when philanthropic organizations are aware of these dangers, they may feel that they have no choice but to participate in crowdfunding. These organizations are aware that online giving is increasingly popular among younger donors and has shifted giving from institutions to individuals, creating pressure for philanthropic organizations to directly compete with individual campaigners for support.[31]

While crowdfunding has the potential to counter the antidemocratic tendencies of philanthropic organizations, the turn toward greater mediation by crowdfunding platforms undermines this potential. These platforms have enormous influence in shaping crowdfunding appeals by individuals and philanthropic organizations, including determining what formats of fundraisers are supported, what content is allowed, and what campaigns will be promoted on their platforms. Whereas norms and laws in various jurisdictions promote some transparency in decision-making and priority setting among philanthropic organizations, the policies of both for-profit and not-for-profit arms of crowdfunding platforms are generally opaque. This opacity extends to how algorithms for promoting specific campaigns are determined, which causes and organizations are partnered with, and how concerns with donor and recipient privacy, the impact of fundraisers, and equity among causes are balanced against simply promoting fundraising for its own sake. Significantly, the visibility of crowdfunding platforms as powerful philanthropic intermediaries is still limited, certainly in comparison with large and powerful philanthropic organizations. As a result of this relative invisibility as an intermediary, crowdfunding platforms have thus far largely escaped the kind of scrutiny other philanthropic intermediaries have been subjected to.

This lack of scrutiny and accountability applies to both for-profit and nonprofit crowdfunding platforms. But it is significant that many of the largest crowdfunding platforms, including in the West, India, and China, are for-profit companies. The reputation of these companies is important to their financial success, including a reputation for filtering out fraudulent campaigns, protecting the security of online donations, and performing other customer service functions. In other respects, the reputation of these companies can lead them in very different directions, as demonstrated by the freedom-loving rhetoric of GiveSendGo as compared with the refusal to host campaigns that are more socially divisive on GoFundMe.

Crucially, these decisions are generally made by leaders who come from the tech rather than the philanthropy world. As noted in Chapter 1, many of these leaders have online marketing and retail backgrounds. While not all crowdfunding platforms are for-profits, even some nonprofits like GoFundMe.org maintain strong ties to their for-profit cousins and may re-quire recipients to maintain campaigns on the for-profit platform.[32] Thus, the values of these for-profit enterprises, their venture capital backers, and their tech-based leadership may differ deeply from those developed in the giving sector. Similarly, the stakeholders of these companies, both publicly and privately held, are generally different from those in philanthropic organizations. While philanthropic organizations are often beholden to corporate donors and wealthy individuals, they are also placed within the norms and regulatory framework of the philanthropy world. This is generally not true of for-profit crowdfunding companies and, in some cases, their not-for-profit cousins.

Conclusion

Traditional philanthropic organizations are increasingly embracing crowd-funding as a means of raising money and diversifying their donor base. Crowdfunding platforms are in turn becoming more like philanthropic intermediaries, shaping how individual campaigns are created, choosing winners and losers among campaigns, and owning the infrastructure that supports online fundraising. Peer-to-peer crowdfunding has been supported as a potential counter to some of the antidemocratic aspects of indirect giving, though, as I have noted, crowdfunding carries with it a large array of costs for donors and recipients. But crowdfunding's turn toward be-coming an intermediary in giving has the potential to maintain many of these costs while eschewing the democratic appeal of crowdfunding. This worst-of-both-worlds outcome and the negative aspects of crowdfunding aren't inherent to this practice, however. In the final chapter of this work, I outline some principles for more ethical crowdfunding combined with practical steps to shaping this practice in a more positive direction in both its direct and indirect forms.

Conclusion: Making crowdfunding more appealing

Throughout this book I have acknowledged the benefits of donation-based crowdfunding and the great good it has done for some people. Where I've criticized the practice of crowdfunding, I have put it in the context of other giving practices, which also have their advantages and limitations, including substantial practical, political, and ethical problems. That said, the large majority of this project has outlined why we should be concerned with the increasing presence of donation-based crowdfunding among giving practices. This concern is not simply based on the evidence that crowdfunding replicates some of the problems found in other giving practices. Rather, its online and social dimensions, coupled with increased mediation between donors and recipients by some crowdfunding platforms, create new and insufficiently acknowledged problems for donors, campaigners, recipients, and the public at large.

Needless to say, however, donation-based crowdfunding isn't going away. The COVID-19 pandemic demonstrated the utility of crowdfunding and showed how increased familiarity with this practice will continue to drive people to crowdfund, especially when public institutions and other forms of giving aren't meeting their needs. Even if increased use of crowdfunding is built on a poor understanding of the success that crowdfunders will likely have, there is clearly massive and ongoing interest in engaging in crowdfunding. This interest is coupled with a desire by crowdfunding platforms to increase their reach into new communities and dimensions of giving.

Given the growing visibility and appeal of donation-based crowdfunding, I don't want to conclude this project by simply shrugging and saying, "That's not great." Rather, I will suggest ways we can better live with crowdfunding, retaining the great good it can do while at least taking some of the bite out of its many downsides. This is a job for a variety of actors, including donors, campaigners, recipients, crowdfunding platforms, and policy makers.

Appealing to the Crowd. Jeremy Snyder, Oxford University Press. © Oxford University Press 2024.
DOI: 10.1093/oso/9780197658130.003.0011

In many cases these actions can be undertaken by a single one of these groups, meaning that there is room for progress in making crowdfunding less ethically, politically, and practically problematic even if not all of those groups implicated in this practice are engaged in shaping it in less negative ways.

Values for guiding crowdfunding

Before suggesting ways to make crowdfunding less problematic, I want to articulate values to guide these suggestions and how these values confirm an idealized and positive role for crowdfunding that complements other giving practices. These values are informed by the substantial benefits of and problems with crowdfunding that were discussed in the previous chapters of this book; thus, this discussion will in part serve as a recap of the book's primary themes. At the same time, I will articulate values that were implicit in the previous chapters or tied to multiple themes from the various chapters.

As discussed in Chapter 1, there are a variety of ethical arguments for why, how, and how much we should *benefit* others. These diverse views on the ethical import of benefits include a principle of utility that directs us to take actions to maximize benefits, a principle of beneficence that allows some discretion in benefitting people, and many other approaches. Putting aside the substantial and important differences between benefits as understood through utilitarianism, beneficence, and other ethical principles, these approaches help to acknowledge the importance of crowdfunding's potential to benefit others; as a result, crowdfunding can have value through the lenses of these approaches. I have shown clearly that crowdfunding might also harm others, including the recipient, donors, and general public alike—a point I will return to shortly. Nonetheless, financial transfers through crowdfunding can provide a straightforward benefit to the recipient even if they don't reach their fundraising goal. These transfers can reduce the debt taken on by medical treatment, for example, or make it less likely that a person will become unhoused because they can't afford their rent. These benefits are often tied to addressing at least some of the recipient's most basic needs, giving them particular value. In addition to these material gifts, crowdfunding can provide emotional and psychological benefits to the recipient through feeling that their needs are being acknowledged, connecting with others through the campaign, and receiving encouragement and other forms of moral support.

A further advantage of crowdfunding is that it can support or enhance *choice* over the direction of one's life and *solidarity* with others in need. Interpretations of the value of choice vary, but here we can understand it as the capacity to lead a self-directed life. One way crowdfunding supports this self-direction is connected to the financial and psychological benefits of crowdfunding—it is difficult to choose how to live one's life if you are unhoused, hungry, and in pain from medical neglect. Beyond this, crowd-funding can embody the values of choice and solidarity by more closely con-necting the campaigner with a community of potential donors, giving the campaigner the ability to seek support without traditional intermediaries including philanthropic institutions and public agencies that can limit how support is used and create other barriers to receiving it. For donors as well, crowdfunding allows relatively direct access to those in need, giving donors greater voice in directing their own and the public's giving priorities. In this vein, support between a community of donors and recipients can mirror the values of mutual aid where giving is not directed by governments and the wealthiest members of the public but rather reflects the priorities of the wider public. Crowdfunding as a form of mutual aid can also emphasize sol-idarity through drawing attention and seeking solutions to the root causes of need and supporting social movements to effect change.[1] In effect, the degree of disintermediation between donor and recipient can enhance choice for the individual and, taken together, solidarity within the wider democratic public. This point shouldn't be oversold, however. As I have demonstrated, crowdfunding platforms have a large role in shaping the choices and options of donors and recipients, meaning that crowdfunding can act both to en-hance and to limit choice and solidarity in different respects.

Turning now more directly to the ethical, political, and practical problems raised by crowdfunding, this practice has very large implications for per-sonal *privacy*. Through crowdfunding, campaigners invite the public into the lives of the campaign recipient, usually including details about their daily experiences, images, videos, and other pieces of information that are typically not publicly available. This value can be interpreted in a variety of ways and has close connections to the value of choice. A key factor in interpreting the implications of crowdfunding for privacy is the degree to which recipients choose to disclose information about themselves to others. Privacy can be undermined when a campaigner discloses personal information about a re-cipient to the public without permission to do so, thus denying the recipient full control over private aspects of their selves. But even when the recipient seemingly knowingly chooses to release this information, crowdfunding platforms and the practice of crowdfunding itself can exert coercive pressure on recipients to make every detail about their lives and needs public to encourage donations. More generally, when the recipient's "choice" is between having their basic needs like shelter, medical care, and education met or not, we can question whether crowdfunding and privacy are at all compatible. Thus, the interests of donors and choices of crowdfunding platforms exert massive pressure on campaigners to trade their privacy for help from others.

Campaigners may forfeit privacy in order to engage in a popularity contest for donations from the wider public. This competition conveys the message that some and only some people deserve help from the crowd. In doing so, it undermines the *dignity* of recipients, particularly when they are seeking help to meet their basic needs. By abandoning the principle that all people are entitled to these basic goods, crowdfunding encourages grading people into groups of more and less deserving of help. In crowdfunding, personal deservingness is not based on shared humanity or some other universal requirement of dignity; rather, one's past deeds, social contributions, innocence (or lack thereof), and other factors are used to assess whether the crowd should support this campaign. As with forgoing privacy, campaigners often choose in a weak sense to participate in this self-degradation. But the preferences of the public and structure of crowdfunding as a practice make it difficult to succeed with crowdfunding while maintaining a sense of equal entitlement and respect. Recipients need not feel degraded by crowdfunding and indeed may experience a substantial degree of affirmation and respect from the support they receive. But at its core, crowdfunding does pressure campaigners to make the case for why they should receive this help and affirmation, often abandoning the idea that we are all deserving.

The contest for donations created by crowdfunding means that the funds raised through this practice are not distributed according to the values of maximizing benefit, helping those with the greatest need, equality, or other plausible interpretations of distributive justice or *equity*. As a result, there is a problem caused by the benefits created through crowdfunding and the choice that is granted to donors over who will receive this benefit. Insofar as these donations are largely undirected by an intermediary or shaped by the requirements of equity, there is no reason to think that these benefits will be equity-supporting. More concerning, there is good reason to think that some of the factors that shape these donor decisions will worsen inequities. Gender, racial, religious, and myriad other forms of discrimination are the basis of much social inequity. These biases factor into the distribution of crowdfunding donations as well, further deepening social differences, even factoring in that most crowdfunding recipients are in a position of genuine financial need. The practice of crowdfunding has other implications for equity as well in terms of who does the work of campaigning and who takes on the costs of crowdfunding, including losses of privacy and dignity and other potential harms.

The outcomes of crowdfunding are often unfair. So, too, is the need to crowdfund for basic needs in the first place. To put it a different way, much of the drive to crowdfund for basic needs is due to a failure of *social justice*. Crowdfunding is clearly a response to social injustices if we take basic needs like housing, education, personal security, and medical care to be entitlements that should be supported by public institutions. There is a temptation to also see crowdfunding as a solution to this injustice in that it can allow some people to meet their basic needs and empowers donors to bypass failed or inadequate public institutions in favor of directly helping others. However, the costs of crowdfunding to the privacy and dignity of recipients, coupled with the deep inequities in how this funding is distributed, show that crowdfunding is, at best, a badly flawed response to these injustices. Furthermore, when it is presented as a solution to social injustice, crowdfunding may make it more difficult to see and address these problems, especially if the public is given a sense that people can simply crowdfund their way out of institutional failures. Furthermore, relatively privileged people experience the most success through crowdfunding. This bias raises the possibility that these people—and their relatively privileged supporters—will be less moved to help those left behind by crowdfunding.

In addition to harms from a loss of privacy or dignity, other people experience harms when fraudsters take advantage of the public's generosity for personal enrichment. Donors are harmed by having their intention to help others thwarted. They may also face a financial loss if they would not have donated otherwise. When fraudsters take these donations, honest recipients who might have benefited from well-intentioned donors are harmed as well. Other harms of crowdfunding are less concrete, as when messages in these campaigns spread hateful attitudes and misinformation to the broader public. While harder to pinpoint, even these harms can have concrete effects on how people are treated, what kinds of medical decisions people make, and what political values are supported. Moreover, this messaging is backed by money that helps to realize its harmful effects. These violations of a value of *non-maleficence* or not harming others include both intentional harm by fraudulent campaigners and unintentional harm by misguided campaigners who may genuinely believe the misinformation they spread through their campaigns. Fraud, hate, and misinformation are harms that predate crowdfunding, of course, but the practice of crowdfunding creates new opportunities for these harms to spread.

While crowdfunding can create a more direct connection between donor and recipient than in more heavily mediated forms of giving, crowdfunding platforms have a substantial and growing role as intermediaries. As a result, these platforms have considerable influence over how the values linked to crowdfunding are implicated by this practice. It is important that these platforms enact truthfulness and transparency around how they pick winners and losers in crowdfunding, engage in the practice of giving more generally, and benefit from institutional failures to meet the public's basic needs. The often-unseen power that these platforms wield creates a need for *accountability* to the public, just as the public in turn demands accountability from political figures and policy makers. Campaigners owe accountability to donors as well, not simply to ward off fraud and misinformation but also to ensure that donations fit with the intentions of their donors and make efficient use of these resources.

The values of benefit and choice suggest an idealized role for online donation-based crowdfunding. This giving practice allows campaigners to quickly voice their needs to friends, family, and, if necessary, the wider public. Even in a fully just society, crowdfunding would offer a potentially effective way of raising funds for nonessential needs like travel or needs that aren't appropriately provided by public institutions, like religious activities. In other cases, a democratic and pluralistic society may engage in debate about whether certain needs count as essential and part of the requirements of a just state, as may be the case for gender-affirming care, for example. In these cases, crowdfunding can both help individuals address these needs and serve as a means of articulating them and shaping ongoing public debates. Crowdfunding also offers a nimble way of identifying emerging needs during emergencies or times of heightened needs like a pandemic. In these cases, crowdfunding can complement state institutions and indirect giving by allowing campaigners to voice their most pressing needs and using crowdfunding as a stopgap while the state, private organizations, insurance, and other institutions step into action.

Ideal conditions also help to reduce the danger of crowdfunding running afoul of the other values listed above. These conditions assume that crowdfunding takes place under fully just conditions where essential needs are met, just institutions are in place, and people live free from intentional fraud, hate, and misinformation. Privacy concerns may be less pressing in crowdfunding campaigns for nonessential needs as they might not touch on one's physical health, living conditions, or experiences with unjust social institutions. Moreover, having one's essential needs met in a just society means that people are less likely to be forced to engage in crowdfunding and make the case that they deserve to be helped. That said, when crowdfunding is used to address emerging or emergency needs, crowdfunding may be seen as a requirement. In these cases, crowdfunding can be treated as a convenient technology that allows campaigners to quickly voice their needs to friends and family without loss of privacy and dignity or where philanthropic organizations can use crowdfunding platforms to fund their operations while acting to shield recipients from public scrutiny. Finally, in ideal contexts crowdfunding can reinforce just institutions by allowing recipients to guide giving, helping to identify emerging needs and direct public conversations about what needs are essential. Thus, crowdfunding in its ideal form and under ideal conditions is a highly valuable giving practice that helps address nonessential needs, identify emerging essential needs, and complement state and private organizations and other forms of giving when they are under strain.

Crowdfunding in an imperfect world

I have articulated nine values for guiding how different actors should engage with donation-based crowdfunding: benefit, choice, solidarity, privacy, dignity, equity, social justice, non-maleficence, and accountability. These values demonstrate how crowdfunding can harm others and how it can feed on and contribute to forms of injustice. They also acknowledge the good that crowdfunding can do and illustrate an idealized form of crowdfunding that is a complementary form of giving under ideal social conditions.

Unfortunately, we do not live under just social conditions; thus, we largely do not and cannot engage in an idealized form of crowdfunding that is not a response to and reflective of social injustice and other harms. Crowdfunding under real-world circumstances raises questions about how to amplify the positives of this practice and dampen its negatives. When we engage in crowdfunding under nonideal circumstances as guided by the nine values, there is no guarantee that we can consistently do so while living up to all of these values. As we have seen, for example, an action that promotes the benefits of crowdfunding may come at a cost to the value of privacy. Therefore, the best we can hope for may be to promote most of these values in real-world circumstances while doing the least to undermine others. With this in mind, I will sketch ways that key actors can use these values to guide their behavior.

As a group, *donors* to crowdfunding campaigns have enormous influence over the practice of crowdfunding and particularly the behavior of campaigners. This influence arises because campaigners are beholden to the priorities and preferences of donors and often must convince them that the campaign is legitimate, deserves their support, and will fulfill donors' aims as benefactors. Crucially, this power is derived from the typical structure of crowdfunding as a popularity contest, where donors are the judges of deservingness and they control the prize of their support. However, if donors *restrict their crowdfunding contributions to close friends and family whom they personally know*, this structure shifts. Instead of a device to choose winners and losers and separate the deserving from the undeserving, crowdfunding between close connections serves largely as a convenience. It retains many of the benefits of this form of giving, where donors can easily transfer funds to campaign recipients, receive updates from the campaigner, and communicate support for the recipient. When campaigns are restricted to close contacts in this way and donors choose not to enter into the wider context of crowdfunding between strangers, the donor does not contribute to an incentive structure where campaigners must sacrifice their privacy and dignity to appeal to potential donors. Alternatively, donors can give within communities of mutual aid where community members help to both coordinate giving, encourage social change, and direct donations to serve both immediate needs and the root causes of these needs. Crowdfunding as mutual aid would tend to look more like crowdfunding campaigns in trans communities than viral competitions among isolated individuals.

Restricting crowdfunding donations in these ways seemingly comes at a cost to the donor's choice over whom to benefit. However, they certainly may and should give to others—just not to crowdfunding campaigns benefiting individual strangers. This form of giving, in addition to incentivizing self-effacing behavior by campaigners, is deeply inequitable and runs contrary to using donations to do the most good for those in need. Focusing giving on close friends and family also typically does not serve the goal of equity but may be justified by an obligation to help those we are specially positioned to help or by commitments to those with whom we have close relationships. Giving to appealing strangers does not have these justifications, and so donors would better serve the values of equity and social justice by aiding causes and organizations that have the capacity to do the most good, help those most in need, and address the structural causes of need and injustice. Giving in this way takes the form of supporting the goals of mutual aid rather than a marketplace of crowdfunders. For example, donors might choose to *use crowdfunding to directly benefit organizations and communities that support the values of equity and social justice*, including existing philanthropies that score well in terms of their impact and efficiency. Donors may also *patronize crowdfunding platforms that curate causes and campaigns that adhere to the goals of equity and social justice*. Importantly, however, there is nothing built into crowdfunding that necessarily supports these ends any more than other means of online electronic transfers or donations—in all cases they allow donors to choose which individuals or causes to support in line with the values they hold.

Crowdfunding *campaigners* may or may not be the recipients of donations to the campaign; regardless, they have a distinct role in shaping the practice of crowdfunding. Campaigners choose what information about the recipient to make public through the campaign, including financial and medical information; insights into the recipient's mental states, experiences, and emotions; photos and videos of the recipient; and aspects of the recipient that make them seemingly deserving of support. Thus, the campaigner has enormous control over the recipient's privacy and dignity through the choices they make in how the campaign is run. Ideally, campaigners can follow the lead of donors in *using crowdfunding largely as a convenience to coordinate giving among the recipient's close friends and family or to support giving as a form of mutual aid*. If this is practical, then the campaigner can limit the amount of sensitive information that is made public and know that their intended audience is largely made up of people who are already knowledgeable about key facts about the recipient. However, whereas donors have a great deal of power to limit their crowdfunding donations to those they have close ties to, campaigners may not have the same power—for example, if the recipient's financial needs are greater than the amount of support their friends and family are likely to be able to provide. This disparity in turn reflects inequities in terms of which campaigners are able to shield crowdfunding recipients from the need to appeal to the wider public.

When campaigners are compelled to appeal to the wider public for support, they should *consult where possible with the recipient about what information should be made public and how the recipient should be portrayed.* This task will be simple when the campaigner and recipient are the same person, of course, and challenging or impossible if the recipient is a very young child, is severely cognitively impaired, or has entrusted the campaigner with making these decisions because of illness or lack of time. In these cases, the campaigner is accountable to the recipient, meaning that they must balance the recipient's interest in protecting their privacy and dignity with their need to benefit from crowdfunding. This accountability extends to the community of potential donors as well, where the campaigner should take care to be clear, accurate, and honest in the campaign so as not to harm the public through fraud or misinformation. Again, this honesty may be in tension with the campaigner's privacy and dignity, but this tension can be managed by leaving details out of the discussion rather than actively misleading potential donors.

The campaigner should also *highlight social injustices that give rise to the need to crowdfund,* such as a lack of publicly funded medical insurance or the exposure of racialized minorities to police violence. There may be a tension between making the recipient seem appealing and calling attention to these structural problems, but they can be put in a relatively positive light and framed less as excuses for the recipient's need and more as calls to action by the recipient's community so that they and others like them need not resort to crowdfunding in the future. Such calls to action take advantage of the online and social nature of crowdfunding that can coordinate giving but also—potentially—coordinate responses to promote social justice in line with the value of solidarity between donors and recipients. When crowdfunding campaigners are choosing to support a cause, philanthropic institution, or community of mutual aid rather than an individual, these campaigns will be particularly well suited to highlighting these injustices and using the campaign as a call to action. Thus, the recipient's needs and context will impact how much values like privacy, dignity, and social justice are implicated by the campaign.

When crowdfunding campaign **recipients** also manage their own crowdfunding campaigns, the issue of consent around what information should be disclosed through the campaign is simple. But even when others are managing the campaign on their behalf, recipients should *consult with campaigners about the content of their campaigns*. This step is important to protect the recipient's choice of what private information to disclose to the public and to ensure that the public presentation of their needs does not undermine their dignity. At the same time, recipients have a role to play in *encouraging campaigners to highlight the social injustices that may be relevant to their needs* and using the campaign as a way to coordinate actions to address these injustices. The recipient can also *review information in the campaign to ensure that it is accurate* and does not contain information that misleads or harms the public.

All of these actions by the recipient in coordination with the campaign manager assumes that the recipient is in a position to take on these duties. As noted above, this coordination may be difficult or impossible because of cognitive limitations, the complications of being unhoused or in pain, or other demands on their time and other resources. Asking recipients to take on these duties when their needs are caused by social injustices may further deepen these injustices as well, as when a person out of work due to discriminatory hiring practices is now tasked with promoting social justice through a crowdfunding campaign while also trying to find new employment, pay their rent, and manage their food budget. Nonetheless, these campaigns are created and made public in the recipient's name and interest. Although the recipient may not be in a position to promote the values tied to crowdfunding, others may be especially well situated to do so on their behalf, contributing their voice to public discussions of the failure of just institutions.

The behaviors of crowdfunding donors, campaigners, and recipients are heavily constrained and shaped by *crowdfunding platforms* and the people who create and manage them. Throughout this book I have given examples of how crowdfunding platforms advise campaigners to act in ways that undermine the values of privacy and dignity. As a first step, then, they can *make supporting privacy and dignity central to their structures and advice to campaigners*. When campaigners seek donations from strangers, they enter into a competition with other campaigners for the public's attention and financial support. Thus, they might feel that they are sabotaging their campaign if they decide to withhold images, video, and information they are told will appeal to potential donors. Platforms can help with this problem by *encouraging all campaigners to be cautious about what information they share with the public and eliminating or making less prominent particularly invasive features like photos and videos*. The case for eliminating these features is strongest in particularly sensitive contexts, such as fundraising for medical needs and for young children. Moreover, platforms can *require that campaigners acting on behalf of others attest to receiving permission to post private information and imagery of others*, again with particular focus on sensitive needs and populations.

The role of crowdfunding platforms in promoting or undermining the values of benefit, equity, solidarity, and social justice depends significantly on their structure and choices. As discussed in detail in the book, a for-profit structure that promotes crowdfunding campaigns largely based on their popularity and ability to appeal to the wider public tends to undermine these values. By comparison, crowdfunding platforms can focus on *partnering with reputable and efficient philanthropic organizations and communities with expertise in addressing the deeper causes of need and inequity*. This focus has the benefit of retaining some of the ease of crowdfunding and its ability to bring in a wider and more representative range of donors to the practice of giving while making this practice less of a free-for-all among campaigns. Similarly, crowdfunding platforms can *curate causes that benefit traditionally disadvantaged groups and work to address social justice more sustainably*, as with platforms like Watsi.org and GoFundMe.org. Importantly, though, more active curation of causes to promote the values of benefit, equity, and social justice must be coupled with accountability. GoFundMe.org works closely with its for-profit arm, often curates causes for individual campaigns that must be hosted on its for-profit arm, and promotes the causes of celebrities and its corporate partners. A more accountable approach would be to *be highly transparent about how decisions are made about what causes and recipients to promote and to have this process driven by the values of benefit, equity, and social justice* rather than the interests of for-profit crowdfunding and corporate groups interested in burnishing their public image.

Even before determining which campaigns to promote, crowdfunding platforms determine what campaigns to host and what messages and claims will be allowed at all. Platforms should ensure that they do not harm others by spreading hate and misinformation. A strategy to this end can include *banning campaigns that support hate groups, promote violence, and support harmful or fraudulent medical treatments and providers*. Where campaigns potentially spread misinformation or touch on sensitive topics, platforms may *append warnings or direct potential donors to vetted sources of information*, as already happens on some platforms around vaccine misinformation. Although campaigners who are prohibited from fundraising on one platform may simply move to another, more permissive platform, these restrictions can reduce the visibility of these campaigns and marginalize platforms that host harmful campaigns. Once again, accountability by these platforms is important, as decisions about what campaigns and causes are restricted should be guided by values of non-maleficence and equity rather than their own interest in avoiding bad press coverage or the ire of politicians. These platforms should *be clear about how these decisions are made, be transparent about what policies and values govern these decisions, and receive input and guidance from other stakeholders* rather than act through a purely self-interested and opaque process.

Some of the actions that crowdfunding platforms can take to self-police their industry will likely benefit them reputationally and financially, but others will come at a cost. Particularly where some or all of these platforms are unwilling to take these actions on their own, public *policy makers* must use regulatory and legal mechanisms to protect donors, recipients, and the wider public. In some cases, regulations already widely exist, particularly in the areas of financial fraud. Another helpful step would be to develop policies around the public disclosure of normally private information without consent. These policies could include regulations *requiring platforms to determine whether campaigners have received consent to disclose personal information through crowdfunding campaigns or creating and enforcing regulations against the disclosure of particularly sensitive information without permission*, such as bank statements and medical records. In each of these cases, policy makers have good reason to be cautious in creating and implementing such regulations, as enforcement can be a blunt instrument that would largely target people already in a position of considerable need. These actions could undermine the values of benefit and choice while doing little to promote other values. The clearest exception to this concern is in cases of fraud, where the campaigner is not genuinely a person in need or is clearly harming the recipient by disclosing sensitive information without permission.

Policy makers also have a role to ensure that crowdfunding does not serve to supercharge hate and misinformation through crowdfunded financial support. As discussed in the previous chapter, anti-vaccine-mandate fundraisers in Canada led to news coverage that credulously reported that these fundraisers demonstrated widespread local support for the campaigners and their goals. In reality, however, more than half of the donors to the GiveSendGo version of the campaign were from the United States.[2] This experience highlights the danger of crowdfunding being used by international political movements and agents to shape domestic politics and policy, spread hate and misinformation, and undermine democratic processes. As a result of this experience, Canada introduced a policy that *requires crowdfunding platforms to register with the national financial tracking regulator, report suspicious and large-volume donations, keep records on transactions, and develop compliance programs.*[3] It is not clear yet whether these new policies will be adequate or need further refinement, but they indicate a direction other countries should follow to mitigate the potential harms of crowdfunding and the ways this practice can be manipulated to undermine democracy. Crucially, this policy puts the burden of reporting on crowdfunding platforms without introducing new limits on the vast majority of campaigners and donors who seek to benefit organizations and individuals in need.

Obviously, the most effective thing policy makers could do to address the potential negatives of crowdfunding would be to reduce the need for it. In donation-based crowdfunding, some people are compelled to appeal to the general public for support in meeting their basic needs. If policy makers did a better job of providing universal medical insurance, adequate housing, guaranteed income, protection from a variety of forms of discrimination and violence, and all other basic needs, the market for donation-based crowdfunding would be much smaller. Just as obviously, however, this is a very tall order. Even under the best of circumstances, democratically elected governments have different priorities around tax burdens, essential services, and nonessential activities. Moreover, there will always be reasonable debates about what needs are essential and whether public institutions are the most efficient and just means of addressing all of them. Short of addressing all of the essential needs that drive donation-based crowdfunding, policy makers can *use information from crowdfunding campaigns to better understand the experiences of campaigners and identify which of their needs are going unmet.* In some cases, these will be fundraisers for interventions like religious missions abroad that are not appropriate for public funding or unproven medical interventions that would not be an efficient use of public resources. In others, policy makers may discover timely evidence to advocate to address specific gaps for renters, people experiencing mental health crises, and those impacted by disasters and other emergencies that may not be well captured by other sources of data or have influential voices in policy debates. This information could be shared voluntarily by crowdfunding platforms, compelled through regulation, or gathered through publicly available crowdfunding campaign pages. If partially anonymized, these data would have a lower impact on the privacy of campaign recipients.

Finally, policy makers should pay careful attention to the turn toward mediation between donors and recipients by crowdfunding platforms and the way this turn is being fueled by tax benefits to nonprofit groups. In some cases, this trend is a continuation of existing practices where nonprofit organizations with tax-exempt status augment their online fundraising activities to include crowdfunding campaigns or partner with crowdfunding platforms to highlight causes for their users to support. These practices, supported through tax exemptions, have been criticized as being inefficient, being antidemocratic, and deepening inequities.[4] The move toward mediation in crowdfunding may continue this pattern by turning crowdfunding platforms more clearly into indirect-giving organizations themselves with an outsized and undemocratic influence on which causes and needs are supported by the public. Moreover, as in the case of GoFundMe.org, some platforms are creating nonprofit entities that, while separate from their for-profit arms, work closely with them to create opportunities for tax exemptions for donors to individual campaigns. Any *reforms targeting tax exemption for donations should be aware of and responsive to the growing role of crowdfunding in giving*.

These suggested responses are necessarily imprecise, as the contexts of donors, campaigners, recipients, platforms, and policy makers will shape what responses are possible and best support the values implicated by crowdfunding. These values can conflict with one another, further complicating attempts to support them. The financial situations, needs, and political and regulatory contexts of these actors will all shape what actions should be taken in response. Those with the least power socially, politically, and economically—individual donors, campaigners, and recipients—collectively have a great deal of power to limit donation-based crowdfunding to what it does best. By focusing on the ease with which crowdfunding can nimbly coordinate giving within an existing community, these actors can help to ensure that the worst forms of crowdfunding are avoided to the greatest extent possible. In this way, people using crowdfunding can treat it as a tool that can be used to promote or undermine the values of benefit, choice, solidarity, privacy, dignity, equity, social justice, non-maleficence, and accountability. Using crowdfunding among people in existing relationships and in the service of mutual aid is much more likely to promote these values insofar as campaigners can draw attention to the root causes of their needs and motivate and coordinate collective actions to address these problems.[5] The deeper reforms needed to address the drive to crowdfund and the more destructive elements of crowdfunding, including the structure of the platforms hosting these campaigns and the unmet needs driving individuals to them, also require participation by more powerful entities and the public to hold them to account. Otherwise, the costs of addressing crowdfunding's worst features will fall largely on those who most need crowdfunding in the first place.

Notes

Introduction

1. Indiana University Lilly Family School of Philanthropy, "The Digital for Good: A Global Study on Emerging Ways of Giving, United Kingdom," May 2022, https://globalindices.iupui.edu/additional-research/united-kingdom.html.
2. GoFundMe, "The Data Behind Donations During the COVID-19 Pandemic," *GoFundMe Stories* (blog), September 24, 2020, https://medium.com/gofundme-stories/the-data-behind-donations-during-the-covid-19-pandemic-c40e0f690bfa.
3. Susan Cahn and Mollie Hertel, "Millions of Americans Continue to Donate to Crowdfunding Sites to Help Others Pay Medical Bills Despite Economic Hardships of the Pandemic" (NORC at the University of Chicago, April 1, 2021), https://www.norc.org/NewsEventsPublications/PressReleases/Pages/millions-of-americans-continue-to-donate-to-crowdfunding-sites-to-help-others-pay-medical-bills-despite-economic-hardships.aspx.
4. Una Osili et al., "Charitable Crowdfunding: Who Gives, to What, and Why?," Working Paper, March 31, 2021, https://scholarworks.iupui.edu/handle/1805/25515.
5. Indiana University Lilly Family School of Philanthropy, "The Digital for Good: A Global Study on Emerging Ways of Giving, Brazil," May 2022, https://globalindices.iupui.edu/additional-research/brazil.html.
6. Indiana University Lilly Family School of Philanthropy, "The Global Philanthropy Environment Index 2022," March 10, 2022, https://scholarworks.iupui.edu/handle/1805/28098.
7. Una Osili et al., "Global Philanthropy Tracker 2020," Working Paper, October 22, 2020, https://scholarworks.iupui.edu/handle/1805/24144.
8. Rob Solomon, "GoFundMe CEO Rob Solomon on the Power of Social Fundraising," *BrainStation* (blog), November 10, 2017, https://brainstation.io/magazine/vanguards-gofundme-rob-solomon.
9. Ben Paynter, "How Will the Rise of Crowdfunding Reshape How We Give to Charity?," *Fast Company*, March 13, 2017, https://www.fastcompany.com/3068534/how-will-the-rise-of-crowdfunding-reshape-how-we-give-to-charity-2.
10. Stephen Marche, "Go Fund Yourself," *Mother Jones*, February 2018, https://www.motherjones.com/politics/2018/01/go-fund-yourself-health-care-popularity-contest/.
11. Cari Romm, "Is It Fair to Ask the Internet to Pay Your Hospital Bill?," *The Atlantic*, March 12, 2015, https://www.theatlantic.com/health/archive/2015/03/is-it-fair-to-ask-the-internet-to-pay-your-hospital-bill/387577/.

12. Ainsley Harris, "How Crowdfunding Platform GoFundMe Has Created a $3 Billion Digital Safety Net," *Fast Company*, February 13, 2017, https://www.fastcompany.com/3067472/how-crowdfunding-platform-gofundme-has-created-a-3-billion-digital.

13. Romm, "Is It Fair to Ask the Internet to Pay Your Hospital Bill?"

14. Rachel Monroe, "When GoFundMe Gets Ugly," *The Atlantic*, October 9, 2019, https://www.theatlantic.com/magazine/archive/2019/11/gofundme-nation/598369/.

15. Harris, "How Crowdfunding Platform GoFundMe Has Created a $3 Billion Digital Safety Net."

16. Nathan Heller, "The Hidden Cost of GoFundMe Health Care," June 24, 2019, https://www.newyorker.com/magazine/2019/07/01/the-perverse-logic-of-gofundme-health-care.

17. Seth Stevenson, "The Dark Side of GoFundMe," *Slate*, December 9, 2020, https://slate.com/business/2020/12/gofundme-dark-side-fraud-social-media-health-care.html.

18. Monroe, "When GoFundMe Gets Ugly."

19. Quentin Fottrell, "GoFundMe Has Revolutionized How We Give, but Is That a Good Thing?," *Town & Country*, June 19, 2019, https://www.townandcountrymag.com/society/money-and-power/a27309524/crowdsourcing-ethics-gofundme-etiquette/.

20. Heller, "The Hidden Cost of GoFundMe Health Care."

21. Monroe, "When GoFundMe Gets Ugly."

22. Ibid.

23. Marche, "Go Fund Yourself."

24. Heller, "The Hidden Cost of GoFundMe Health Care."

25. Monroe, "When GoFundMe Gets Ugly."

26. Marche, "Go Fund Yourself."

27. Stevenson, "The Dark Side of GoFundMe."

Chapter 1

1. Aristotle, *Nicomachean Ethics*, trans. Harris Rackham (Cambridge, MA: Harvard University Press, 1926).

2. Ibid., 1121b.

3. Philippa Foot, *Virtues and Vices and Other Essays in Moral Philosophy* (Oxford: Clarendon Press, 2002).

4. Nancy E. Snow, "Neo-Aristotelian Virtue Ethics," in *The Oxford Handbook of Virtue* (Oxford: Oxford University Press, 2018), 321–42.

5. David Hume, *An Enquiry Concerning the Principles of Morals*, ed. Tom L. Beauchamp, Revised edition (Oxford/New York: Oxford University Press, 1998), 81.

6. John Stuart Mill, *Utilitarianism* (Milton Park, UK: Routledge, 2016).

7. Peter Singer, *The Most Good You Can Do: How Effective Altruism Is Changing Ideas About Living Ethically* (New Haven: Yale University Press, 2015).

8. Elizabeth Ashford, "Severe Poverty as an Unjust Emergency," in *The Ethics of Giving*, ed. Paul Woodruff (Oxford: Oxford University Press, 2018), 103–48.

9. T. E. Hill, "Duties and Choices in Philanthropic Giving: Kantian Perspectives," in *The Ethics of Giving: Philosophers' Perspectives on Philanthropy*, ed. Paul Woodruff (Oxford: Oxford University Press, 2018), 13–39.

10. Immanuel Kant, *Lectures on Ethics*, ed. Peter Heath and J. B. Schneewind, trans. Peter Heath, *The Cambridge Edition of the Works of Immanuel Kant* (Cambridge: Cambridge University Press, 1997), 27: 456.

11. Hill, "Duties and Choices in Philanthropic Giving: Kantian Perspectives."

12. Clare Chambers and Philip Parvin, "Coercive Redistribution and Public Agreement: Re-Evaluating the Libertarian Challenge of Charity," *Critical Review of International Social and Political Philosophy* 13, no. 1 (2010): 93–114.

13. Lucius Caviola, Stefan Schubert, and Joshua D. Greene, "The Psychology of (In)Effective Altruism," *Trends in Cognitive Sciences* 25, no. 7 (2021): 596–607.

14. Jonas Nagel and Michael R. Waldmann, "Deconfounding Distance Effects in Judgments of Moral Obligation," *Journal of Experimental Psychology: Learning, Memory, and Cognition* 39, no. 1 (2013): 237–52.

15. Murat Genç, Stephen Knowles, and Trudy Sullivan, "In Search of Effective Altruists," *Applied Economics* 53, no. 7 (2021): 805–19.

16. Lucius Caviola, Stefan Schubert, and Jason Nemirow, "The Many Obstacles to Effective Giving," *Judgment and Decision Making* 15, no. 2 (2020): 159–72.

17. Lila Corwin Berman, "How Americans Give: The Financialization of American Jewish Philanthropy," *American Historical Review* 122, no. 5 (2017): 1459–89.

18. Marcel Mauss, *The Gift: The Form and Reason for Exchange in Archaic Societies*, trans. W. D. Halls (New York: W. W. Norton & Company, 2000).

19. Shauna Mottiar and Mvuselelo Ngcoya, "Indigenous Philanthropy: Challenging Western Preconceptions," in *The Routledge Companion to Philanthropy*, ed. Tobias Jung, Susan Phillips, and Jenny Harrow (Milton Park, UK: Routledge, 2016), 171–81.

20. John A. Grim, "A Comparative Study in Native American Philanthropy," in *Philanthropy in the World's Traditions*, ed. Warren F. Ilchman, Stanley N. Katz, and Edward L. Queen II (Bloomington: Indiana University Press, 1998), 25–53.

21. Peter Kropotkin, *Mutual Aid: A Factor in Evolution* (London: McClure, Philips & Company, 1902).

22. Dean Spade, *Mutual Aid: Building Solidarity During This Crisis (and the Next)* (New York: Verso Books, 2020).

23. Peter Brown, *Through the Eye of a Needle: Wealth, the Fall of Rome, and the Making of Christianity in the West, 350–550 AD* (Princeton: Princeton University Press, 2012).

24. Lucius Annaeus Seneca, *On Benefits*, trans. Miriam Griffin and Brad Inwood (Chicago: University of Chicago Press, 2011), II.19.

25. Leviticus, 19:9–10.

26. Deuteronomy, 24:19–22.

27. Deuteronomy, 14:28–29.

28. Deuteronomy, 15:8.

29. Aaron L. Mackler, "Judaism, Justice, and Access to Health Care," *Kennedy Institute of Ethics Journal* 1, no. 2 (1991): 143–61.

30. Scott Davis, "Philanthropy as a Virtue in Late Antiquity and the Middle Ages," in *Giving: Western Ideas of Philanthropy*, ed. Jerome B. Schneewind (Bloomington: Indiana University Press, 1996), 1–23.

31. Brown, *Through the Eye of a Needle*.

32. Saint Ambrose, *De Officiis*, trans. Ivor J. Davidson, Oxford Early Christian Studies (New York: Oxford University Press, 2001), XVI 76.

33. Suzanne Roberts, "Contexts of Charity in the Middle Ages: Religious, Social, and Civic," in *Giving: Western Ideas of Philanthropy*, ed. Jerome B. Schneewind (Bloomington: Indiana University Press, 1996), 24–53.

34. J. B Schneewind, "Philosophical Ideas of Charity: Some Historical Reflections," in *Giving: Western Ideas of Philanthropy*, ed. J. B Schneewind (Bloomington: Indiana University Press, 1996), 54–75.

35. John Calvin, *Institutes of the Christian Religion*, trans. Henry Beveridge (Grand Rapids: Christian Classics Ethereal Library; NetLibrary, 1990), II.VII.5.

36. Abdul Hameed Siddiqui, ed., *The Holy Qur'ān: English Translation and Explanatory Notes* (Chicago: Islamic Book Centre, 1977), 2: 83.

37. Amy Singer, "Giving Practices in Islamic Societies," *Social Research: An International Quarterly* 80, no. 2 (2013): 341–58.

38. Thierry Kochuyt, "God, Gifts and Poor People: On Charity in Islam," *Social Compass* 56, no. 1 (March 1, 2009): 98–116.

39. Swami Tapasyananda, *Bhagavadgītā* (Madras: Sri Ramakrishna Math, 1984), 17:20–22

40. Maria Heim, *Theories of the Gift in South Asia: Hindu, Buddhist, and Jain Reflections on Dana* (New York: Taylor & Francis Group, 2004).

41. Kant, *Lectures on Ethics*, 27:456.

42. Mackler, "Judaism, Justice, and Access to Health Care."

43. Peter Singer, "Famine, Affluence, and Morality," *Philosophy & Public Affairs* 1, no. 3 (1972): 235.

44. Davis, "Philanthropy as a Virtue in Late Antiquity and the Middle Ages."

45. James Brodman, *Charity and Religion in Medieval Europe* (Washington, DC: CUA Press, 2009).

46. Derek Penslar, "The Origins of Modern Jewish Philanthropy," in *Philanthropy in the World's Traditions*, ed. Warren F. Ilchman, Stanley N. Katz, and Edward L. Queen (Bloomington: Indiana University Press, 1998), 197–214.

47. Amy Singer, "Giving Practices in Islamic Societies."

48. Mark S. LeClair, *Philanthropy in Transition* (New York: Palgrave Macmillan US, 2014).

49. Mark Sidel, "Philanthropy in Asia: Evolving Public Policy," in *The Routledge Companion to Philanthropy*, ed. Tobias Jung, Susan Phillips, and Jenny Harrow (Milton Park, UK: Routledge, 2016), 280–92.

50. Arthur Gautier, "Historically Contested Concepts: A Conceptual History of Philanthropy in France, 1712–1914," *Theory and Society* 48, no. 1 (2019): 95–129.

51. Eric Beerbohm, "The Free-Provider Problem: Private Provision of Public Responsibilities," in *Philanthropy in Democratic Societies*, ed. Rob Reich, Chiara Cordelli, and Lucy Bernholz (Chicago: University of Chicago Press, 2016), 225.

52. Rob Reich, *Just Giving: Why Philanthropy Is Failing Democracy and How It Can Do Better* (Princeton: Princeton University Press, 2018).

53. Ibid.

54. Julian Wolpert, "Redistributional Effects of America's Private Foundations," in *The Legitimacy of Philanthropic Foundations: United States and European Perspectives*, ed. Kenneth Prewitt, Mattei Dogan, Steven Heydemann, and Stefan Toepler (New York: Russell Sage Foundation, 2006), 123–49.

55. Reich, *Just Giving*, 93.

56. Aidan Hollis and Arthur Sweetman, "The Life-Cycle of a Microfinance Institution: The Irish Loan Funds," *Journal of Economic Behavior & Organization* 46, no. 3 (2001): 291–311.

57. Vincent Rouzé, "Crowdsourcing and Crowdfunding: The Origins of a New System?," in *Cultural Crowdfunding: Platform Capitalism, Labour and Globalization*, vol. 12 (London: University of Westminster Press, 2019), 15–33.

58. Carolina Dalla Chiesa and Christian Handke, "Crowdfunding," in *Handbook of Cultural Economics*, 3rd edition (Cheltenham, UK: Edward Elgar Publishing, 2020), 158–67.

59. Knowledge at Wharton Staff, "Can You Spare a Quarter? Crowdfunding Sites Turn Fans into Patrons of the Arts," Knowledge@Wharton, December 8, 2010, https://knowledge.wharton.upenn.edu/article/can-you-spare-a-quarter-crowdfunding-sites-turn-fans-into-patrons-of-the-arts/.

60. Andy Baio, "Kickstarter Launches Another Social Fundraising Platform," *TechCrunch* (blog), April 29, 2009, https://social.techcrunch.com/2009/04/29/kickstarter-launches-another-social-fundraising-platform/.

61. Ryan Lawler, "Crowdfunding Startup GoFundMe, Which Is Like KickStarter for the Rest of Us, Is Pulling in $2 Million a Month," *TechCrunch* (blog), June 29, 2012, https://social.techcrunch.com/2012/06/29/gofundme/.

62. Ibid.

63. Sarah Max, "A Plucky Startup Ditches 'Coin Piggy' Roots and Finds Its Mission," *NBC News*, July 1, 2013, https://www.nbcnews.com/id/wbna52363496.

64. Lawler, "Crowdfunding Startup GoFundMe, Which Is Like KickStarter for the Rest of Us, Is Pulling in $2 Million a Month."

65. Ryan Lawler, "Crowdfunding Startup GoFundMe Launches Member Network Program, Now Sharing Revenue with Partners," *TechCrunch* (blog), September 25, 2012, https://social.techcrunch.com/2012/09/25/gofundme-partner-program/.

66. Haje Jan Kamps, "GoFundMe Hits 25m Donors and $2b Raised on Its Giving Platform," *TechCrunch* (blog), May 10, 2016, https://social.techcrunch.com/2016/05/10/gofundme-2bn-raised/.

67. Ingrid Lunden, "GoFundMe Passes $3B Raised on Its Platform, Adding $1B in Only the Last 5 Months," *TechCrunch* (blog), October 18, 2016, https://social.techcrunch.com/2016/10/18/gofundme-raises-3b-on-its-platform-raising-1b-in-only-the-last-5-months/.

68. Ingrid Lunden, "GoFundMe, Now with $4B in Donations from 40M Donors, Plots Euro Expansion," *TechCrunch* (blog), June 9, 2017, https://social.techcrunch.com/2017/06/09/gofundme-europe-expansion/.

69. Jennifer Van Grove, "GoFundMe Founders Get Big Payday," *San Diego Union-Tribune*, August 24, 2016, https://www.sandiegouniontribune.com/sdut-gofundme-founders-sell-company-to-investors-2015jun24-story.html.

70. Lunden, "GoFundMe, Now with $4B in Donations from 40M Donors, Plots Euro Expansion."

71. Seth Stevenson, "The Tithes Are Turning: The GoFundMe Story," *Slate* (blog), June 7, 2022, https://slate.com/transcripts/K2wrN0tGYzFoNTlJZlRBa2tVTkE3STVoNGVo NHlKeUNOUkowY0MwenFlTT0=.

72. Phillip Inman, "Charities Go Online to Stay in the Running and Reach the Next Generation of Givers," *The Guardian*, March 25, 2008, sec. Society, https://www.theg uardian.com/society/2008/mar/25/voluntarysector.charitablegiving.

73. Howard Lake, "JustGiving Total Raised Passes $4 Billion," *UK Fundraising* (blog), June 6, 2016, https://fundraising.co.uk/2016/06/06/justgiving-total-raised-passes-4-billion/.

74. Andy Ricketts, "Blackbaud Completes Its £95m Takeover of JustGiving," *Third Sector* (blog), October 4, 2017, https://www.thirdsector.co.uk/article/1446437.

75. JustGiving, "About," JustGiving, accessed March 24, 2022, https://justgiving.blackb aud.com/about.

76. Meg Graham, "Competitor Acquires Chicago-Based Crowdfunding Site GiveForward," *Chicago Tribune*, March 29, 2017, https://www.chicagotribune.com/business/blue-sky/ct-giveforward-youcaring-acquisition-bsi-20170329-story.html.

77. Thomas Knowlton, "Exclusive Interview: Vancouver's FundRazr Raises the Bar with Monumental PayPal and Facebook Collaboration," *BrainStation* (blog), August 8, 2010, https://brainstation.io/magazine/exclusive-interview-vancouvers-fundrazr-rai ses-the-bar-with-monumental-paypal-and-facebook-collaboration.

78. Stephen Marche, "Go Fund Yourself," *Mother Jones*, February 2018, https://www.moth erjones.com/politics/2018/01/go-fund-yourself-health-care-popularity-contest/.

79. Ingrid Lunden, "GoFundMe Acquires CrowdRise to Expand to Fundraising for Charities," *TechCrunch* (blog), January 10, 2017, https://social.techcrunch.com/2017/01/10/gofundme-buys-crowdrise-to-expand-to-fundraising-for-charities/.

80. Ingrid Lunden, "GoFundMe Acquires YouCaring as Charitable Crowdfunding Continues to Consolidate," *TechCrunch* (blog), April 3, 2018, https://social.techcru nch.com/2018/04/03/gofundme-acquires-youcaring-as-charitable-crowdfunding-continues-to-consolidate/.

81. GoFundMe, "GoFundMe 2022 Year in Help," *GoFundMe* (blog), December 2022, https://www.gofundme.com/c/gofundme-2022-year-in-help.

82. Lhendup Bhutia, "'If You Give People the Right to Information, They Will Be Ready to Donate,'" *Open: The Magazine*, November 1, 2018, https://openthemagazine.com/cover-stories/wealth-issue-2018/if-you-give-people-the-right-to-information-they-will-be-ready-to-donate/.

83. Indulekha Aravind, "How Milaap Tweaked Crowdfunding Model to Raise Money for Medical Care," *Economic Times*, March 1, 2020, https://economictimes.indiatimes.com/industry/healthcare/biotech/healthcare/how-milaap-tweaked-crowdfunding-model-to-raise-money-for-medical-care/articleshow/74420753.cms.

84. Brinda Sarkar, "Ketto Looks to Double Its Headcount in 2021," *Economic Times*, December 24, 2020, https://economictimes.indiatimes.com/tech/startups/ketto-looks-to-double-its-headcount-in-2021/articleshow/79940566.cms.

85. Bhutia, " 'If You Give People the Right to Information, They Will Be Ready to Donate.' "

86. Milaap, "The Journey So Far of Crowdfunding in India," accessed March 22, 2022, https://milaap.org/about-us/overview.

87. Aravind, "How Milaap Tweaked Crowdfunding Model to Raise Money for Medical Care."

88. Disha Sharma, "Crowdfunding Platform Impact Guru Gets Seed Funding," *VCCircle*, April 28, 2016, https://www.vccircle.com/crowdfunding-platform-impact-guru-gets-seed-funding.

89. ImpactGuru, "About Us," *ImpactGuru.com*, accessed March 24, 2022, https://www.impactguru.com/about-us.

90. United Nations Development Programme China Poverty, Equity, and Governance, "Internet Philanthropy in China" (Beijing: United Nations Development Programme, 2016).

91. Pingyue Jin, "Medical Crowdfunding in China: Empirics and Ethics," *Journal of Medical Ethics* 45, no. 8 (2019): 538–44.

92. Lydia Willgress, "JustGiving Accused of Taking £20m from Donations While Paying Staff up to £200,000," *The Telegraph*, February 7, 2017, https://www.telegraph.co.uk/news/2017/02/07/justgiving-accused-taking-20m-donations-paying-staff-200000/.

93. Ainsley Harris, "How Crowdfunding Platform GoFundMe Has Created a $3 Billion Digital Safety Net," *Fast Company*, February 13, 2017, https://www.fastcompany.com/3067472/how-crowdfunding-platform-gofundme-has-created-a-3-billion-digital.

94. GoFundMe, "What Is Crowdfunding? The Clear and Simple Answer," *GoFundMe (CA)* (blog), accessed March 28, 2022, https://www.gofundme.com/en-ca/c/crowdfunding.

95. Fundly, "Personal Fundraising: How Individuals Can Raise Money Online," *Fundly* (blog), accessed March 28, 2022, https://blog.fundly.com/personal-fundraising/.

96. Lazar Finker, "What Crowdfunding Means For Philanthropy," *Lazar Finker's Philanthropy Blog* (blog), April 2, 2018, https://web.archive.org/web/20210506182125/http://lazarfinker.com/what-crowdfunding-means-for-philanthropy/.

97. Carolyn Victoria McKechnie, "What Is a Crowdfunding Platform?," *Inside Philanthropy* (blog), accessed March 28, 2022, https://www.insidephilanthropy.com/explainers/what-is-a-crowdfunding-platform.

98. Ketto, "Who Benefits from Crowdfunding?," March 24, 2022, https://www.ketto.org/blog/who-benefits-from-crowdfunding.

99. Fundly, "Personal Fundraising: How Individuals Can Raise Money Online."

100. David Gelles, "The GoFundMe C.E.O. Wants You to Ask: 'How Can I Help?,'" *New York Times*, March 4, 2022, sec. Business, https://www.nytimes.com/2022/03/04/business/tim-cadogan-gofundme-corner-office.html.

101. Rebecca TeKoltse, "Crowdfunding Research and Impact on the Philanthropic Sector," *Lilly Family School of Philanthropy* (blog), December 2, 2019, https://blog.philanthropy.iupui.edu/2019/12/02/crowdfunding-research-and-impact-on-the-philanthropic-sector/.

102. Jacqueline Ackerman and Jon Bergdoll, "4 New Revelations on How People Give to Charity Crowdfunding Campaigns," *Fast Company,* June 5, 2021, https://www.fastcompany.com/90643893/4-new-revelations-on-how-people-give-to-charity-crowdfunding-campaigns.

103. Finker, "What Crowdfunding Means For Philanthropy."

104. McKechnie, "What Is a Crowdfunding Platform?"

105. Una Osili et al., "Charitable Crowdfunding: Who Gives, to What, and Why?," Working Paper (Indianapolis: Indiana University Lilly Family School of Philanthropy, March 31, 2021), https://scholarworks.iupui.edu/handle/1805/25515.

106. Lauren V. Ghazal et al., "'Both a Life Saver and Totally Shameful': Young Adult Cancer Survivors' Perceptions of Medical Crowdfunding," *Journal of Cancer Survivorship: Research and Practice* (2022), https://doi.org/10.1007/s11764-022-01188-x.

107. Gordon Burtch and Jason Chan, "Investigating the Relationship Between Medical Crowdfunding and Personal Bankruptcy in the United States: Evidence of a Digital Divide," *MIS Quarterly* 43, no. 1 (2019): 237–62.

Chapter 2

1. Rachel Monroe, "When GoFundMe Gets Ugly," *The Atlantic*, November 2019, https://www.theatlantic.com/magazine/archive/2019/11/gofundme-nation/598369/.

2. Edmund D. Pellegrino, "The Relationship of Autonomy and Integrity in Medical Ethics," *Bulletin of the Pan American Health Organization* 24, no. 4 (1990): 361–71.

3. Samuel D. Warren and Louis D. Brandeis, "The Right to Privacy," *Harvard Law Review* 4, no. 5 (1890): 193–220, 207.

4. W. A. Parent, "Privacy, Morality, and the Law," *Philosophy & Public Affairs* 12, no. 4 (1983): 269–88.

5. Charles Fried, *An Anatomy of Values: Problems of Personal and Social Choice* (Cambridge, MA: Harvard University Press, 1970).

6. Omer Tene and Jules Polonetsky, "A Theory of Creepy: Technology, Privacy and Shifting Social Norms," *Yale Journal of Law and Technology* 16 (2013): 59–102.

7. Michel Mollat, *The Poor in the Middle Ages: An Essay in Social History* (New Haven: Yale University Press, 1986).

8. Aaron L. Mackler, "Judaism, Justice, and Access to Health Care," *Kennedy Institute of Ethics Journal* 1, no. 2 (1991): 143–61.

9. Alice Fothergill, "The Stigma of Charity: Gender, Class, and Disaster Assistance," *Sociological Quarterly* 44, no. 4 (September 1, 2003): 659–80.

10. John Gilliom, *Overseers of the Poor: Surveillance, Resistance, and the Limits of Privacy* (Chicago: University of Chicago Press, 2001).

11. Warren and Brandeis, "The Right to Privacy."

12. Gilliom, *Overseers of the Poor.*

13. Mary Madden et al., "Privacy, Poverty, and Big Data: A Matrix of Vulnerabilities for Poor Americans," *Washington University Law Review* 95, no. 1 (2017): 53–126.

14. Michele Estrin Gilman, "The Return of the Welfare Queen," *American University Journal of Gender, Social Policy & the Law* 22, no. 2 (2014): 247–79.

15. Michael B. Katz, *In the Shadow of the Poorhouse: A Social History of Welfare in America* (New York: Basic Books, 1996), 83.

16. Ibid.

17. Deborah S. Skok, "Organized Almsgiving: Scientific Charity and the Society of St. Vincent de Paul in Chicago, 1871–1918," *U.S. Catholic Historian* 16, no. 4 (1998): 19–35.

18. Marco H. D. Van Leeuwen, Elise van Nederveen Meerkerk, and Lex Heerma van Voss, "Provisions for the Elderly in North-Western Europe: An International Comparison of Almshouses, Sixteenth–Twentieth Centuries," *Scandinavian Economic History Review* 62, no. 1 (2014): 1–16.

19. Chak Kwan Chan, "Caring for the Poor versus Degrading the Poor—the Case of Hong Kong Newspaper Charity," *International Journal of Social Welfare* 13, no. 3 (2004): 266–75.

20. GoFundMe, "How GoFundMe Protects Donors from Fraudulent Campaigns," *GoFundMe* (blog), accessed June 15, 2021, https://www.gofundme.com/c/safety/fraudulent-campaigns.

21. Laura Daily, "Is That Crowdfunding Charity Campaign Legit? Here Are Some Ways to Protect Your Donation," *Washington Post*, October 2, 2018, https://www.washingtonpost.com/lifestyle/home/is-that-crowdfunding-charity-campaign-legit-here-are-some-ways-to-protect-your-donation/2018/10/01/3cb97a6a-bdd2-11e8-8792-78719177250f_story.html.

22. GoFundMe, "The Complete Guide to Writing Your GoFundMe Fundraiser Story," *GoFundMe* (blog), May 3, 2021, https://www.gofundme.com/c/blog/campaign-story.

23. Ibid.

24. Bradley Rife, "How Internet Fundraisers Can Help You Cover Emergency Medical Bills," Oprah.com, December 2017, https://www.oprah.com/health_wellness/crowdfunding-tips-for-emergency-medical-bills.

25. GoFundMe, "Raise More Money with This Medical Crowdfunding Guide," *GoFundMe* (blog), May 12, 2021, https://www.gofundme.com/c/blog/medical-crowdfunding-guide.

26. GoFundMe, "Want a Successful Fundraiser? Avoid These Common Mistakes," *GoFundMe* (blog), January 4, 2021, https://ca.gofundme.com/c/blog/mistakes-successful-fundraisers-avoid.

27. GoFundMe, "Starting Your First Fundraiser? Here's How to Ask for Donations," *GoFundMe* (blog), February 16, 2021, https://www.gofundme.com/c/blog/ask-for-donations.

28. GoFundMe, "Raise More Money with This Medical Crowdfunding Guide."

29. GoFundMe, "Medical Fundraising Tips: Financial Support When You Need It," *GoFundMe* (blog), accessed June 1, 2021, https://www.gofundme.com/c/fundraising-tips/medical.

30. GoFundMe, "Tips to Create a Powerful Fundraising Video," *GoFundMe* (blog), accessed June 1, 2021, https://www.gofundme.com/c/fundraising-tips/video.

31. GoFundMe, "Why the Right Images for Your Fundraiser Are the Key to Success," *GoFundMe* (blog), accessed June 1, 2021, https://www.gofundme.com/c/fundraising-tips/image.

32. GoFundMe, "Tips to Create a Powerful Fundraising Video."

33. GoFundMe, "The Complete Guide to Writing Your GoFundMe Fundraiser Story."

34. GoFundMe, "These Social Media Tips Make It Easy to Promote Your Fundraiser," *GoFundMe* (blog), accessed June 1, 2021, https://www.gofundme.com/c/fundraising-tips/social-media.

35. GoFundMe, "25 Fundraiser Sharing Tips to Increase Donations," *GoFundMe* (blog), accessed June 2, 2021, https://www.gofundme.com/c/fundraising-tips/sharing.

36. GoFundMe, "How to Get Local Media to Cover Your Fundraiser," *GoFundMe* (blog), accessed January 10, 2023, https://www.gofundme.com/en-ca/c/fundraising-tips/local-media.

37. GoFundMe, "Five Simple Steps to Creating a Foolproof Fundraising Plan," *GoFundMe* (blog), December 19, 2019, https://www.gofundme.com/c/blog/fundraising-plan.

38. GoFundMe, "Gender Confirmation Surgery Costs and Fundraising Guide," *GoFundMe* (blog), May 24, 2021, https://www.gofundme.com/c/blog/gender-confirmation-surgery.

39. GoFundMe, "Five Cancer Fundraising Tips to Help You Raise More Money," *GoFundMe*, accessed June 1, 2021, https://www.gofundme.com/c/fundraising-tips/cancer.

40. GoFundMe, "The Complete Guide to Writing Your GoFundMe Fundraiser Story."

41. Ibid.

42. Ana Sanfilippo, *Crowdfunding Best Practices: Steps & Stories to Help You Launch a Successful Campaign* (Pennsauken: BookBaby, 2016).

43. GoFundMe, "The Complete Guide to Writing Your GoFundMe Fundraiser Story."

44. GoFundMe, "Medical Fundraising Tips: Financial Support When You Need It."

45. GoFundMe, "Why the Right Images for Your Fundraiser Are the Key to Success."

46. GoFundMe, "How to Get Local Media to Cover Your Fundraiser."

47. GoFundMe, "Raise More Money with This Medical Crowdfunding Guide."

48. Jennifer G. Kim et al., "The Power of Collective Endorsements: Credibility Factors in Medical Crowdfunding Campaigns," in *Proceedings of the 2016 CHI Conference on Human Factors in Computing Systems*, 2016, 4538–49.

49. Lauren S. Berliner and Nora J. Kenworthy, "Producing a Worthy Illness: Personal Crowdfunding amidst Financial Crisis," *Social Science & Medicine* 187 (2017): 233–42.

50. Zhichao Ba et al., "Understanding the Determinants of Online Medical Crowdfunding Project Success in China," *Information Processing & Management* 58, no. 2 (2021): 102465.

51. Chris A. Barcelos and Stephanie L. Budge, "Inequalities in Crowdfunding for Transgender Health Care," *Transgender Health* 4, no. 1 (2019): 81–8.

52. Amy L Gonzales et al., "'Better Everyone Should Know Our Business than We Lose Our House': Costs and Benefits of Medical Crowdfunding for Support, Privacy, and Identity," *New Media & Society* 20, no. 2 (2018): 641–58, 651.

53. Jennifer G. Kim, Hwajung Hong, and Karrie Karahalios, "Understanding Identity Presentation in Medical Crowdfunding," in *Proceedings of the 2018 CHI Conference on Human Factors in Computing Systems*, 2018, 1–12, 6.

54. Jennifer G. Kim et al., "'Not by Money Alone' Social Support Opportunities in Medical Crowdfunding Campaigns," in *Proceedings of the 2017 ACM Conference on Computer Supported Cooperative Work and Social Computing*, 2017, 1997–2009.

55. Varsha Palad and Jeremy Snyder, "'We Don't Want Him Worrying About How He Will Pay to Save His Life': Using Medical Crowdfunding to Explore Lived Experiences with Addiction Services in Canada," *International Journal of Drug Policy* 65 (March 1, 2019): 73–7.

56. Adam Faletsky et al., "Crowdfunding for Gender-Affirming Mastectomy: Balancing Fundraising With Loss of Privacy," *Annals of Plastic Surgery* 88, no. 4 (April 1, 2022): 372–4, https://doi.org/10.1097/SAP.0000000000002953.

57. Niki Fritz and Amy Gonzales, "Privacy at the Margins| Not the Normal Trans Story: Negotiating Trans Narratives While Crowdfunding at the Margins," *International Journal of Communication* 12 (2018): 1189–208.

58. Will Marler, "'You Can Connect with Like, the World!': Social Platforms, Survival Support, and Digital Inequalities for People Experiencing Homelessness," *Journal of Computer-Mediated Communication* 27, no. 1 (January 1, 2022): 1–19, https://doi.org/10.1093/jcmc/zmab020.

59. Jon Woodward, "Ontario Government Staffer out of a Job after $100 Donation to Ottawa Blockade, Others under Scrutiny." *CTV News*, February 16, 2022. https://toronto.ctvnews.ca/ontario-government-staffer-out-of-a-job-after-100-donation-to-ottawa-blockade-others-under-scrutiny-1.5784390.

60. GoFundMe, "Raise More Money with This Medical Crowdfunding Guide."

61. GoFundMe, "Fundraising Team—How to Build in Four Easy Steps," *GoFundMe* (blog), April 14, 2021, https://www.gofundme.com/c/blog/build-fundraising-team.

62. Trena M. Paulus and Katherine R. Roberts, "Crowdfunding a 'Real-Life Superhero': The Construction of Worthy Bodies in Medical Campaign Narratives," *Discourse, Context & Media* 21 (2018): 64–72.

63. Hannah S. Thomas et al., "Characterizing Online Crowdfunding Campaigns for Patients with Kidney Cancer," *Cancer Medicine* 10, no. 13 (2021): 4564–74.

64. Palad and Snyder, "'We Don't Want Him Worrying About How He Will Pay to Save His Life.'"

65. Lauren V. Ghazal et al., "'Both a Life Saver and Totally Shameful': Young Adult Cancer Survivors' Perceptions of Medical Crowdfunding," *Journal*

of *Cancer Survivorship: Research and Practice* (2022), https://doi.org/10.1007/s11 764-022-01188-x.

66. Thomas et al., "Characterizing Online Crowdfunding Campaigns for Patients with Kidney Cancer."

67. Ba et al., "Understanding the Determinants of Online Medical Crowdfunding Project Success in China."

68. Pingyue Jin, "Medical Crowdfunding in China: Empirics and Ethics," *Journal of Medical Ethics* 45, no. 8 (2019): 538–44.

69. GoFundMe, "The Complete Guide to Writing Your GoFundMe Fundraiser Story."

70. Sanfillipo, *Crowdfunding Best Practices*, 20.

71. Ibid., 45.

72. Jeremy Snyder and Valorie A. Crooks, "Is There Room for Privacy in Medical Crowdfunding?," *Journal of Medical Ethics* 47, no. 12 (2021): e49.

73. Anika Vassell, Valorie Crooks, and Jeremy Snyder, "Responsibilities to the Story, Campaign(er), and Profession: Exploring Important Considerations Shaping Canadian Print Journalists' Coverage of Medical Crowdfunding Campaigns," *Canadian Journal of Communication*, In Press. https://summit.sfu.ca/_flysystem/fed ora/sfu_migrate/19937/etd20683.pdf.

74. Jeremy Snyder and Leigh Turner, "Crowdfunding for Stem Cell-Based Interventions to Treat Neurologic Diseases and Injuries," *Neurology* 93, no. 6 (August 6, 2019): 252–8.

75. Ágnes Lublóy, "Medical Crowdfunding in a Healthcare System with Universal Coverage: An Exploratory Study," *BMC Public Health* 20, no. 1 (November 9, 2020): 1672.

Chapter 3

1. Danielle Cinone, "As Border Wall GoFundMe Rakes in Millions, Here Are Six Other Campaigns You Should Check Out," *New York Daily News*, December 21, 2018, sec. News, U.S., https://www.nydailynews.com/news/national/ny-news-gofundme-bor der-wall-top-gofundme-20181221-story.html.

2. Nathan Heller, "The Hidden Cost of GoFundMe Health Care," *New Yorker*, June 24, 2019, https://www.newyorker.com/magazine/2019/07/01/the-perverse-logic-of-gofundme-health-care.

3. JPost.com Staff, "Israeli Parents Crowd-Fund to Save Twin-Babies," *Jerusalem Post*, December 17, 2018, https://m.jpost.com/israel-news/israeli-parents-crowd-fund-to-save-twin-babies-574545/amp.

4. Heller, "The Hidden Cost of GoFundMe Health Care."

5. Gabi Ilinetsky, "Save Yoel and Yael," gofundme.com, accessed August 8, 2021, https://www.gofundme.com/f/cper2x-save-yoel-and-yael.

6. Heller, "The Hidden Cost of GoFundMe Health Care."

7. Jessica Field, "Charitable Giving," in *The Routledge Companion to Humanitarian Action*, ed. Roger Mac Ginty and Jenny H. Peterson (Milton Park, UK: Routledge, 2015), 429–39, https://doi.org/10.4324/9780203753422.

8. Hugh Cunningham, "The Multi-Layered History of Western Philanthropy," in *The Routledge Companion to Philanthropy*, ed. Tobias Jung, Susan D. Phillips, and Jenny Harrow (Milton Park, UK: Routledge, 2016), 42–55, https://doi.org/10.4324/978131 5740324.

9. Shauna Mottiar and Mvuselelo Ngcoya, "Indigenous Philanthropy: Challenging Western Preconceptions," in *The Routledge Companion to Philanthropy*, ed. Tobias Jung, Susan Phillips, and Jenny Harrow (Milton Park, UK: Routledge, 2016), 171–81.

10. Lucius Annaeus Seneca, *On Benefits*, trans. Miriam Griffin and Brad Inwood (Chicago: University of Chicago Press, 2011), 2.18.3; 2.18.5.

11. Cunningham, "The Multi-Layered History of Western Philanthropy."

12. Donileen R. Loseke and Kirsten Fawcett, "Appealing Appeals: Constructing Moral Worthiness, 1912–1917," *Sociological Quarterly* 36, no. 1 (1995): 61–77.

13. Donileen R. Loseke, "'The Whole Spirit of Modern Philanthropy': The Construction of the Idea of Charity, 1912–1992," *Social Problems* 44, no. 4 (1997): 425–44.

14. Ibid.

15. Wim van Oorschot, "Making the Difference in Social Europe: Deservingness Perceptions Among Citizens of European Welfare States," *Journal of European Social Policy* 16, no. 1 (February 1, 2006): 23–42, https://doi.org/10.1177/095892870 6059829.

16. Loseke, "'The Whole Spirit of Modern Philanthropy,'" 429.

17. Ibid.

18. Ibid.

19. Loseke and Fawcett, "Appealing Appeals: Constructing Moral Worthiness, 1912–1917."

20. Loseke, "'The Whole Spirit of Modern Philanthropy.'"

21. Steve Hindle, "Dependency, Shame and Belonging: Badging the Deserving Poor, c.1550–1750," *Cultural and Social History* 1, no. 1 (January 1, 2004): 6–35, https://doi.org/10.1191/1478003804cs0003oa.

22. Robert Humphreys, "Scientific Charity in Victorian London. Claims and Achievements of the Charity Organisation Society, 1869–1890," *London School of Economics and Political Science, Working Papers* 14 (1993): 1–38.

23. Annie Skinner and Nigel Thomas, "'A Pest to Society': The Charity Organisation Society's Domiciliary Assessments into the Circumstances of Poor Families and Children," *Children & Society* 32, no. 2 (2018): 133–44.

24. GoFundMe, "How to Get Rid of Debt: Know Your Options," GoFundMe, December 11, 2018, https://ca.gofundme.com/c/blog/how-to-get-rid-of-debt.

25. Leo Aquino, "6 Tips for Crowdfunding Your Gender-Affirming Surgery, from Someone with Experience," *Business Insider*, June 30, 2021, https://www.businessinsi der.com/personal-finance/tips-for-crowdfunding-gender-affirming-surgery-2021-6.

26. GoFundMe, "The Beginner's Guide to Viral Fundraising," GoFundMe, January 25, 2017, https://uk.gofundme.com/c/blog/viral-fundraising?lang=en.

27. Mycause, "Your Essential Crowdfunding Page Checklist," Mycause, February 29, 2016, https://www.mycause.com.au/blog/your-essential-crowdfunding-page-checklist.

28. GoFundMe, "How to Get Local Media to Cover Your Fundraiser," *GoFundMe* (blog), accessed August 13, 2021, https://www.gofundme.com/c/fundraising-tips/local-media.

29. GoFundMe, "Fundraising for Individuals: Simple Steps for Success," *GoFundMe* (blog), accessed August 3, 2021, https://ca.gofundme.com/c/fundraising-tips/fundraising-for-individuals.

30. Jenna Davis, "How to Ask for Help with Money: Five Tips to Make It Easy," *GoFundMe* (blog), October 23, 2019, https://ca.gofundme.com/c/blog/how-to-ask-for-help-with-money.

31. GoFundMe, "How to Ask for Donations for Funeral Expenses: 3 Templates," *GoFundMe* (blog), June 10, 2019, https://ca.gofundme.com/c/blog/ask-donations-funeral-expenses.

32. Jenna Davis, "Finding Financial Help for Pregnant Women," *GoFundMe* (blog), October 1, 2018, https://ca.gofundme.com/c/blog/financial-help-pregnant-women.

33. Ann-Marie D'arcy-Sharpe, "How GoGetFunding Campaigns Are Helping the Homeless," *GoGetFunding*, April 5, 2021, https://gogetfunding.com/blog/how-gogetfunding-campaigns-are-helping-the-homeless/.

34. Chiara Milton, "3 Life Lessons That Autistic Children Teach Us," *ImpactGuru*, July 17, 2021, https://web.archive.org/web/20220707064035/https://www.impactguru.com/blog/3_lessons_to_learn_from_autistic_children_and_see_the_world_differently.

35. Diamond Milton, "Kudos to These Kids for Putting Up a Brave Fight," *ImpactGuru*, July 28, 2021, https://web.archive.org/web/20220819164636/https://www.impactguru.com/blog/How-These-Kids-Are-Putting-Up-A-Brave-Fight-Against-Cancer.

36. GoFundMe, "Fundraising for Individuals."

37. GoFundMe, "Six Online Fundraising Challenges and How to Overcome Them," *GoFundMe* (blog), February 13, 2018, https://ca.gofundme.com/c/blog/online-fundraising-challenges.

38. Davis, "How to Ask for Help with Money."

39. GoFundMe, "How to Write a Fundraiser Update," *GoFundMe* (blog), accessed August 3, 2021, https://www.gofundme.com/c/fundraising-tips/update.

40. GoFundMe, "Write a Thank You Letter for a Donation From a Sponsor," *GoFundMe* (blog), March 10, 2016, https://www.gofundme.com/c/blog/donation-thank-you-letter.

41. Trena M. Paulus and Katherine R. Roberts, "Crowdfunding a 'Real-Life Superhero': The Construction of Worthy Bodies in Medical Campaign Narratives," *Discourse, Context & Media* 21 (2018): 64–72.

42. Jeremy Snyder et al., "Appealing to the Crowd: Ethical Justifications in Canadian Medical Crowdfunding Campaigns," *Journal of Medical Ethics* 43, no. 6 (June 1, 2017): 364–7, https://doi.org/10.1136/medethics-2016-103933.

43. Lauren S. Berliner and Nora J. Kenworthy, "Producing a Worthy Illness: Personal Crowdfunding amidst Financial Crisis," *Social Science & Medicine* 187 (August 1, 2017): 233–42, https://doi.org/10.1016/j.socscimed.2017.02.008.

44. Snyder et al., "Appealing to the Crowd."

45. Paulus and Roberts, "Crowdfunding a 'Real-Life Superhero.'"

46. Ibid.

47. Snyder et al., "Appealing to the Crowd."

48. Pingyue Jin, "Medical Crowdfunding in China: Empirics and Ethics," *Journal of Medical Ethics* 45, no. 8 (2019): 538–44.

49. Paulus and Roberts, "Crowdfunding a 'Real-Life Superhero.'"

50. Celeste Watkins-Hayes and Elyse Kovalsky, "The Discourse of Deservingness: Morality and the Dilemmas of Poverty Relief in Debate and Practice," in *The Oxford Handbook of the Social Science of Poverty*, ed. David Brady and Linda Burton (New York: Oxford University Press, 2016), 193–220.

51. Michael B. Katz, *The Undeserving Poor: America's Enduring Confrontation with Poverty: Fully Updated and Revised*, 2nd edition (Oxford: Oxford University Press, 2013).

Chapter 4

1. Giving USA Foundation, *Giving USA 2021 Annual Report* (Chicago: Giving USA Foundation, 2021).

2. Rob Reich, *Just Giving: Why Philanthropy Is Failing Democracy and How It Can Do Better* (Princeton: Princeton University Press, 2018).

3. Lina Sonne and Divya Chopra, "Global Philanthropy Tracker: India" (Indianapolis: Indiana University Lilly Family School of Philanthropy, October 2020), https://scholarworks.iupui.edu/bitstream/handle/1805/24848/india-repor t21-1.pdf?sequence=4&isAllowed=y.

4. Charities Aid Foundation, *"UK Giving 2019"* (Kent/London: Charities Aid Foundation, 2019), https://www.cafonline.org/docs/default-source/about-us-publi cations/caf-uk-giving-2019-report-an-overview-of-charitable-giving-in-the-uk.pdf?sfvrsn=c4a29a40_4.

5. Giving Japan White Paper Research Society, "Giving Japan 2015" Japan Fundraising Association, 2015, https://www.jnpoc.ne.jp/en/reports/selected-translation-of-giv ing-japan-2015-2/.

6. Clair Null, "Warm Glow, Information, and Inefficient Charitable Giving," *Journal of Public Economics*, Charitable Giving and Fundraising Special Issue, 95, no. 5 (2011): 455–65, https://doi.org/10.1016/j.jpubeco.2010.06.018.

7. Cassandra M. Chapman, Barbara M. Masser, and Winnifred R. Louis, "Identity Motives in Charitable Giving: Explanations for Charity Preferences from a Global Donor Survey," *Psychology & Marketing* 37, no. 9 (2020): 1277–91, https://doi.org/ 10.1002/mar.21362.

8. Una Osili et al., "The Impact of Diversity: Understanding How Nonprofit Board Diversity Affects Philanthropy, Leadership, and Board Engagement" (Indianapolis: Indiana University Lilly Family School of Philanthropy, February 20, 2018), https://scholarworks.iupui.edu/handle/1805/15239.

9. Jordan van Rijn, Esteban J. Quiñones, and Bradford L. Barham, "Empathic Concern for Children and the Gender-Donations Gap," *Journal of Behavioral and Experimental Economics* 82 (October 1, 2019): 101462, https://doi.org/10.1016/j.socec.2019.101462.

10. Elizabeth J. Dale et al., "Giving to Women and Girls: An Emerging Area of Philanthropy," *Nonprofit and Voluntary Sector Quarterly* 47, no. 2 (April 1, 2018): 241–61, https://doi.org/10.1177/0899764017744674.

11. Debra Mesch et al., "Where Do Men and Women Give? Gender Differences in the Motivations and Purposes for Charitable Giving," Working Paper (Indianapolis: Indiana University Lilly Family School of Philanthropy, September 2015), https://scholarworks.iupui.edu/handle/1805/6985.

12. Robb Willer, Christopher Wimer, and Lindsay A. Owens, "What Drives the Gender Gap in Charitable Giving? Lower Empathy Leads Men to Give Less to Poverty Relief," *Social Science Research* 52 (July 1, 2015): 83–98, https://doi.org/10.1016/j.ssresearch.2014.12.014.

13. Debra Mesch et al., "How and Why Women Give: Current and Future Directions for Research on Women's Philanthropy," Working Paper (Indianapolis: Indiana University Lilly Family School of Philanthropy, May 2015), https://scholarworks.iupui.edu/handle/1805/6983.

14. Christina M. Fong and Erzo F. P. Luttmer, "Do Fairness and Race Matter in Generosity? Evidence from a Nationally Representative Charity Experiment," *Journal of Public Economics*, Charitable Giving and Fundraising Special Issue, 95, no. 5 (June 1, 2011): 372–94, https://doi.org/10.1016/j.jpubeco.2010.07.010.

15. Daniel M. Hungerman, "Race and Charitable Church Activity," *Economic Inquiry* 46, no. 3 (2008): 380–400, https://doi.org/10.1111/j.1465-7295.2007.00104.x.

16. C. Dorsey et al., "Overcoming the Racial Bias in Philanthropic Funding," *Stanford Social Innovation Review* (blog), May 4, 2020, https://ssir.org/articles/entry/overcoming_the_racial_bias_in_philanthropic_funding.

17. Meghan Elizabeth Kallman, "Allocative Failures: Networks and Institutions in International Grantmaking Relationships," *VOLUNTAS: International Journal of Voluntary and Nonprofit Organizations* 28, no. 2 (2017): 745–72, https://doi.org/10.1007/s11266-017-9827-3.

18. Mairi Maclean et al., "Elite Philanthropy in the United States and United Kingdom in the New Age of Inequalities," *International Journal of Management Reviews* 23, no. 3 (2021): 330–52, https://doi.org/10.1111/ijmr.12247.

19. Christopher Marquis, Mary Ann Glynn, and Gerald F. Davis, "Community Isomorphism and Corporate Social Action," *Academy of Management Review* 32, no. 3 (2007): 925–45.

20. Bryan W. Husted, Dima Jamali, and Walid Saffar, "Near and Dear? The Role of Location in CSR Engagement," *Strategic Management Journal* 37, no. 10 (2016): 2050–70, https://doi.org/10.1002/smj.2437.

21. Charles T. Clotfelter, "Tax-Induced Distortions in the Voluntary Sector Symposium: What Is Charity," *Case Western Reserve Law Review* 39, no. 3 (1989): 663–94.

22. Muhammad Umar Boodoo, Irene Henriques, and Bryan W. Husted, "Putting the 'Love of Humanity' Back in Corporate Philanthropy: The Case of Health Grants by Corporate Foundations," *Journal of Business Ethics* 178, no. 2 (April 10, 2021): 415–28, https://doi.org/10.1007/s10551-021-04807-2.

23. Anthony J. Spires, "Organizational Homophily in International Grantmaking: US-Based Foundations and Their Grantees in China," *Journal of Civil Society* 7, no. 3 (2011): 305–31, https://doi.org/10.1080/17448689.2011.605005.

24. Boodoo, Glynn, and Davis, "Putting the 'Love of Humanity' Back in Corporate Philanthropy."

25. Tim Cadogan, "A New Chapter in GoFundMe's Story," *GoFundMe Stories* (blog), August 5, 2021, https://medium.com/gofundme-stories/a-new-chapter-in-gofund mes-story-b4cef13a7b73.

26. Milaap, "Milaap: The Journey So Far of Crowdfunding in India," Milaap, accessed September 20, 2021, https://milaap.org/about-us/overview.

27. Nora Kenworthy et al., "A Cross-Sectional Study of Social Inequities in Medical Crowdfunding Campaigns in the United States," *PLOS ONE* 15, no. 3 (March 5, 2020): e0229760, https://doi.org/10.1371/journal.pone.0229760.

28. Lauren S. Berliner and Nora J. Kenworthy, "Producing a Worthy Illness: Personal Crowdfunding amidst Financial Crisis," *Social Science & Medicine* 187 (2017): 233–42.

29. Pingyue Jin, "Medical Crowdfunding in China: Empirics and Ethics," *Journal of Medical Ethics* 45, no. 8 (2019): 538–44.

30. Isabel Pifarré Coutrot, Richard Smith, and Laura Cornelsen, "Is the Rise of Crowdfunding for Medical Expenses in the United Kingdom Symptomatic of Systemic Gaps in Health and Social Care?," *Journal of Health Services Research & Policy* 25, no. 3 (July 1, 2020): 181–6, https://doi.org/10.1177/1355819619897949.

31. Mark Igra et al., "Crowdfunding as a Response to COVID-19: Increasing Inequities at a Time of Crisis," *Social Science & Medicine* 282 (August 1, 2021): 114105, https://doi.org/10.1016/j.socscimed.2021.114105.

32. Wesley M. Durand et al., "Medical Crowdfunding for Organ Transplantation," *Clinical Transplantation* 32, no. 6 (2018): e13267.

33. Sarah J. Pol, Jeremy Snyder, and Samantha J. Anthony, "'Tremendous Financial Burden': Crowdfunding for Organ Transplantation Costs in Canada," *PLOS ONE* 14, no. 12 (December 20, 2019): e0226686, https://doi.org/10.1371/journal.pone.0226686.

34. Andrew J. Cohen et al., "Use of an Online Crowdfunding Platform for Unmet Financial Obligations in Cancer Care," *JAMA Internal Medicine* 179, no. 12 (2019): 1717–20, https://doi.org/10.1001/jamainternmed.2019.3330.

35. Hannah S. Thomas et al., "Characterizing Online Crowdfunding Campaigns for Patients with Kidney Cancer," *Cancer Medicine* 10, no. 13 (2021): 4564–74.

36. Jeremy Snyder, Marco Zenone, and Timothy Caulfield, "Crowdfunding for Complementary and Alternative Medicine: What Are Cancer Patients Seeking?," *PLOS ONE* 15, no. 11 (November 20, 2020): e0242048, https://doi.org/10.1371/journal.pone.0242048.

37. Varsha Palad and Jeremy Snyder, "'We Don't Want Him Worrying About How He Will Pay to Save His Life': Using Medical Crowdfunding to Explore Lived Experiences with Addiction Services in Canada," *International Journal of Drug Policy* 65 (2019): 73–7.

38. Marco Antonio Zenone and Jeremy Snyder, "Crowdfunding Abortion: An Exploratory Thematic Analysis of Fundraising for a Stigmatized Medical Procedure," *BMC Women's Health* 20, no. 90 (May 4, 2020), https://doi.org/10.1186/s12905-020-00938-2.

39. Michael T. Solotke et al., "Exploring Crowdfunding Campaigns for Abortion Services," *Contraception* 102, no. 1 (July 1, 2020): 18–22, https://doi.org/10.1016/j.contraception.2020.02.008.

40. Chris A. Barcelos, "Go Fund Inequality: The Politics of Crowdfunding Transgender Medical Care," *Critical Public Health* 30, no. 3 (May 26, 2020): 330–9, https://doi.org/10.1080/09581596.2019.1575947.

41. Gordon Burtch and Jason Chan, "Investigating the Relationship Between Medical Crowdfunding and Personal Bankruptcy in the United States: Evidence of a Digital Divide," *MIS Quarterly* 43, no. 1 (2019): 237–62.

42. Kenworthy et al., "A Cross-Sectional Study of Social Inequities in Medical Crowdfunding Campaigns in the United States."

43. Martin Lukk, Erik Schneiderhan, and Joanne Soares, "Worthy? Crowdfunding the Canadian Health Care and Education Sectors," *Canadian Review of Sociology/Revue Canadienne de Sociologie* 55, no. 3 (2018): 404–24.

44. Igra et al., "Crowdfunding as a Response to COVID-19."

45. Mark Igra, "Donor Financial Capacity Drives Racial Inequality in Medical Crowdsourced Funding," *Social Forces* 100, no. 4 (2022): 1856–83, https://doi.org/10.1093/sf/soab076.

46. Barcelos, "Go Fund Inequality."

47. Kenworthy et al., "A Cross-Sectional Study of Social Inequities in Medical Crowdfunding Campaigns in the United States."

48. Barcelos, "Go Fund Inequality."

49. Kenworthy et al., "A Cross-Sectional Study of Social Inequities in Medical Crowdfunding Campaigns in the United States."

50. Ibid.

51. Lukk, Schneiderhan, and Soares, "Worthy? Crowdfunding the Canadian Health Care and Education Sectors."

52. Durand et al., "Medical Crowdfunding for Organ Transplantation."

53. Pol, Snyder, and Anthony, "'Tremendous Financial Burden.'"

54. Burtch and Chan, "Investigating the Relationship between Medical Crowdfunding and Personal Bankruptcy in the United States."

55. Alysha van Duynhoven et al., "Spatially Exploring the Intersection of Socioeconomic Status and Canadian Cancer-Related Medical Crowdfunding Campaigns," *BMJ Open* 9, no. 6 (2019): e026365, https://doi.org/10.1136/bmjopen-2018-026365.

56. Sumin Lee and Vili Lehdonvirta, "New Digital Safety Net or Just More 'Friendfunding'? Institutional Analysis of Medical Crowdfunding in the United States," *Information,*

Communication & Society, 25, no. 8 (2020): 1151–75, https://doi.org/10.1080/13691 18X.2020.1850838.

57. Matthew R. Sisco and Elke U. Weber, "Examining Charitable Giving in Real-World Online Donations," *Nature Communications* 10, no. 1 (2019): 3968, https://doi.org/ 10.1038/s41467-019-11852-z.

58. Kenworthy et al., "A Cross-Sectional Study of Social Inequities in Medical Crowdfunding Campaigns in the United States."

59. Una Osili et al., *Charitable Crowdfunding: Who Gives, to What, and Why?* (Indianapolis: Indiana University Lilly Family School of Philanthropy, 2021), https:// scholarworks.iupui.edu/bitstream/handle/1805/25515/crowdfunding210331-1.pdf.

60. Will Marler, "'You Can Connect with Like, the World!': Social Platforms, Survival Support, and Digital Inequalities for People Experiencing Homelessness," *Journal of Computer-Mediated Communication* 27, no. 1 (2022): 1–19, https://doi.org/10.1093/ jcmc/zmab020.

61. Amy L Gonzales et al., "'Better Everyone Should Know Our Business than We Lose Our House': Costs and Benefits of Medical Crowdfunding for Support, Privacy, and Identity," *New Media & Society* 20, no. 2 (2018): 641–58, https://doi.org/10.1177/ 1461444816667723.

62. Igra et al., "Crowdfunding as a Response to COVID-19."

63. Lee and Lehdonvirta, "New Digital Safety Net or Just More 'Friendfunding'?"

64. Igra, "Donor Financial Capacity Drives Racial Inequality in Medical Crowdsourced Funding."

65. Igra et al., "Crowdfunding as a Response to COVID-19."

66. van Duynhoven et al., "Spatially Exploring the Intersection of Socioeconomic Status and Canadian Cancer-Related Medical Crowdfunding Campaigns."

67. Osili et al., "Charitable Crowdfunding."

68. Berliner and Kenworthy, "Producing a Worthy Illness."

69. Gonzales et al., "'Better Everyone Should Know Our Business than We Lose Our House.'"

70. Dave Lee, "GoFundMe: Hope, but No Solution, for the Needy," *BBC News*, February 12, 2019, sec. Technology, https://www.bbc.com/news/technology-47156142.

71. Igra et al., "Crowdfunding as a Response to COVID-19."

72. Amy Costello, "Inequalities in Crowdfunding: An 'American Struggle,'" *Nonprofit Quarterly* (blog), December 7, 2018, https://nonprofitquarterly.org/inequalities-in-crowdfunding-an-american-struggle/.

73. Rachel Monroe, "When GoFundMe Gets Ugly," *The Atlantic*, November 2019, https:// www.theatlantic.com/magazine/archive/2019/11/gofundme-nation/598369/.

74. Gary Rider, "Help Us Find Gabby," GoFundMe, accessed June 15, 2022, https://www. gofundme.com/f/help-us-find-gabby.

75. GoFundMe, "The Internet Banded Together in the Search for Gabby Petito—Let's Do the Same for People of Color Who Need Our Support. Here Is a Thread of Verified Fundraisers for Some of Their Families," Tweet, *Twitter*, September 22, 2021, https:// twitter.com/gofundme/status/1440736064998572037.

Chapter 5

1. Kelly Anne Smith, "How Crowdfunding Changed These People's Lives," *Forbes Advisor*, December 19, 2020, https://www.forbes.com/advisor/personal-finance/how-crowdfunding-changed-these-peoples-lives/.

2. Nathan Heller, "The Hidden Cost of GoFundMe Health Care," *New Yorker*, June 24, 2019, https://www.newyorker.com/magazine/2019/07/01/the-perverse-logic-of-gofundme-health-care.

3. Neil Levy, "Against Philanthropy, Individual and Corporate," *Business & Professional Ethics Journal* 21, no. 3/4 (2002): 95–108.

4. Theodore Lechterman, *The Tyranny of Generosity: Why Philanthropy Corrupts Our Politics and How We Can Fix It* (New York: Oxford University Press, 2021).

5. Jennifer C. Rubenstein, "The Lessons of Effective Altruism," *Ethics & International Affairs* 30, no. 4 (2016): 511–26, https://doi.org/10.1017/S0892679416000484.

6. Brian Berkey, "The Institutional Critique of Effective Altruism," *Utilitas* 30, no. 2 (2018): 143–71, https://doi.org/10.1017/S0953820817000176.

7. Rubenstein, "The Lessons of Effective Altruism."

8. Dean Spade, *Mutual Aid: Building Solidarity During This Crisis (and the Next)* (New York: Verso Books, 2020).

9. Anne Robert Jacques Turgot, *The Turgot Collection*, ed. David Gordon (Auburn, AL: Mises Institute, 2011), 464–5.

10. Anand Giridharadas, *Winners Take All: The Elite Charade of Changing the World* (New York: Knopf, 2018), 30.

11. Ibid., 52.

12. Ryan Pevnick, "Democratizing the Nonprofit Sector" *Journal of Political Philosophy* 21, no. 3 (2013): 260–82.

13. Emma Saunders-Hastings, *Private Virtues, Public Vices: Philanthropy and Democratic Equality* (Chicago: University of Chicago Press, 2022).

14. GoFundMe, "Use Psychology to Boost Your Fundraiser," *GoFundMe* (blog), June 26, 2021, https://www.gofundme.com/en-ca/c/blog/psychology-of-giving.

15. GoFundMe, "How to Write a Fundraiser Update," *GoFundMe* (blog), accessed October 25, 2021, https://www.gofundme.com/c/fundraising-tips/update.

16. GoFundMe, "Find Financial Support with These Four Medical Fundraising Tips," *GoFundMe* (blog), accessed October 25, 2021, https://www.gofundme.com/c/fundraising-tips/medical.

17. GoFundMe, "Use Psychology to Boost Your Fundraiser."

18. Jennifer G. Kim, Hwajung Hong, and Karrie Karahalios, "Understanding Identity Presentation in Medical Crowdfunding," in *Proceedings of the 2018 CHI Conference on Human Factors in Computing Systems*, 2018, 1–12.

19. Wesley M. Durand et al., "Medical Crowdfunding for Organ Transplantation," *Clinical Transplantation* 32, no. 6 (2018): e13267.

20. Kexin Zhao, Lina Zhou, and Xia Zhao, "Multi-Modal Emotion Expression and Online Charity Crowdfunding Success," *Decision Support Systems*, 163 (2022): 113842, https://doi.org/10.1016/j.dss.2022.113842.

21. Lauren V. Ghazal et al., "'Both a Life Saver and Totally Shameful': Young Adult Cancer Survivors' Perceptions of Medical Crowdfunding," *Journal of Cancer Survivorship: Research and Practice* (2022), https://doi.org/10.1007/s11 764-022-01188-x.

22. Jeremy Snyder et al., "Appealing to the Crowd: Ethical Justifications in Canadian Medical Crowdfunding Campaigns," *Journal of Medical Ethics* 43, no. 6 (2017): 364–7, https://doi.org/10.1136/medethics-2016-103933.

23. Sarah J. Pol, Jeremy Snyder, and Samantha J. Anthony, "'Tremendous Financial Burden': Crowdfunding for Organ Transplantation Costs in Canada," *PLOS ONE* 14, no. 12 (2019): e0226686, https://doi.org/10.1371/journal.pone.0226686.

24. Pingyue Jin, "Medical Crowdfunding in China: Empirics and Ethics," *Journal of Medical Ethics* 45, no. 8 (2019): 538–44.

25. Nora J. Kenworthy, "Crowdfunding and Global Health Disparities: An Exploratory Conceptual and Empirical Analysis," *Globalization and Health* 15, no. 1 (2019): 71, https://doi.org/10.1186/s12992-019-0519-1.

26. Seth Stevenson, "The Dark Side of GoFundMe," *Slate*, December 9, 2020, https://slate. com/business/2020/12/gofundme-dark-side-fraud-social-media-health-care.html.

27. Turgot, *The Turgot Collection*, 462.

28. Oscar Wilde, "The Soul of Man Under Socialism," in *The Spirit of the Age*, ed. Gertrude Himmelfarb (New Haven: Yale University Press, 2007), 294–310.

29. GoFundMe, "About GoFundMe," *GoFundMe* (blog), accessed June 16, 2022, https:// www.gofundme.com/en-ca/c/about-us.

30. Heller, "The Hidden Cost of GoFundMe Health Care."

31. Divya Kilikar, "How to Write a Medical Fundraising Story," ImpactGuru, March 19, 2018, https://web.archive.org/web/20220527025354/https://www.impactguru.com/ blog/donation-appeal-for-medical-fundraiser .

32. Jasmine Marfatia, "Easy Ways to Raise Funds for Cancer Treatment in India," ImpactGuru, July 24, 2018, https://web.archive.org/web/20220627111451/https:// www.impactguru.com/blog/cancer-treatment-in-india .

33. Tim Cadogan, "GoFundMe CEO: Hello Congress, Americans Need Help and We Can't Do Your Job for You," *USA Today*, February 11, 2021, https://www.usatoday. com/story/opinion/voices/2021/02/11/gofundme-ceo-congress-pass-covid-relief-desperate-americans-column/4440425001/.

34. Saunders-Hastings, *Private Virtues, Public Vices*.

35. Una Osili et al., "Charitable Crowdfunding: Who Gives, to What, and Why?" (Indianapolis: Indiana University Lilly Family School of Philanthropy, 2021).

36. Fuguo Zhang et al., "Effect of Textual Features on the Success of Medical Crowdfunding: Model Development and Econometric Analysis from the Tencent Charity Platform," *Journal of Medical Internet Research* 23, no. 6 (2021): e22395, https://doi.org/10.2196/22395.

37. Varsha Palad and Jeremy Snyder, "'We Don't Want Him Worrying About How He Will Pay to Save His Life': Using Medical Crowdfunding to Explore Lived Experiences with Addiction Services in Canada," *International Journal of Drug Policy* 65 (2019): 73–7.

38. Anika Vassell, Valorie A. Crooks, and Jeremy Snyder, "What Was Lost, Missing, Sought and Hoped for: Qualitatively Exploring Medical Crowdfunding Campaign Narratives for Lyme Disease," *Health* 25, no. 6 (November 1, 2021): 707–21, https://doi.org/10.1177/1363459320912808.

39. Niki Fritz and Amy Gonzales, "Privacy at the Margins| Not the Normal Trans Story: Negotiating Trans Narratives While Crowdfunding at the Margins," *International Journal of Communication* 12 (2018): 20.

40. Chris A. Barcelos, "'Bye-Bye Boobies': Normativity, Deservingness and Medicalisation in Transgender Medical Crowdfunding," *Culture, Health & Sexuality* 21, no. 12 (2019): 1394–408.

41. Fritz and Gonzales, "Privacy at the Margins."

42. Ana Sanfilippo, *Crowdfunding Best Practices: Steps & Stories to Help You Launch a Successful Campaign* (Pennsauken: BookBaby, 2016), 57.

43. Amy Gonzales and Nicole Fritz, "Prioritizing Flexibility and Intangibles: Medical Crowdfunding for Stigmatized Individuals," in *Proceedings of the 2017 CHI Conference on Human Factors in Computing Systems*, CHI '17 (New York: Association for Computing Machinery, 2017), 2371–5, https://doi.org/10.1145/3025453.3025647.

44. Sam Guy, "Access to Justice on the Market: An Empirical Case Study on the Dynamics of Crowdfunding Judicial Reviews," *Public Law*, no. 4 (October 2021): 678–87, 680.

45. Rossalyn Warren, "Meet the Lawyer-Turned-Tech Entrepreneur Trying to Make Justice Available to All," *The Guardian*, August 29, 2019, sec. Guardian Careers, https://www.theguardian.com/careers/2019/aug/29/meet-the-lawyer-turned-tech-entrepreneur-trying-to-make-justice-available-to-all.

46. Guy, "Access to Justice on the Market," 680.

Chapter 6

1. Elizabeth McSheffrey, "Here's How to Support BC Residents Impacted by Floods, Landslides," *Global News*, November 16, 2021, https://globalnews.ca/news/8378542/help-bc-residents-flooding-landslides/.

2. GoFundMe, "How to Help Those Affected by the BC Flooding," *GoFundMe* (blog), accessed December 2, 2021, https://www.gofundme.com/en-ca/c/act/bc-flooding.

3. Daniel S. Goldberg, "Doubt & Social Policy: The Long History of Malingering in Modern Welfare States," *Journal of Law, Medicine & Ethics* 49, no. 3 (2021): 385–93, https://doi.org/10.1017/jme.2021.58.

4. Daniel Siegel, *Charity and Condescension: Victorian Literature and the Dilemmas of Philanthropy* (Athens: Ohio University Press, 2012), http://muse.jhu.edu/book/13711.

5. Charles E. Trevelyan, *Three Letters from Sir Charles Trevelyan to "The Times" on London Pauperism: With the Leading Article upon Them and Extracts from "How to Relieve the Poor of Edinburgh and Other Great Cities, without Increasing Pauperism: A Tried Successful, and Economical Plan, 1867" and from the "Report on the Condition of*

the Poorer Classes of Edinburgh, and of Their Dwellings, Neighbourhoods, and Families, 1868." Talbot Collection of British Pamphlets (London: Longmans, Green, and Co., 1870), http://www.archive.org/details/threelettersfrom00trev, 15.

6. Michael Roberts, "Reshaping the Gift Relationship: The London Mendicity Society and the Suppression of Begging in England 1818–1869," *International Review of Social History* 36, no. 2 (1991): 201–31, https://doi.org/10.1017/S0020859000110508.

7. Trevelyan, *Three Letters from Sir Charles Trevelyan.*

8. Spencer Headworth, *Policing Welfare: Punitive Adversarialism in Public Assistance* (Chicago: University of Chicago Press, 2021).

9. Goldberg, "Doubt & Social Policy."

10. Paul Fredericks and Matthew Rowe, "Charity Fraud," in *Fraud*, ed. Alan Doig (New York: Routledge, 2016), 245–64.

11. David Horton Smith, Sharon Eng, and Kelly Albertson, "The Darker Side of Philanthropy," in *The Routledge Companion to Philanthropy*, ed. Tobias Jung, Susan D. Phillips, and Jenny Harrow (New York: Routledge, 2016), 273–86.

12. Rob Reich, *Just Giving: Why Philanthropy Is Failing Democracy and How It Can Do Better* (Princeton: Princeton University Press, 2018).

13. Smith, Eng, and Albertson, "The Darker Side of Philanthropy."

14. Gideon Lewis-Kraus, "Sam Bankman-Fried, Effective Altruism, and the Question of Complicity," *The New Yorker*, December 1, 2022. https://www.newyorker.com/news/annals-of-inquiry/sam-bankman-fried-effective-altruism-and-the-question-of-complicity.

15. Fredericks and Rowe, "Charity Fraud."

16. GoFundMe, "The GoFundMe Guarantee," *GoFundMe* (blog), accessed January 13, 2022, https://www.gofundme.com/c/safety/gofundme-guarantee.

17. Adrienne Gonzalez, "GoFraudMe: GoFundMe Fraud, Scams, Crowdfunding Ethics, GoFundMe News," *GoFraudMe*, accessed June 21, 2022, http://gofraudme.com/.

18. GoFundMe, "How GoFundMe Protects Donors From Fraudulent Campaigns," *GoFundMe* (blog), accessed January 12, 2022, https://www.gofundme.com/c/safety/fraudulent-campaigns.

19. Paul Oommen, "Fake Fundraising Campaigns Tarnish Growing Crowdfunding Concept in India," *The News Minute*, August 3, 2021, https://www.thenewsminute.com/article/fake-fundraising-campaigns-tarnish-growing-crowdfunding-concept-india-153349.

20. Marco Zenone and Jeremy Snyder, "Fraud in Medical Crowdfunding: A Typology of Publicized Cases and Policy Recommendations," *Policy & Internet* 11, no. 2 (2019): 215–34, https://doi.org/10.1002/poi3.188.

21. Nicole O'Reilly, "Burlington Woman Accused of Faking Rare Illness for Money," *InsideHalton.Com*, May 8, 2015, https://www.insidehalton.com/news-story/5607038-burlington-woman-accused-of-faking-rare-illness-for-money/.

22. Zenone and Snyder, "Fraud in Medical Crowdfunding."

23. David Gambacorta and Barbara Boyer, "The Truth About the GoFundMe Campaign for a Homeless Veteran: It Was All a Scam," *Philadelphia Inquirer*, November 15, 2018, sec. News, https://www.inquirer.com/philly/news/homeless-gofun

dme-scam-kate-mcclure-johnny-bobitt-jr-mark-damico-arrests-charges-20181
115.html.

24. Robin Simmons, "Claims of Fake GoFundMe Accounts to Help Surfside Victims
Prompt Call for Federal Probe," *7 News Miami*, October 19, 2021, https://wsvn.com/
news/local/claims-of-fake-gofundme-accounts-to-help-surfside-victims-prompt-
call-for-federal-probe/.

25. Jillian Pikora, "Fake GoFundMe Removed as Community Rallies for School Bus
Driver Dad Killed in I79 Crash," *Cumberland Daily Voice*, November 5, 2021, https://
dailyvoice.com/pennsylvania/cumberland/news/fake-gofundme-removed-as-
community-rallies-for-school-bus-driver-dad-killed-in-i79-crash/819552/.

26. Zenone and Snyder, "Fraud in Medical Crowdfunding."

27. Caitlin Neuwelt-Kearns et al., "Getting the Crowd to Care: Marketing Illness Through
Health-Related Crowdfunding in Aotearoa New Zealand," *Environment and Planning
A: Economy and Space* (2021), 1–19, https://doi.org/10.1177/0308518X211009535.

28. Katherine Skiba, "Beware of Phony Online Fundraisers on GoFundMe," *AARP*
(blog), August 16, 2021, https://www.aarp.org/money/scams-fraud/info-2021/bew
are-of-phony-fundraisers-on-gofundme.html.

29. Michael Tedder, "GoFundMe Helps Struggling Americans Raise Cash. It Also Has a
Huge Fraud Problem," *Money*, January 25, 2021, https://money.com/fake-gofundme/.

30. Ross McLaughlin and Espe Currie, "Donating Online? Here's How to Make Sure the
Campaign Isn't Fake," *CTV News*, January 22, 2020, https://bc.ctvnews.ca/donating-
online-here-s-how-to-make-sure-the-campaign-isn-t-fake-1.4772754.

31. BBC News, "Here's How to Spot a Fake Crowdfunding Page," *BBC News*, April 3,
2017, sec. Newsbeat, https://www.bbc.com/news/newsbeat-39478846.

32. GoFundMe, "Determining If a Fundraiser Is Trustworthy," *GoFundMe*, October 27,
2021, https://support.gofundme.com/hc/en-us/articles/115015913668-Determin
ing-if-a-fundraiser-is-trustworthy.

33. Tedder, "GoFundMe Helps Struggling Americans Raise Cash."

34. Kathleen Felton, "Crowdfunding Scams Are Growing. Here's How to Tell Which
Cases Are Real," *Health*, February 24, 2016, https://www.health.com/mind-body/
crowdfunding-scams-are-growing-heres-how-to-tell-which-cases-are-real.

35. GoFundMe, "GoFundMe Verification Guidelines," *GoFundMe*, accessed January 13,
2022, https://www.gofundme.com/en-ca/c/safety/verification-guidelines.

36. Stephanie Gosk and Conor Ferguson, "GoFundMe Says It Has an Answer for Fraud,"
NBC News, April 8, 2019, https://www.nbcnews.com/news/us-news/after-new-jer
sey-scam-gofundme-says-it-has-answer-fraud-n992086.

37. JustGiving, "I Have Concerns About a Crowdfunding Page, What Should I Do?,"
JustGiving, accessed January 12, 2022, https://help.justgiving.com/hc/en-us/articles/
202871602-I-have-concerns-about-a-Crowdfunding-Page-what-should-I-do-.

38. Oommen, "Fake Fundraising Campaigns Tarnish Growing Crowdfunding Concept
in India."

39. Kim Lyons, "Indiegogo Switches Gears to More Closely Screen Crowdfunding
Campaigns," *The Verge* (blog), November 3, 2021, https://www.theverge.com/2021/
11/3/22757421/indiegogo-crowdfunding-campaign-screening-fraud-gofundme.

40. GoFundMe, "Behind the Scenes: A Look at How We Verify Fundraisers During a US Crisis," *GoFundMe Stories*, October 15, 2021, https://medium.com/gofundme-stor ies/behind-the-scenes-a-look-at-how-we-verify-fundraisers-during-a-u-s-crisis-b54a4a26fef6.

41. Lyons, "Indiegogo Switches Gears."

42. Jennifer G. Kim et al., "'The Power of Collective Endorsements: Credibility Factors in Medical Crowdfunding Campaigns," in *Proceedings of the 2016 CHI Conference on Human Factors in Computing Systems*, 2016, 4538–49.

43. Kim et al., "The Power of Collective Endorsements."

44. GoFundMe, "Behind the Scenes."

45. Ibid.

Chapter 7

1. Truth and Reconciliation Commission of Canada, *Canada's Residential Schools: The Final Report of the Truth and Reconciliation Commission of Canada* (Montreal/Kingston: McGill-Queen's University Press, 2015).

2. Alex Reed, "Subsidizing Hate: A Proposal to Reform the Internal Revenue Service's Methodology Test," *Fordham Journal of Corporate and Financial Law* 17, no. 3 (2012): 823–70.

3. Ibid.

4. Theodore Lechterman, *The Tyranny of Generosity: Why Philanthropy Corrupts Our Politics and How We Can Fix It* (New York: Oxford University Press, 2021).

5. Eric Franklin Amarante, "Why Don't Some White Supremacist Groups Pay Taxes?," *Emory Law Journal Online* 67 (2018): 2045–68.

6. Michelle Smith, "How a Kennedy Built an Anti-Vaccine Juggernaut amid COVID-19," *AP News*, December 15, 2021, sec. Coronavirus pandemic, https://apnews.com/ article/how-rfk-jr-built-anti-vaccine-juggernaut-amid-covid-4997be1bcf591fe8b 7f1f90d16c9321e.

7. Kevin Roose, "How 'Save the Children' Is Keeping QAnon Alive," *New York Times*, September 28, 2020, sec. Technology, https://www.nytimes.com/2020/09/28/technol ogy/save-the-children-qanon.html.

8. Abbas Barzegar and Arain Zainab, "Hijacked by Hate: American Philanthropy and the Islamophobia Network" (Anaheim: Council on American-Islamic Relations, 2019), https://ca.cair.com/losangeles/publications/hijacked-by-hate-american-phila nthropy-and-the-islamophobia-network/.

9. Jay Greene, "Amazon Values Same-Sex Equality, but Its Charitable-Giving Plan Clashes," *Seattle Times*, December 2, 2014, sec. Business, https://www.seattletimes. com/business/amazon-values-same-sex-equality-but-its-charitable-giving-plan-clas hes-1/.

10. Jay Greene and Jeremy Merrill, "This Amazon Program Has Funneled Thousands to Anti-Vax Activists During the Pandemic," *Washington Post*, December 11, 2021,

https://www.washingtonpost.com/technology/2021/12/11/amazon-anti-vaccine-charity/.

11. Deborah Hastings, "N.J. Deli Owner Who Ignited Fury with 'White History Month' Goes out of Business," *New York Daily News*, April 17, 2015, sec. U.S., https://www.nydailynews.com/news/national/n-man-business-white-history-month-article-1.2189508.

12. Rachel Monroe, "When GoFundMe Gets Ugly," *The Atlantic*, November 2019, https://www.theatlantic.com/magazine/archive/2019/11/gofundme-nation/598369/.

13. Seth Stevenson, "The Dark Side of GoFundMe," *Slate*, December 9, 2020, https://slate.com/business/2020/12/gofundme-dark-side-fraud-social-media-health-care.html.

14. Monroe, "When GoFundMe Gets Ugly."

15. Ed Pilkington, "Capitol Attack Insurrectionists Flock to Fundraising Websites to Raise Defense Funds," *The Guardian*, December 17, 2021, sec. US news, https://www.theguardian.com/us-news/2021/dec/17/capitol-attack-insurrectionists-fundraising-defense-money.

16. Carter Sherman, "Anti-LGTBQ 'Conversion Therapy' Fundraisers Are Still Alive and Well on GoFundMe," *Vice* (blog), September 4, 2020, https://www.vice.com/en/article/jgx9g7/gofundme-is-hosting-anti-lgbtq-conversion-therapy-fundraisers.

17. Aneesha Bedi, "BJP Leader Kapil Mishra Runs Crowdfunding Campaign for Hindu Victims of Delhi Riots," *The Print* (blog), March 17, 2020, https://theprint.in/india/bjp-leader-kapil-mishra-runs-crowdfunding-campaign-for-hindu-victims-of-delhi-riots/382709/.

18. Akanksha Singh, "Medical Crowdfunding Has Become Essential in India, but It's Leaving Many Behind," Rest of World, August 4, 2021, https://restofworld.org/2021/crowdfunded-healthcare-in-india/.

19. Greg Elmer and Sabrina Ward-Kimola, "Political Crowdfunding and Campaigning on GoFundMe," *Canadian Journal of Communication* 46, no. 4 (2021): 803–20, https://doi.org/10.22230/cjc.2021v46n4a3935.

20. Jeremy Snyder, Leigh Turner, and Valorie A. Crooks, "Crowdfunding for Unproven Stem Cell–Based Interventions," *Journal of the American Medical Association* 319, no. 18 (2018): 1935–6.

21. Jeremy Snyder, Marco Zenone, and Timothy Caulfield, "Crowdfunding for Complementary and Alternative Medicine: What Are Cancer Patients Seeking?," *PLOS ONE* 15, no. 11 (2020): e0242048, https://doi.org/10.1371/journal.pone.0242048.

22. Ford Vox et al., "Medical Crowdfunding for Scientifically Unsupported or Potentially Dangerous Treatments," *Journal of the American Medical Association* 320, no. 16 (2018): 1705–6.

23. Pew Charitable Trusts, "Harms Linked to Unapproved Stem Cell Interventions Highlight Need for Greater FDA Enforcement," The Pew Charitable Trusts (June 1, 2021), https://pew.org/3fKASu5.

24. Jeremy Snyder and Leigh Turner, "Crowdfunding for Stem Cell-Based Interventions to Treat Neurologic Diseases and Injuries," *Neurology* 93, no. 6 (2019): 252–8.

25. Vox et al., "Medical Crowdfunding for Scientifically Unsupported or Potentially Dangerous Treatments."

26. Snyder, Zenone, and Caulfield, "Crowdfunding for Complementary and Alternative Medicine."

27. Gabrielle Dressler and Sarah A. Kelly, "Ethical Implications of Medical Crowdfunding: The Case of Charlie Gard," *Journal of Medical Ethics* 44, no. 7 (2018): 453–7, https://doi.org/10.1136/medethics-2017-104717.

28. Jeremy Snyder, Leigh Turner, and Valorie A. Crooks, "Crowdfunding for Unproven Stem Cell Procedures Spreads Misinformation," *STAT*, August 6, 2018, https://www.statnews.com/2018/08/06/crowdfunding-for-unproven-stem-cell-procedures-was tes-money-and-spreads-misinformation/.

29. Snyder, Zenone, and Caulfield, "Crowdfunding for Complementary and Alternative Medicine."

30. Snyder and Turner, "Crowdfunding for Stem Cell-Based Interventions to Treat Neurologic Diseases and Injuries."

31. Jeremy Snyder and Timothy Caulfield, "Patients' Crowdfunding Campaigns for Alternative Cancer Treatments," *Lancet Oncology* 20, no. 1 (2019): 28–9.

32. Marco Zenone, Jeremy Snyder, and Timothy Caulfield, "Crowdfunding Cannabidiol (CBD) for Cancer: Hype and Misinformation on GoFundMe," *American Journal of Public Health* 110, no. S3 (2020): S294–9, https://doi.org/10.2105/AJPH.2020.305768.

33. Snyder, Turner, and Crooks, "Crowdfunding for Unproven Stem Cell–Based Interventions."

34. Zenone, Snyder, and Caulfield, "Crowdfunding Cannabidiol (CBD) for Cancer."

35. Jeremy Snyder and Leigh Turner, "Crowdfunding, Stem Cell Interventions and Autism Spectrum Disorder: Comparing Campaigns Related to an International 'Stem Cell Clinic' and US Academic Medical Center," *Cytotherapy* 23, no. 3 (2021): 198–202, https://doi.org/10.1016/j.jcyt.2020.09.002.

36. Abby Ohlheiser, "After GoFundMe Shuts down Christian Bakery Crowdfunding, It Bans 'Discriminatory' Campaigns," *Washington Post*, May 1, 2015, https://www.was hingtonpost.com/news/acts-of-faith/wp/2015/05/01/after-gofundme-shuts-down-christian-bakery-crowdfunding-it-bans-discriminatory-fundraising-campaigns/.

37. GoFundMe, "Terms of Service," *GoFundMe* (blog), May 12, 2022, https://www.gofun dme.com/c/terms.

38. Milaap, "Terms and Conditions of Milaap," *Milaap*, February 8, 2019, https://milaap. org/about-us/terms-and-conditions.

39. Ketto, "Disclaimer," *Ketto*, accessed February 2, 2022, https://www.ketto.org/terms-of-use.php.

40. Givealittle, "Givealittle Terms & Conditions," *Givealittle*, September 7, 2020, https:// givealittle.co.nz/content/howgivealittleworks/terms.

41. Milaap, "Terms and Conditions of Milaap."

42. Ketto, "Disclaimer."

43. GoFundMe, "Terms of Service."

44. Caitlin Dewey, "GoFundMe, the Site That Has Raised Money for Convicted Murderers, Will Draw the Line at Abortion and 'Sorcery,'" *Washington Post*, September 9, 2014, https://www.washingtonpost.com/news/the-intersect/wp/2014/ 09/09/gofundme-the-site-that-has-raised-money-for-convicted-murderers-will-draw-the-line-at-abortion-and-sorcery/.

45. Milaap, "Terms and Conditions of Milaap."
46. GoFundMe, "Terms of Service."
47. Martin Coulter, "GoFundMe Blocks Cash Appeals for Controversial Cancer Clinic," *Financial Times*, March 20, 2019, https://www.ft.com/content/f2c17eaa-4afb-11e9-bbc9-6917dce3dc62.
48. Julia Arciga, "GoFundMe Bans Anti-Vaxxers Who Raise Money to Spread Misinformation," *The Daily Beast*, March 22, 2019, sec. science, https://www.thedailybeast.com/gofundme-bans-anti-vaxxers-who-raise-money-to-spread-misinformation.
49. Ben Paynter, "Can GoFundMe Be the Future of Philanthropy If the Alt-Right Uses It to Raise Funds?," *Fast Company*, January 20, 2017, https://www.fastcompany.com/3067237/can-gofundme-be-the-future-of-philanthropy-if-the-alt-right-uses-it-r.
50. Stevenson, "The Dark Side of GoFundMe."
51. Julia Reinstein, Rosie Gray, and Salvador Hernandez, "Former Top Trump Aide Stephen Bannon and 'Build the Wall' Founder Brian Kolfage Have Been Charged with Fraud," *BuzzFeed News*, August 20, 2020, https://www.buzzfeednews.com/article/juliareinstein/stephen-bannon-brian-kolfage-wall-charged.
52. Siladitya Ray, "The Far-Right Is Flocking to These Alternate Social Media Apps—Not All of Them Are Thrilled," *Forbes*, January 14, 2021, https://www.forbes.com/sites/siladityaray/2021/01/14/the-far-right-is-flocking-to-these-alternate-social-media-apps—-not-all-of-them-are-thrilled/.
53. GiveSendGo, "GiveSendGo," *GiveSendGo.com*, accessed June 7, 2022, http://givesendgo.com/.
54. GiveSendGo, "Terms and Conditions," *GiveSendGo.com*, April 7, 2022, http://givesendgo.com/terms-of-use.
55. GiveSendGo, "New York Post Says Crowdfunding Site Was Created for Rittinghouse Campaign. A Blatant Misrepresentation," *GiveSendGo.com*, October 2020, http://givesendgo.com/site/press?v=Oct.
56. GoFundMe, "GoFundMe Policy on Fundraisers for the Legal Defense of Violent Crimes," *GoFundMe Stories* (blog), November 19, 2021, https://medium.com/gofundme-stories/gofundme-policy-on-fundraisers-for-the-legal-defense-of-violent-crimes-975aff8ba5f6.
57. Talia Lavin, "Crowdfunding Hate in the Name of Christ," *The Nation*, April 5, 2021, https://www.thenation.com/article/society/givesendgo-crowdfunding-extremism/.
58. Ibid.

Chapter 8

1. Lilly Family School of Philanthropy, "Crowdfunding," Lilly Family School of Philanthropy, accessed February 22, 2022, https://philanthropy.iupui.edu/research/covid/crowdfunding.html.

2. Sarah Kinosian, "Venezuelans Rely on the Kindness of Strangers to Pay for COVID-19 Treatment," *Reuters*, October 4, 2021, sec. Americas, https://www.reuters.com/world/americas/venezuelans-rely-kindness-strangers-pay-COVID-19-treatment-2021-10-04/.

3. Krutika Pathi and Yirmiyan Arthur, "Pandemic Leaves Indians Mired in Massive Medical Debts," *US News & World Report*, July 26, 2021, https://www.usnews.com/news/world/articles/2021-07-26/pandemic-leaves-indians-mired-in-massive-medical-debts.

4. Manu Balachandran, "COVID-19: Crowdfunding to the Rescue," *Forbes India*, November 26, 2020, https://www.forbesindia.com/article/heroes-of-philanthropy/covid19-crowdfunding-to-the-rescue/64499/1.

5. Tim Cadogan, "Helping Our Community During the Coronavirus Pandemic," *GoFundMe Stories* (blog), March 21, 2020, https://medium.com/gofundme-stories/helping-our-community-during-the-coronavirus-pandemic-147dccd07403.

6. Nathaniel Popper and Taylor Lorenz, "GoFundMe Confronts Coronavirus Demand," *New York Times*, March 26, 2020, sec. Style, https://www.nytimes.com/2020/03/26/style/gofundme-coronavirus.html.

7. GoFundMe, "The Data Behind Donations During the COVID-19 Pandemic," *GoFundMe Stories* (blog), September 24, 2020, https://medium.com/gofundme-stories/the-data-behind-donations-during-the-COVID-19-pandemic-c40e0f690bfa.

8. Mark Igra et al., "Crowdfunding as a Response to COVID-19: Increasing Inequities at a Time of Crisis," *Social Science & Medicine* 282 (2021): 114105, https://doi.org/10.1016/j.socscimed.2021.114105.

9. Sameh Nagui Saleh, Christoph U. Lehmann, and Richard J. Medford, "Early Crowdfunding Response to the COVID-19 Pandemic: Cross-Sectional Study," *Journal of Medical Internet Research* 23, no. 2 (2021): e25429, https://doi.org/10.2196/25429.

10. Lilly Family School of Philanthropy, "Crowdfunding."

11. Milaap, "COVID-19: The Only Way to Fight This, Is Together," *Milaap*, accessed February 22, 2022, https://milaap.org/communities/COVID-19.

12. Ketto, "Ketto's Impact During the Coronavirus (COVID-19) Pandemic," *Ketto*, May 31, 2021, https://www.ketto.org/blog/kettos-impact-during-the-coronavirus-pandemic.

13. ImpactGuru, "Raise Funds for Covid Patients Online in India," ImpactGuru, accessed February 22, 2022, https://www.impactguru.com/fight-covid.

14. Saleh, Lehmann, and Medford, "Early Crowdfunding Response to the COVID-19 Pandemic."

15. Pawel Rajwa et al., "Online Crowdfunding Response to Coronavirus Disease 2019," *Journal of General Internal Medicine* 35, no. 8 (2020): 2482–4, https://doi.org/10.1007/s11606-020-05896-x.

16. Matthew McKitrick et al., "Spatial and Temporal Patterns in Canadian COVID-19 Crowdfunding Campaigns," *PLOS ONE* 16, no. 8 (2021): e0256204, https://doi.org/10.1371/journal.pone.0256204.

17. JustGiving, "COVID-19," JustGiving, accessed February 22, 2022, https://justgiving.blackbaud.com/inspiration/how-to-help/COVID-19.

18. Alix Moine and Daphnée Papiasse, "Evidence from France: How Crowdfunding Is Being Used to Support the Response to COVID-19," *LSE European Politics and Policy (EUROPP) Blog* (blog), April 24, 2020, http://eprints.lse.ac.uk/105226/1/europpblog_2020_04_24_evidence_from_france_how_crowdfunding_is_being.pdf.

19. Ella Robinson and Susan Wardell, "Effects of the COVID-19 Lockdown on the Healthcare Experiences of Medical Crowdfunders in Aotearoa New Zealand" (University of Otago, December 23, 2020), https://ourarchive.otago.ac.nz/handle/10523/10615.

20. McKitrick et al., "Spatial and Temporal Patterns in Canadian COVID-19 Crowdfunding Campaigns."

21. GoFundMe, "The Data Behind Donations During the COVID-19 Pandemic."

22. GoFundMe, "Our New Fundraising Category—Rent, Food + Monthly Bills—Helps Address the Increase in Urgent Needs," *GoFundMe Stories* (blog), October 22, 2020, https://medium.com/gofundme-stories/our-new-fundraising-category-rent-food-monthly-bills-helps-address-the-increase-in-urgent-4dcd9d941178.

23. Sushant Peshkar, "Indians Embrace Crowdfunding to Help Covid-Related Campaigns," Ketto, September 8, 2020, https://www.ketto.org/blog/indians-embrace-crowdfunding-to-help-covid-related-campaigns.

24. Chiara Taqdees, "Fundraisers You Should Start During COVID-19," ImpactGuru, November 16, 2020, https://www.impactguru.com/blog/three-types-of-fundraisers-you-should-start-during-COVID-19.

25. Tim Cadogan, "GoFundMe CEO: Hello Congress, Americans Need Help and We Can't Do Your Job for You," *USA Today*, February 11, 2021, https://www.usatoday.com/story/opinion/voices/2021/02/11/gofundme-ceo-congress-pass-covid-relief-desperate-americans-column/4440425001/.

26. Cadogan, "Helping Our Community During the Coronavirus Pandemic."

27. WXYZ, "More Families Relying on Crowdfunding for Funeral Costs amid COVID-19 Pandemic," *WXYZ*, October 11, 2021, https://www.wxyz.com/news/more-families-relying-on-crowdfunding-for-funeral-costs-amid-COVID-19-pandemic.

28. Chad Richard, "Yelp Teams Up with GoFundMe to Make It Easy for People to Support the Local Businesses They Love," *Yelp—Official Blog* (blog), March 24, 2020, https://blog.yelp.com/news/yelp-teams-up-with-gofundme-to-make-it-easy-for-people-to-support-the-local-businesses-they-love/.

29. Ibid.

30. Nick Statt, "Yelp to Stop Auto-Creating Fundraisers After Outrage from Business Owners," *The Verge*, March 26, 2020, https://www.theverge.com/2020/3/26/21196446/yelp-gofundme-coronavirus-automatic-opt-in-fundraiser-pause.

31. Michael Klein, "Yelp Backs Down After Creating Restaurant GoFundMe Campaigns Without Consent," *The Philadelphia Inquirer*, March 27, 2020, sec. Coronavirus, health, coronavirus, https://www.inquirer.com/health/coronavirus/yelp-gofundme-restaurants-contribution-campaign-unauthorized-automatic-20200327.html.

32. Ingrid Lunden and Anthony Ha, "Yelp Pauses GoFundMe COVID-19 Fundraising After Opt-out Outcry," *TechCrunch* (blog), March 27, 2020, https://social.techcrunch.com/2020/03/27/yelp-pauses-gofundme-COVID-19-fundraising-after-opt-out-outcry/.

33. Statt, "Yelp to Stop Auto-Creating Fundraisers After Outrage from Business Owners."

34. Lunden and Ha, "Yelp Pauses GoFundMe COVID-19 Fundraising After Opt-out Outcry."

35. Susan Wardell, "To Wish You Well: The Biopolitical Subjectivities of Medical Crowdfunders During and After Aotearoa New Zealand's COVID-19 Lockdown," *BioSocieties*, September 22, 2021, https://doi.org/10.1057/s41292-021-00251-7.

36. Lindsay William-Ross, "'We Are Going to Survive This Closure': Customers Pitch in over $21k to Save Vancouver Restaurant," *Vancouver Is Awesome*, April 20, 2021, https://www.vancouverisawesome.com/food-and-drink/we-are-going-to-survive-this-closure-customers-pitch-in-over-21k-to-save-vancouver-restaurant-3648681.

37. Wardell, "To Wish You Well."

38. Saleh, Lehmann, and Medford, "Early Crowdfunding Response to the COVID-19 Pandemic."

39. Igra et al., "Crowdfunding as a Response to COVID-19: Increasing Inequities at a Time of Crisis."

40. GoFundMe, "Small Business Relief Fund," *GoFundMe*, accessed February 21, 2022, https://www.gofundme.com/f/smallbusinessrelieffund.

41. Flexport, "Frontline Responders Fund," *GoFundMe*, accessed February 21, 2022, https://www.gofundme.com/f/frontlineresponsersfund.

42. Ketto, "Acknowledging Our Frontline COVID-19 Warriors on India's 75th Independence Day," *Ketto*, August 16, 2021, https://www.ketto.org/blog/acknowledging-our-frontline-COVID-19-warriors-on-indias-75th-independence-day.

43. Imperial Health Charity, "Support Our COVID-19 Relief Fund," *JustGiving*, accessed February 22, 2022, https://www.justgiving.com/campaign/help-our-nhs.

44. Peter Hum, "Fundraiser Seeks to Feed Ottawa Front-Line Medical Staff with Restaurant Meals," *Ottawa Citizen*, January 12, 2022, https://ottawacitizen.com/news/local-news/fundraiser-seeks-to-feed-ottawa-front-line-medical-staff-with-restaurant-meals.

45. Igra et al., "Crowdfunding as a Response to COVID-19: Increasing Inequities at a Time of Crisis."

46. Ibid.

47. Saleh, Lehmann, and Medford, "Early Crowdfunding Response to the COVID-19 Pandemic."

48. Igra et al., "Crowdfunding as a Response to COVID-19: Increasing Inequities at a Time of Crisis."

49. GoFundMe, "The Data Behind Donations During the COVID-19 Pandemic."

50. Igra et al., "Crowdfunding as a Response to COVID-19: Increasing Inequities at a Time of Crisis."

51. Popper and Lorenz, "GoFundMe Confronts Coronavirus Demand."

52. Igra et al., "Crowdfunding as a Response to COVID-19: Increasing Inequities at a Time of Crisis."

53. Susan J Roe and Ryan P. Smith, "Asking for Help: Restaurant Crowdfunding During COVID-19," *Journal of Foodservice Business Research* (2021): 1–22, https://doi.org/10.1080/15378020.2021.2006038.

54. Popper and Lorenz, "GoFundMe Confronts Coronavirus Demand."

55. GoFundMe, "The Data Behind Donations During the COVID-19 Pandemic."

56. Igra et al., "Crowdfunding as a Response to COVID-19: Increasing Inequities at a Time of Crisis."

57. Saleh, Lehmann, and Medford, "Early Crowdfunding Response to the COVID-19 Pandemic."

58. Rajwa et al., "Online Crowdfunding Response to Coronavirus Disease 2019."

59. Ketto, "The Role of Crowdfunding in Pandemic," *Ketto*, January 19, 2022, https://www.ketto.org/blog/role-of-crowdfunding-in-pandemic.

60. Imperial Health Charity, "Support Our COVID-19 Relief Fund."

61. Ketto, "The Role of Crowdfunding in Pandemic."

62. Popper and Lorenz, "GoFundMe Confronts Coronavirus Demand."

63. Moine and Papiasse, "Evidence from France."

64. Popper and Lorenz, "GoFundMe Confronts Coronavirus Demand."

65. GoFundMe Trust & Safety Team, "Guidance: COVID-19 Vaccine Fundraising on GoFundMe," *GoFundMe Stories* (blog), October 8, 2021, https://medium.com/gofundme-stories/guidance-COVID-19-vaccine-fundraising-on-gofundme-4e480d7ed17d.

66. Sara Dorn, "The Sneaky New Way Vaccine Conspiracists Are Raising Cash," *The Daily Beast*, July 16, 2021, sec. US news, https://www.thedailybeast.com/the-sneaky-new-way-vaccine-conspiracists-are-raising-cash.

67. Aaron Mak, "The Lucrative Business of Stoking Vaccine Skepticism," *Slate*, August 6, 2021, https://slate.com/technology/2021/08/givesendgo-gofundme-vaccine-skeptics-covid-misinformation.html.

68. Haschal Thompson, "Vaccine Police," *GiveSendGo*, accessed February 23, 2022, http://givesendgo.com/vaccinepolicenews.

69. Janice Dickson and Salmaan Farooqui, "Ottawa Police Probe Desecration of Monuments by Trucker Convoy Protesters," *The Globe and Mail*, January 30, 2022, https://www.theglobeandmail.com/canada/article-ottawa-police-investigate-desecration-of-monuments-by-trucker-convoy/.

70. Tamara Lich, "Taking Back Our Freedom Convoy 2022," *GoFundMe*, January 15, 2022, https://web.archive.org/web/20220115003941/https://www.gofundme.com/f/taking-back-our-freedom-convoy-2022.

71. Tamara Lich, "Freedom Convoy 2022," *GoFundMe*, January 20, 2022, https://web.archive.org/web/20220120205555/https://www.gofundme.com/f/taking-back-our-freedom-convoy-2022.

72. Christopher Reynolds, "GoFundMe Withholding $4.7M from Trucker Convoy until Plan Presented," *CBC*, January 25, 2022, https://www.cbc.ca/news/canada/manitoba/gofundme-withhold-millions-trucker-convoy-1.6327665.

73. Catharine Tunney, "GoFundMe Has Released $1M of More than $6M Raised for Protest Convoy," *CBC*, January 27, 2022, https://www.cbc.ca/news/politics/gofundme-money-released-convoy-1.6328029.

74. Lich, "Freedom Convoy 2022."

75. Canadian Anti-Hate Network, "The 'Freedom Convoy' Is Nothing but a Vehicle for the Far Right," *Canadian Anti-Hate Network*, January 27, 2022, https://www.antihate.ca/the_freedom_convoy_is_nothing_but_a_vehicle_for_the_far_right.

76. Sarah Anderson, "'Vile, Violent, and Hateful': Leaders Denounce Nazi, Confederate Flags at Ottawa Protest," *Daily Hive*, January 30, 2022, https://dailyhive.com/vancouver/nazi-confederate-flags-ottawa-protest.

77. Jeremy Snyder, "Is GoFundMe Violating Its Own Terms of Service on the 'Freedom Convoy?,'" *The Conversation*, February 2, 2022, http://theconversation.com/is-gofundme-violating-its-own-terms-of-service-on-the-freedom-convoy-176147.

78. GoFundMe, "UPDATE: GoFundMe to Refund All Freedom Convoy 2022 Donations (2/5/2022)," *GoFundMe Stories* (blog), February 5, 2022, https://medium.com/gofundme-stories/update-gofundme-statement-on-the-freedom-convoy-2022-fundraiser-4ca7e9714e82.

79. GiveSendGo, "GoFundMe Withholds $5.2 Million from Canadian Truckers Convoy and Campaign Donors," *GiveSendGo*, January 26, 2022, http://www.givesendgo.com/site/press?v=Jan26.

80. GiveSendGo, "GiveSendGo Issues Public Statement Regarding Freedom Convoy 2022 Campaign," *GiveSendGo*, February 7, 2022, https://www.givesendgo.com/site/pressrelease?v=Feb22.

81. Costanza Musu and Patrick Leblond, "How Authorities Are Targeting the 'Freedom Convoy' Money via the Emergencies Act," *The Conversation*, accessed February 24, 2022, http://theconversation.com/how-authorities-are-targeting-the-freedom-convoy-money-via-the-emergencies-act-177204.

82. Snyder, "Is GoFundMe Violating Its Own Terms of Service on the 'Freedom Convoy?'"

83. Elizabeth Thompson, Roberto Rocha, and Albert Leung, "Hacked Convoy Data Shows More than Half of Donations Came from US," *CBC*, February 14, 2022, https://www.cbc.ca/news/politics/convoy-protest-donations-data-1.6351292.

84. Freedom 2022 Human Rights and Freedoms, "Freedom Convoy 2022," *GiveSendGo*, accessed February 24, 2022, http://www.givesendgo.com/FreedomConvoy2022.

Chapter 9

1. Benjamin Soskis, "Norms and Narratives That Shape US Charitable and Philanthropic Giving" (Washington, DC: Urban Institute, March 2021), https://www.urban.org/sites/default/files/publication/103772/norms-and-narratives-that-shape-us-charitable-and-philanthropic-giving_0.pdf.

2. Evie Lucas, "Reinventing the Rattling Tin: How UK Charities Use Facebook in Fundraising," *International Journal of Nonprofit and Voluntary Sector Marketing* 22, no. 2 (2017): e1576, https://doi.org/10.1002/nvsm.1576.

3. Lucy Bernholz, "Wiring a New Social Economy: Reflections on Philanthropy in the Digital Age," in *The Routledge Companion to Philanthropy*, ed. Tobias Jung, Susan D. Phillips, and Jenny Harrow (Milton Park, UK: Routledge, 2016), 458–71.

4. Susan Adams, "Free Market Philanthropy: GoFundMe Is Changing the Way People Give to Causes Big and Small," *Forbes*, October 19, 2016, https://www.forbes.com/sites/susanadams/2016/10/19/free-market-philanthropy-gofundme-is-changing-the-way-people-give-to-causes-big-and-small/.

5. Milaap, "The Journey So Far of Crowdfunding in India," *Milaap*, accessed March 22, 2022, https://milaap.org/about-us/overview.

6. GoFundMe, "GoFundMe Announces GoFundMe Charity," *GoFundMe Stories* (blog), October 15, 2019, https://medium.com/gofundme-stories/gofundme-announces-gofundme-charity-21f9efd2e947.

7. Tim Cadogan, "How GoFundMe Will Accelerate Progress Towards Our Vision to Be the Most Helpful Place in the World," *GoFundMe Stories* (blog), January 13, 2022, https://medium.com/gofundme-stories/how-gofundme-will-accelerate-progress-towards-our-vision-to-be-the-most-helpful-place-in-the-world-b1e60c95009e.

8. Zhichao Ba et al., "Exploring the Donation Allocation of Online Charitable Crowdfunding Based on Topical and Spatial Analysis: Evidence from the Tencent GongYi," *Information Processing & Management* 57, no. 6 (2020): 102322, https://doi.org/10.1016/j.ipm.2020.102322.

9. Chuffed, "Our Story | Non-Profit Charity and Social Enterprise Fundraising," *Chuffed*, accessed April 27, 2022, https://chuffed.org/about.

10. Watsi, "FAQ," *Watsi*, accessed April 27, 2022, https://watsi.org/faq.

11. ImpactGuru, "Donate Monthly to Support Patients with Critical Illness," ImpactGuru, accessed April 27, 2022, https://www.impactguru.com/monthly/save-patients-with-critical-illness.

12. Erin Morgan Gore and Breanna DiGiammarino, "Crowdfunding for Nonprofits," *Stanford Social Innovation Review*, May 22, 2014, https://ssir.org/articles/entry/crowdfunding_for_nonprofits.

13. Bobby Whitmore, "It's Time to Act: Help American Families Struggling to Make Ends Meet," *GoFundMe Stories* (blog), December 21, 2020, https://medium.com/gofundme-stories/its-time-to-act-help-american-families-struggling-to-make-ends-meet-fdc19dbd1992.

14. GoFundMe, "UPDATE: Mila Kunis and Ashton Kutcher Have Reached Their $30M Fundraising Goal. #StandWithUkraine Https://T.Co/OH85S0c4Px," Tweet, *Twitter*, March 17, 2022, https://twitter.com/gofundme/status/1504491231417536513.

15. Matthew Wade, "'The Giving Layer of the Internet': A Critical History of GoFundMe's Reputation Management, Platform Governance, and Communication Strategies in Capturing Peer-to-Peer and Charitable Giving Markets," *Journal of Philanthropy and Marketing* e1777 (2022).

16. Ingrid Lunden, "GoFundMe Rebrands the Direct Impact Fund as GoFundMe.Org for Wider Charitable Giving," *TechCrunch* (blog), April 11, 2019, https://social.techcru nch.com/2019/04/11/gofundme-rebrands-the-direct-impact-fund-as-gofundme-org-for-wider-charitable-giving/.

17. GoFundMe.Org, "Frequently Asked Questions," *GoFundMe.Org* (blog), accessed April 22, 2022, https://www.gofundme.org/faq/.

18. Watsi, "FAQ."

19. Ketto, "Charitable Donations as a Means of Tax Deduction," *Ketto*, July 6, 2021, https://www.ketto.org/blog/how-to-maximize-your-tax-deduction.

20. Kean Birch and Kelly Bronson, "Big Tech," *Science as Culture* 31, no. 1 (2022): 1–14, https://doi.org/10.1080/09505431.2022.2036118.

21. Blake Masters, "Reclaiming Our Independence from Big Tech," *Wall Street Journal*, September 6, 2021, sec. Opinion, https://www.wsj.com/articles/big-tech-regulation-apple-google-facebook-twitter-amazon-addiction-antitrust-censorship-content-moderation-section-230-11630959185.

22. Mike Isaac and Kellen Browning, "Fact-Checked on Facebook and Twitter, Conservatives Switch Their Apps," *New York Times*, November 11, 2020, sec. Technology, https://www.nytimes.com/2020/11/11/technology/parler-rumble-news max.html.

23. Aaron Mak, "The Lucrative Business of Stoking Vaccine Skepticism," *Slate*, August 6, 2021, https://slate.com/technology/2021/08/givesendgo-gofundme-vaccine-skept ics-covid-misinformation.html.

24. Paulina Villegas and Reis Thebault, "Frozen out of GoFundMe, Canadian Protest Convoy Raises Millions on Christian Site," *Washington Post*, February 7, 2022, https://www.washingtonpost.com/world/2022/02/07/canada-protesters-fundraising-platform/.

25. Wade, "'The Giving Layer of the Internet.'"

26. GiveSendGo, "GiveSendGo," *GiveSendGo.com*, accessed June 7, 2022, http://givesen dgo.com/.

27. Jacob Lorinc, "The Big Business of GiveSendGo: U.S. Crowdfunding Site Earned at Least $735,000 on Ottawa Protests Alone, Leaked Data Shows," *Toronto Star*, February 25, 2022, sec. Business, https://www.thestar.com/business/2022/02/25/the-big-busin ess-of-givesendgo-us-crowdfunding-site-earned-at-least-735000-on-ottawa-prote sts-alone-leaked-data-shows.html.

28. Canada Helps, "The Giving Report 2018" (Toronto: Canada Helps, 2018), https://www.canadahelps.org/media/The-Giving-Report-2018.pdf.

29. GlobalGiving, "Crowdfundamentals: A Beginner's Guide To Crowdfunding Success" (GlobalGiving, November 30, 2016), https://www.globalgiving.org/learn/beginners-guide-crowdfunding-success/.

30. Chuffed, "How It Works—Running a Campaign," Chuffed, accessed May 10, 2022, https://chuffed.org/how-it-works-crowdfunding/create-your-page.

31. Gerry Bellet and Matthew Robinson, "United Way Suffers from Competition for Donation Dollars," *Vancouver Sun*, April 6, 2014, https://vancouversun.com/news/metro/united-way-suffers-from-online-crowdfundings-competition-for-donation-dollars.

32. Jeremy Snyder, "GoFundMe Is Becoming a Social Safety Net—an Inequitable One," *Undark Magazine*, April 8, 2021, https://undark.org/2021/04/08/gofundme-inequita ble-social-safety-net/.

Conclusion: Making crowdfunding more appealing

1. Dean Spade, *Mutual Aid: Building Solidarity During This Crisis (and the Next)* (New York: Verso Books, 2020).
2. Elizabeth Thompson, Roberto Rocha, and Albert Leung, "Hacked Convoy Data Shows More than Half of Donations Came from US," *CBC*, February 14, 2022, https:// www.cbc.ca/news/politics/convoy-protest-donations-data-1.6351292.
3. Elizabeth Thompson, "Crowdfunding Platforms Now Required to Report Transactions, After Truck Convoy Protests," *CBC*, May 4, 2022, https://www.cbc.ca/ news/politics/convoy-finance-crowdfunding-fintrac-1.6440671.
4. Theodore Lechterman, *The Tyranny of Generosity: Why Philanthropy Corrupts Our Politics and How We Can Fix It* (New York: Oxford University Press, 2021).
5. Tamara Kneese, "Pay It Forward: Crowdfunding Is Not Mutual Aid", *Real Life*, June 22, 2020, https://reallifemag.com/pay-it-forward/.

Bibliography

Ackerman, Jacqueline, and Jon Bergdoll. "4 New Revelations on How People Give to Charity Crowdfunding Campaigns." Fast Company, June 5, 2021. https://www.fast company.com/90643893/4-new-revelations-on-how-people-give-to-charity-crowd funding-campaigns.

Adams, Susan. "Free Market Philanthropy: GoFundMe Is Changing the Way People Give to Causes Big and Small." *Forbes*, October 19, 2016. https://www.forbes.com/sites/sus anadams/2016/10/19/free-market-philanthropy-gofundme-is-changing-the-way-peo ple-give-to-causes-big-and-small/.

Amarante, Eric Franklin. "Why Don't Some White Supremacist Groups Pay Taxes?" *Emory Law Journal Online* 67 (2018): 2045–68.

Ambrose, Saint. *De Officiis*. Translated by Ivor J. Davidson. Oxford Early Christian Studies. New York: Oxford University Press, 2001. http://dx.doi.org/10.1093/0199245 789.001.0001.

Anderson, Sarah. "'Vile, Violent, and Hateful': Leaders Denounce Nazi, Confederate Flags at Ottawa Protest." Daily Hive, January 30, 2022. https://dailyhive.com/vancouver/ nazi-confederate-flags-ottawa-protest.

Aquino, Leo. "6 Tips for Crowdfunding Your Gender-Affirming Surgery, from Someone with Experience." *Business Insider*, June 30, 2021. https://www.businessinsider.com/ personal-finance/tips-for-crowdfunding-gender-affirming-surgery-2021-6.

Aravind, Indulekha. "How Milaap Tweaked Crowdfunding Model to Raise Money for Medical Care." *Economic Times*, March 1, 2020. https://economictimes.indiatimes. com/industry/healthcare/biotech/healthcare/how-milaap-tweaked-crowdfunding-model-to-raise-money-for-medical-care/articleshow/74420753.cms?from=mdr.

Arciga, Julia. "GoFundMe Bans Anti-Vaxxers Who Raise Money to Spread Misinformation." *The Daily Beast*, March 22, 2019, sec. science. https://www.thedailybe ast.com/gofundme-bans-anti-vaxxers-who-raise-money-to-spread-misinformation.

Aristotle. *Nicomachean Ethics*. Translated by Harris Rackham. Cambridge, MA: Harvard University Press, 1926.

Ashford, Elizabeth. "Severe Poverty as an Unjust Emergency." In *The Ethics of Giving*, edited by Paul Woodruff, 103–48.Oxford: Oxford University Press, 2018.

Ba, Zhichao, Yuxiang (Chris) Zhao, Shijie Song, and Qinghua Zhu. "Understanding the Determinants of Online Medical Crowdfunding Project Success in China." *Information Processing & Management* 58, no. 2 (2021): 102465. https://doi.org/ 10.1016/j.ipm.2020.102465.

Ba, Zhichao, Yuxiang (Chris) Zhao, Liqin Zhou, and Shijie Song. "Exploring the Donation Allocation of Online Charitable Crowdfunding Based on Topical and Spatial Analysis: Evidence from the Tencent GongYi." *Information Processing & Management* 57, no. 6 (November 1, 2020): 102322. https://doi.org/10.1016/j.ipm.2020.102322.

Baio, Andy. "Kickstarter Launches Another Social Fundraising Platform." *TechCrunch* (blog), April 29, 2009. https://social.techcrunch.com/2009/04/29/kickstarter-launc hes-another-social-fundraising-platform/.

Balachandran, Manu. "COVID-19: Crowdfunding to the Rescue." *Forbes India*, November 26, 2020. https://www.forbesindia.com/article/heroes-of-philanthropy/ covid19-crowdfunding-to-the-rescue/64499/1.

Barcelos, Chris A. "'Bye-Bye Boobies': Normativity, Deservingness and Medicalisation in Transgender Medical Crowdfunding." *Culture, Health & Sexuality* 21, no. 12 (2019): 1394–1408.

Barcelos, Chris A. "Go Fund Inequality: The Politics of Crowdfunding Transgender Medical Care." *Critical Public Health* 30, no. 3 (May 26, 2020): 330–39. https://doi.org/ 10.1080/09581596.2019.1575947.

Barcelos, Chris A., and Stephanie L. Budge. "Inequalities in Crowdfunding for Transgender Health Care." *Transgender Health* 4, no. 1 (2019): 81–88.

Barzegar, Abbas, and Arain Zainab. "Hijacked by Hate: American Philanthropy and the Islamophobia Network." Anaheim: Council on American-Islamic Relations, 2019. https://ca.cair.com/losangeles/publications/hijacked-by-hate-american-philanthr opy-and-the-islamophobia-network/.

BBC News. "Here's How to Spot a Fake Crowdfunding Page," April 3, 2017, sec. Newsbeat. https://www.bbc.com/news/newsbeat-39478846.

Bedi, Aneesha. "BJP Leader Kapil Mishra Runs Crowdfunding Campaign for Hindu Victims of Delhi Riots." *ThePrint* (blog), March 17, 2020. https://theprint.in/india/bjp-leader-kapil-mishra-runs-crowdfunding-campaign-for-hindu-victims-of-delhi-riots/ 382709/.

Beerbohm, Eric. "The Free-Provider Problem: Private Provision of Public Responsibilities." In *Philanthropy in Democratic Societies*, edited by Rob Reich, Chiara Cordelli, and Lucy Bernholz, 207–25. Chicago: University of Chicago Press, 2016.

Bellet, Gerry, and Matthew Robinson. "United Way Suffers from Competition for Donation Dollars." *Vancouver Sun*, April 6, 2014. https://vancouversun.com/news/ metro/united-way-suffers-from-online-crowdfundings-competition-for-donation-dollars.

Berkey, Brian. "The Institutional Critique of Effective Altruism." *Utilitas* 30, no. 2 (June 2018): 143–71. https://doi.org/10.1017/S0953820817000176.

Berliner, Lauren S., and Nora J. Kenworthy. "Producing a Worthy Illness: Personal Crowdfunding Amidst Financial Crisis." *Social Science & Medicine* 187 (August 1, 2017): 233–42. https://doi.org/10.1016/j.socscimed.2017.02.008.

Bernholz, Lucy. "Wiring a New Social Economy: Reflections on Philanthropy in the Digital Age." In *The Routledge Companion to Philanthropy*, edited by Tobias Jung, Susan D. Phillips, and Jenny Harrow, 458–71. Milton Park, UK: Routledge, 2016.

Bhutia, Lhendup. "'If You Give People the Right to Information, They Will Be Ready to Donate.'" *Open The Magazine*, November 1, 2018. https://openthemagazine.com/ cover-stories/wealth-issue-2018/if-you-give-people-the-right-to-information-they-will-be-ready-to-donate/.

Birch, Kean, and Kelly Bronson. "Big Tech." *Science as Culture* 31, no. 1 (January 2, 2022): 1–14. https://doi.org/10.1080/09505431.2022.2036118.

Boodoo, Muhammad Umar, Irene Henriques, and Bryan W. Husted. "Putting the 'Love of Humanity' Back in Corporate Philanthropy: The Case of Health Grants by Corporate

Foundations." *Journal of Business Ethics* 178, no. 2 (April 10, 2021): 415–28. https://doi. org/10.1007/s10551-021-04807-2.

Brodman, James. *Charity and Religion in Medieval Europe*. Washington, DC: CUA Press, 2009.

Brown, Peter. *Through the Eye of a Needle: Wealth, the Fall of Rome, and the Making of Christianity in the West, 350–550 AD*. Princeton: Princeton University Press, 2012. http://ebookcentral.proquest.com/lib/sfu-ebooks/detail.action?docID=980041.

Burtch, Gordon, and Jason Chan. "Investigating the Relationship between Medical Crowdfunding and Personal Bankruptcy in the United States: Evidence of a Digital Divide." *MIS Quarterly* 43, no. 1 (2019): 237–62.

Cadogan, Tim. "A New Chapter in GoFundMe's Story." *GoFundMe Stories* (blog), August 5, 2021. https://medium.com/gofundme-stories/a-new-chapter-in-gofundmes-story-b4cef13a7b73.

Cadogan, Tim. "GoFundMe CEO: Hello Congress, Americans Need Help and We Can't Do Your Job for You." *USA Today*, February 11, 2021. https://www.usatoday.com/story/opinion/voices/2021/02/11/gofundme-ceo-congress-pass-covid-relief-desperate-americans-column/4440425001/.

Cadogan, Tim. "Helping Our Community During the Coronavirus Pandemic." *GoFundMe Stories* (blog), March 21, 2020. https://medium.com/gofundme-stories/helping-our-community-during-the-coronavirus-pandemic-147dccd07403.

Cadogan, Tim. "How GoFundMe Will Accelerate Progress Towards Our Vision to Be the Most Helpful Place in the World." *GoFundMe Stories* (blog), January 13, 2022. https://medium.com/gofundme-stories/how-gofundme-will-accelerate-progress-towards-our-vision-to-be-the-most-helpful-place-in-the-world-b1e60c95009e.

Cahn, Susan, and Mollie Hertel. "Millions of Americans Continue to Donate to Crowdfunding Sites to Help Others Pay Medical Bills Despite Economic Hardships of the Pandemic | NORC.Org." NORC at the University of Chicago, April 1, 2021. https://www.norc.org/NewsEventsPublications/PressReleases/Pages/millions-of-americans-continue-to-donate-to-crowdfunding-sites-to-help-others-pay-medical-bills-despite-economic-hardships.aspx.

Calvin, John. *Institutes of the Christian Religion*. Translated by Henry Bevridge. Grand Rapids: Christian Classics Ethereal Library; NetLibrary, 1990. https://search.ebscohost.com/login.aspx?direct=true&scope=site&db=nlebk&db=nlabk&AN=2008386.

Canada Helps. "The Giving Report 2018." Toronto: Canada Helps, 2018. https://www.canadahelps.org/media/The-Giving-Report-2018.pdf.

Canadian Anti-Hate Network. "The 'Freedom Convoy' Is Nothing But a Vehicle for the Far Right." Canadian Anti-Hate Network, January 27, 2022. https://www.antihate.ca/the_freedom_convoy_is_nothing_but_a_vehicle_for_the_far_right.

Caviola, Lucius, Stefan Schubert, and Joshua D. Greene. "The Psychology of (In)Effective Altruism." *Trends in Cognitive Sciences* 25, no. 7 (2021): 596–607. https://doi.org/10.1016/j.tics.2021.03.015.

Caviola, Lucius, Stefan Schubert, and Jason Nemirow. "The Many Obstacles to Effective Giving." *Judgment and Decision Making* 15, no. 2 (2020): 159–72.

Chambers, Clare, and Philip Parvin. "Coercive Redistribution and Public Agreement: Re-Evaluating the Libertarian Challenge of Charity." *Critical Review of International Social and Political Philosophy* 13, no. 1 (2010): 93–114.

Chan, Chak Kwan. "Caring for the Poor Versus Degrading the Poor: The Case of Hong Kong Newspaper Charity." *International Journal of Social Welfare* 13, no. 3 (2004): 266–75. https://doi.org/10.1111/j.1369-6866.2004.00320.x.

Chapman, Cassandra M., Barbara M. Masser, and Winnifred R. Louis. "Identity Motives in Charitable Giving: Explanations for Charity Preferences from a Global Donor Survey." *Psychology & Marketing* 37, no. 9 (2020): 1277–91. https://doi.org/10.1002/mar.21362.

Charities Aid Foundation. "UK Giving 2019." Kent/London: Charities Aid Foundation, 2019. https://www.cafonline.org/docs/default-source/about-us-publications/caf-uk-giving-2019-report-an-overview-of-charitable-giving-in-the-uk.pdf?sfvrsn=c4a29a40_4.

Chiesa, Carolina Dalla, and Christian Handke. "Crowdfunding." In *Handbook of Cultural Economics, Third Edition*, edited by Ruth Towse and Trilce Navarrete Hernandez, 158–67. Cheltenham, UK: Edward Elgar Publishing, 2020. https://www-elgaronline-com.proxy.lib.sfu.ca/view/edcoll/9781788975797/9781788975797.00023.xml.

Chuffed. "How It Works—Running a Campaign." Chuffed. Accessed May 10, 2022. https://chuffed.org/how-it-works-crowdfunding/create-your-page.

Chuffed. "Our Story | Non-Profit Charity and Social Enterprise Fundraising." Chuffed. Accessed April 27, 2022. https://chuffed.org/about.

Cinone, Danielle. "As Border Wall GoFundMe Rakes in Millions, Here Are Six Other Campaigns You Should Check Out." *New York Daily News*, December 21, 2018, sec. News, U.S. https://www.nydailynews.com/news/national/ny-news-gofundme-border-wall-top-gofundme-20181221-story.html.

Clotfelter, Charles T. "Tax-Induced Distortions in the Voluntary Sector Symposium: What Is Charity." *Case Western Reserve Law Review* 39, no. 3 (1989 1988): 663–94.

Cohen, Andrew J., Hartley Brody, German Patino, Medina Ndoye, Aron Liaw, Christi Butler, and Benjamin N. Breyer. "Use of an Online Crowdfunding Platform for Unmet Financial Obligations in Cancer Care." *JAMA Internal Medicine* 179, no. 12 (December 1, 2019): 1717–20. https://doi.org/10.1001/jamainternmed.2019.3330.

Corwin Berman, Lila. "How Americans Give: The Financialization of American Jewish Philanthropy." *American Historical Review* 122, no. 5 (2017): 1459–89.

Costello, Amy. "Inequalities In Crowdfunding: An 'American Struggle.'" *Nonprofit Quarterly* (blog), December 7, 2018. https://nonprofitquarterly.org/inequalities-in-crowdfunding-an-american-struggle/.

Coulter, Martin. "GoFundMe Blocks Cash Appeals for Controversial Cancer Clinic." *Financial Times*, March 20, 2019. https://www.ft.com/content/f2c17eaa-4afb-11e9-bbc9-6917dce3dc62.

Coutrot, Isabel Pifarré, Richard Smith, and Laura Cornelsen. "Is the Rise of Crowdfunding for Medical Expenses in the United Kingdom Symptomatic of Systemic Gaps in Health and Social Care?" *Journal of Health Services Research & Policy* 25, no. 3 (July 1, 2020): 181–86. https://doi.org/10.1177/1355819619897949.

Cunningham, Hugh. "The Multi-Layered History of Western Philanthropy." In *The Routledge Companion to Philanthropy*, edited by Tobias Jung, Susan D. Phillips, and Jenny Harrow, 42–55. Milton Park, UK: Routledge, 2016. https://doi.org/10.4324/9781315740324.

Daily, Laura. "Is That Crowdfunding Charity Campaign Legit? Here Are Some Ways to Protect Your Donation." *Washington Post*, October 2, 2018. https://www.washingtonpost.com/lifestyle/home/is-that-crowdfunding-charity-campa

ign-legit-here-are-some-ways-to-protect-your-donation/2018/10/01/3cb97a6a-bdd2-11e8-8792-78719177250f_story.html.

Dale, Elizabeth J., Jacqueline Ackerman, Debra J. Mesch, Una Okonkwo Osili, and Silvia Garcia. "Giving to Women and Girls: An Emerging Area of Philanthropy." *Nonprofit and Voluntary Sector Quarterly* 47, no. 2 (April 1, 2018): 241–61. https://doi.org/10.1177/0899764017744674.

D'arcy-Sharpe, Ann-Marie. "How GoGetFunding Campaigns Are Helping the Homeless." GoGetFunding, April 5, 2021. https://gogetfunding.com/blog/how-gogetfunding-campaigns-are-helping-the-homeless/.

Davis, Jenna. "Finding Financial Help for Pregnant Women." GoFundMe (CA), October 1, 2018. https://ca.gofundme.com/c/blog/financial-help-pregnant-women.

Davis, Jenna. "How to Ask for Help with Money: Five Tips to Make It Easy." GoFund Me, October 23, 2019. https://ca.gofundme.com/c/blog/how-to-ask-for-help-with-money.

Davis, Scott. "Philanthropy as a Virtue in Late Antiquity and the Middle Ages." In *Giving: Western Ideas of Philanthropy*, edited by Jerome B. Schneewind, 1–23. Bloomington: Indiana University Press, 1996.

Dewey, Caitlin. "GoFundMe, the Site That Has Raised Money for Convicted Murderers, Will Draw the Line at Abortion and 'Sorcery.'" *Washington Post*, September 9, 2014. https://www.washingtonpost.com/news/the-intersect/wp/2014/09/09/gofundme-the-site-that-has-raised-money-for-convicted-murderers-will-draw-the-line-at-abortion-and-sorcery/.

Dickson, Janice, and Salmaan Farooqui. "Ottawa Police Probe Desecration of Monuments by Trucker Convoy Protesters." *The Globe and Mail*, January 30, 2022. https://www.theglobeandmail.com/canada/article-ottawa-police-investigate-desecration-of-monuments-by-trucker-convoy/.

Dorn, Sara. "The Sneaky New Way Vaccine Conspiracists Are Raising Cash." *The Daily Beast*, July 16, 2021, sec. us-news. https://www.thedailybeast.com/the-sneaky-new-way-vaccine-conspiracists-are-raising-cash.

Dorsey, C., P. Kim, C. Daniels, L. Sakaue, and B. Savage. "Overcoming the Racial Bias in Philanthropic Funding." *Stanford Social Innovation Review* (blog), May 4, 2020. https://ssir.org/articles/entry/overcoming_the_racial_bias_in_philanthropic_funding.

Dressler, Gabrielle, and Sarah A. Kelly. "Ethical Implications of Medical Crowdfunding: The Case of Charlie Gard." *Journal of Medical Ethics* 44, no. 7 (July 1, 2018): 453–57. https://doi.org/10.1136/medethics-2017-104717.

Durand, Wesley M., Jillian L. Peters, Adam E. M. Eltorai, Saisanjana Kalagara, Adena J. Osband, and Alan H. Daniels. "Medical Crowdfunding for Organ Transplantation." *Clinical Transplantation* 32, no. 6 (2018): e13267.

Duynhoven, Alysha van, Anthony Lee, Ross Michel, Jeremy Snyder, Valorie Crooks, Peter Chow-White, and Nadine Schuurman. "Spatially Exploring the Intersection of Socioeconomic Status and Canadian Cancer-Related Medical Crowdfunding Campaigns." *BMJ Open* 9, no. 6 (June 1, 2019): e026365. https://doi.org/10.1136/bmjopen-2018-026365.

Elmer, Greg, and Sabrina Ward-Kimola. "Political Crowdfunding and Campaigning on GoFundMe." *Canadian Journal of Communication* 46, no. 4 (November 30, 2021): 803–20. https://doi.org/10.22230/cjc.2021v46n4a3935.

Faletsky, Adam, Jane J. Han, Karen J. Lee, Guohai Zhou, Sean Singer, Simon G. Talbot, and Arash Mostaghimi. "Crowdfunding for Gender-Affirming Mastectomy: Balancing

Fundraising with Loss of Privacy." *Annals of Plastic Surgery* 88, no. 4 (April 1, 2022): 372–74. https://doi.org/10.1097/SAP.0000000000002953.

Felton, Kathleen. "Crowdfunding Scams Are Growing. Here's How to Tell Which Cases Are Real." *Health*, February 24, 2016. https://www.health.com/mind-body/crowdfund ing-scams-are-growing-heres-how-to-tell-which-cases-are-real.

Field, Jessica. "Charitable Giving." In *The Routledge Companion to Humanitarian Action*, edited by Roger Mac Ginty and Jenny H. Peterson, 429–39. Milton Park, UK: Routledge, 2015. https://doi.org/10.4324/9780203753422.

Finker, Lazar. "What Crowdfunding Means for Philanthropy." *Lazar Finker's Philanthropy Blog* (blog), April 2, 2018. https://web.archive.org/web/20210506182125/http://laza rfinker.com/what-crowdfunding-means-for-philanthropy/.

Flexport. "Frontline Responders Fund." GoFundMe. Accessed February 21, 2022. https:// www.gofundme.com/f/frontlinerespondersfund.

Fong, Christina M., and Erzo F. P. Luttmer. "Do Fairness and Race Matter in Generosity? Evidence from a Nationally Representative Charity Experiment." *Journal of Public Economics*, Charitable Giving and Fundraising Special Issue, 95, no. 5 (June 1, 2011): 372–94. https://doi.org/10.1016/j.jpubeco.2010.07.010.

Foot, Philippa. *Virtues and Vices and Other Essays in Moral Philosophy*. Oxford: Clarendon Press, 2002.

Fothergill, Alice. "The Stigma of Charity: Gender, Class, and Disaster Assistance." *Sociological Quarterly* 44, no. 4 (September 1, 2003): 659–80. https://doi.org/10.1111/ j.1533-8525.2003.tb00530.x.

Fottrell, Quentin. "GoFundMe Has Revolutionized How We Give, But Is That a Good Thing?" *Town & Country*, June 19, 2019. https://www.townandcountrymag.com/soci ety/money-and-power/a27309524/crowdsourcing-ethics-gofundme-etiquette/.

Fredericks, Paul, and Matthew Rowe. "Charity Fraud." In *Fraud*, edited by Alan Doig, 245–64. New York: Routledge, 2016.

Freedom 2022 Human Rights and Freedoms. "Freedom Convoy 2022." GiveSendGo. Accessed February 24, 2022. http://www.givesendgo.com/FreedomConvoy2022.

Fried, Charles. *An Anatomy of Values: Problems of Personal and Social Choice*. Cambridge, MA: Harvard University Press, 1970.

Fritz, Niki, and Amy Gonzales. "Privacy at the Margins| Not the Normal Trans Story: Negotiating Trans Narratives While Crowdfunding at the Margins." *International Journal of Communication* 12 (March 1, 2018): 1189–1208.

Fundly. "Personal Fundraising: How Individuals Can Raise Money Online." *Fundly* (blog). Accessed March 28, 2022. https://blog.fundly.com/personal-fundraising/.

Gambacorta, David, and Barbara Boyer. "The Truth About the GoFundMe Campaign for a Homeless Veteran: It Was All a Scam." *Philadelphia Inquirer*, November 15, 2018, sec. News, news, news. https://www.inquirer.com/philly/news/homeless-gofundme-scam-kate-mcclure-johnny-bobitt-jr-mark-damico-arrests-charges-20181115.html.

Gautier, Arthur. "Historically Contested Concepts: A Conceptual History of Philanthropy in France, 1712–1914." *Theory and Society* 48, no. 1 (2019): 95–129.

Gelles, David. "The GoFundMe C.E.O. Wants You to Ask: 'How Can I Help?'" *New York Times*, March 4, 2022, sec. Business. https://www.nytimes.com/2022/03/04/business/ tim-cadogan-gofundme-corner-office.html.

Genç, Murat, Stephen Knowles, and Trudy Sullivan. "In Search of Effective Altruists." *Applied Economics* 53, no. 7 (2021): 805–19.

Ghazal, Lauren V., Samantha E. Watson, Brooke Gentry, and Sheila J. Santacroce. "'Both a Life Saver and Totally Shameful': Young Adult Cancer Survivors' Perceptions of Medical Crowdfunding." *Journal of Cancer Survivorship: Research and Practice* 17, no. 2 (February 16, 2022): 332–41. https://doi.org/10.1007/s11764-022-01188-x.

Gilliom, John. *Overseers of the Poor: Surveillance, Resistance, and the Limits of Privacy.* Chicago: University of Chicago Press, 2001.

Gilman, Michele Estrin. "The Return of the Welfare Queen." *The American University Journal of Gender, Social Policy & the Law* 22, no. 2 (2014): 247–79.

Giridharadas, Anand. *Winners Take All: The Elite Charade of Changing the World.* New York: Knopf, 2018.

Givealittle. "Givealittle Terms & Conditions." Givealittle, September 7, 2020. https://give alittle.co.nz/content/howgivealittleworks/terms.

GiveSendGo. "GiveSendGo." GiveSendGo.com. Accessed June 7, 2022. http://givesen dgo.com/.

GiveSendGo. "GiveSendGo Issues Public Statement Regarding Freedom Convoy 2022 Campaign." GiveSendGo, February 7, 2022. https://www.givesendgo.com/site/press release?v=Feb22.

GiveSendGo. "GoFundMe Withholds $5.2 Million from Canadian Truckers Convoy and Campaign Donors." GiveSendGo, January 26, 2022. http://www.givesendgo.com/site/ pressrelease?v=Jan26.

GiveSendGo. "New York Post Says Crowdfunding Site Was Created for Rittinghouse Campaign. A Blatant Misrepresentation." GiveSendGo.com, October 2020. http://giv esendgo.com/site/pressrelease?v=Oct.

GiveSendGo. "Terms and Conditions." GiveSendGo.com, April 7, 2022. http://givesen dgo.com/terms-of-use.

Giving Japan White Paper Research Society. "Giving Japan 2015." Japan Fundraising Association, 2015. https://www.jnpoc.ne.jp/en/reports/selected-translation-of-giving-japan-2015-2/.

Giving USA Foundation. *Giving USA 2021 Annual Report.* Chicago: Giving USA Foundation, 2021.

GlobalGiving. "Crowdfundamentals: A Beginner's Guide to Crowdfunding Success." GlobalGiving, November 30, 2016. https://www.globalgiving.org/learn/beginners-guide-crowdfunding-success/.

GoFundMe. "25 Fundraiser Sharing Tips to Increase Donations." GoFundMe. Accessed June 2, 2021. https://www.gofundme.com/c/fundraising-tips/sharing.

GoFundMe. "About GoFundMe." *GoFundMe* (blog). Accessed June 16, 2022. https://www.gofundme.com/en-ca/c/about-us.

GoFundMe. "Behind the Scenes: A Look at How We Verify Fundraisers During a U.S. Crisis." GoFundMe Stories, October 15, 2021. https://medium.com/gofundme-stories/behind-the-scenes-a-look-at-how-we-verify-fundraisers-during-a-u-s-crisis-b54a4 a26fef6.

GoFundMe. "Determining If a Fundraiser Is Trustworthy." GoFundMe, October 27, 2021. https://support.gofundme.com/hc/en-us/articles/115015913668-Determining-if-a-fundraiser-is-trustworthy.

GoFundMe. "Find Financial Support with These Four Medical Fundraising Tips." *GoFundMe* (blog). Accessed October 25, 2021. https://www.gofundme.com/c/fundrais ing-tips/medical.

GoFundMe. "Five Cancer Fundraising Tips to Help You Raise More Money." GoFundMe. Accessed June 1, 2021. https://www.gofundme.com/c/fundraising-tips/cancer.

GoFundMe. "Five Simple Steps to Creating a Foolproof Fundraising Plan." GoFundMe, December 19, 2019. https://www.gofundme.com/c/blog/fundraising-plan.

GoFundMe. "Fundraising for Individuals: Simple Steps for Success." GoFundMe. Accessed August 3, 2021. https://ca.gofundme.com/c/fundraising-tips/fundraising-for-individuals.

GoFundMe. "Fundraising Team—How to Build in Four Easy Steps." GoFundMe, April 14, 2021. https://www.gofundme.com/c/blog/build-fundraising-team.

GoFundMe. "Gender Confirmation Surgery Costs and Fundraising Guide." GoFundMe, May 24, 2021. https://www.gofundme.com/c/blog/gender-confirmation-surgery.

GoFundMe. "GoFundMe 2022 Year in Help." *GoFundMe* (blog), December 2022. https://www.gofundme.com/c/gofundme-2022-year-in-help.

GoFundMe. "GoFundMe Announces GoFundMe Charity™." *GoFundMe Stories* (blog), October 15, 2019. https://medium.com/gofundme-stories/gofundme-announces-gofundme-charity-21f9efd2e947.

GoFundMe. "GoFundMe Policy on Fundraisers for the Legal Defense of Violent Crimes." *GoFundMe Stories* (blog), November 19, 2021. https://medium.com/gofundme-stor ies/gofundme-policy-on-fundraisers-for-the-legal-defense-of-violent-crimes-975af f8ba5f6.

GoFundMe. "GoFundMe Verification Guidelines." GoFundMe. Accessed January 13, 2022. https://www.gofundme.com/en-ca/c/safety/verification-guidelines.

GoFundMe. "How GoFundMe Protects Donors From Fraudulent Campaigns." *GoFundMe* (blog). Accessed January 12, 2022. https://www.gofundme.com/c/safety/fraudulent-campaigns.

GoFundMe. "How to Ask for Donations for Funeral Expenses: 3 Templates." GoFundMe, June 10, 2019. https://ca.gofundme.com/c/blog/ask-donations-funeral-expenses.

GoFundMe. "How to Get Local Media to Cover Your Fundraiser." *GoFundMe* (blog). Accessed August 13, 2021. https://www.gofundme.com/c/fundraising-tips/local-media.

GoFundMe. "How to Get Rid of Debt: Know Your Options." GoFundMe, December 11, 2018. https://ca.gofundme.com/c/blog/how-to-get-rid-of-debt.

GoFundMe. "How to Help Those Affected by the BC Flooding." *GoFundMe* (blog). Accessed December 2, 2021. https://www.gofundme.com/en-ca/c/act/bc-flooding.

GoFundMe. "How to Write a Fundraiser Update." *GoFundMe* (blog). Accessed October 25, 2021. https://www.gofundme.com/c/fundraising-tips/update.

GoFundMe. "Medical Fundraising Tips: Financial Support When You Need It." GoFundMe. Accessed June 1, 2021. https://www.gofundme.com/c/fundraising-tips/medical.

GoFundMe. "Our New Fundraising Category — Rent, Food + Monthly Bills — Helps Address the Increase in Urgent . . . ." *GoFundMe Stories* (blog), October 22, 2020. https://medium.com/gofundme-stories/our-new-fundraising-category-rent-food-monthly-bills-helps-address-the-increase-in-urgent-4dcd9d941178.

GoFundMe. "Raise More Money with This Medical Crowdfunding Guide." GoFundMe, May 12, 2021. https://www.gofundme.com/c/blog/medical-crowdfunding-guide.

GoFundMe. "Six Online Fundraising Challenges and How to Overcome Them." GoFundMe, February 13, 2018. https://ca.gofundme.com/c/blog/online-fundraising-challenges.

GoFundMe. "Small Business Relief Fund." GoFundMe. Accessed February 21, 2022. https://www.gofundme.com/f/smallbusinessrelieffund.

GoFundMe. "Starting Your First Fundraiser? Here's How to Ask for Donations." GoFundMe, February 16, 2021. https://www.gofundme.com/c/blog/ask-for-donations.

GoFundMe. "Terms of Service." *GoFundMe* (blog), May 12, 2022. https://www.gofundme.com/c/terms.

GoFundMe. "The Beginner's Guide to Viral Fundraising." GoFundMe, January 25, 2017. https://uk.gofundme.com/c/blog/viral-fundraising?lang=en.

GoFundMe. "The Complete Guide to Writing Your GoFundMe Fundraiser Story." GoFundMe, May 3, 2021. https://www.gofundme.com/c/blog/campaign-story.

GoFundMe. "The Data Behind Donations During the COVID-19 Pandemic." *GoFundMe Stories* (blog), September 24, 2020. https://medium.com/gofundme-stories/the-data-behind-donations-during-the-covid-19-pandemic-c40e0f690bfa.

GoFundMe. "The GoFundMe Guarantee." *GoFundMe* (blog). Accessed January 13, 2022. https://www.gofundme.com/c/safety/gofundme-guarantee.

GoFundMe. "The Internet Banded Together in the Search for Gabby Petito—Let's Do the Same for People of Color Who Need Our Support. Here Is a Thread of Verified Fundraisers for Some of Their Families:" Tweet. *Twitter*, September 22, 2021. https://twitter.com/gofundme/status/1440736064998572037.

GoFundMe. "These Social Media Tips Make It Easy to Promote Your Fundraiser." GoFundMe. Accessed June 1, 2021. https://www.gofundme.com/c/fundraising-tips/social-media.

GoFundMe. "Tips to Create a Powerful Fundraising Video." GoFundMe. Accessed June 1, 2021. https://www.gofundme.com/c/fundraising-tips/video.

GoFundMe. "UPDATE: GoFundMe to Refund All Freedom Convoy 2022 Donations (2/5/2022)." *GoFundMe Stories* (blog), February 5, 2022. https://medium.com/gofundme-stories/update-gofundme-statement-on-the-freedom-convoy-2022-fundraiser-4ca7e9714e82.

GoFundMe. "UPDATE: Mila Kunis and Ashton Kutcher Have Reached Their $30M Fundraising Goal. StandWithUkraine Https://T.Co/OH85S0c4Px." Tweet. *Twitter*, March 17, 2022. https://twitter.com/gofundme/status/1504491231417536513.

GoFundMe."Use Psychology to Boost Your Fundraiser." *GoFundMe* (blog), June 26, 2021. https://www.gofundme.com/en-ca/c/blog/psychology-of-giving.

GoFundMe. "Want a Successful Fundraiser? Avoid These Common Mistakes." GoFundMe, January 4, 2021. https://ca.gofundme.com/c/blog/mistakes-successful-fundraisers-avoid.

GoFundMe. "What Is Crowdfunding? The Clear and Simple Answer." *GoFundMe (CA)* (blog). Accessed March 28, 2022. https://www.gofundme.com/en-ca/c/crowdfunding.

GoFundMe. "Why the Right Images for Your Fundraiser Are the Key to Success." GoFundMe. Accessed June 1, 2021. https://www.gofundme.com/c/fundraising-tips/image.

GoFundMe. "Write a Thank You Letter for a Donation From a Sponsor." *GoFundMe* (blog), March 10, 2016. https://www.gofundme.com/c/blog/donation-thank-you-letter.

GoFundMe Trust & Safety Team. "Guidance: COVID-19 Vaccine Fundraising on GoFundMe." *GoFundMe Stories* (blog), October 8, 2021. https://medium.com/gofundme-stories/guidance-covid-19-vaccine-fundraising-on-gofundme-4e480d7ed17d.

GoFundMe.Org. "Frequently Asked Questions." *GoFundMe.Org* (blog). Accessed April 22, 2022. https://www.gofundme.org/faq/.

Goldberg, Daniel S. "Doubt & Social Policy: The Long History of Malingering in Modern Welfare States." *Journal of Law, Medicine & Ethics* 49, no. 3 (2021): 385–93. https://doi.org/10.1017/jme.2021.58.

Gonzales, Amy, and Nicole Fritz. "Prioritizing Flexibility and Intangibles: Medical Crowdfunding for Stigmatized Individuals." In *Proceedings of the 2017 CHI Conference on Human Factors in Computing Systems*, 2371–75. CHI '17. New York: Association for Computing Machinery, 2017. https://doi.org/10.1145/3025453.3025647.

Gonzales, Amy L., Elizabeth Y. Kwon, Teresa Lynch, and Nicole Fritz. "'Better Everyone Should Know Our Business than We Lose Our House': Costs and Benefits of Medical Crowdfunding for Support, Privacy, and Identity." *New Media & Society* 20, no. 2 (February 1, 2018): 641–58. https://doi.org/10.1177/1461444816667723.

Gonzalez, Adrienne. "GoFraudMe | GoFundMe Fraud, Scams, Crowdfunding Ethics, GoFundMe News." GoFraudMe. Accessed June 21, 2022. http://gofraudme.com/.

Gosk, Stephanie, and Conor Ferguson. "GoFundMe Says It Has an Answer for Fraud." *NBC News*, April 8, 2019. https://www.nbcnews.com/news/us-news/after-new-jersey-scam-gofundme-says-it-has-answer-fraud-n992086.

Graham, Meg. "Competitor Acquires Chicago-Based Crowdfunding Site GiveForward." *Chicago Tribune*, March 29, 2017. https://www.chicagotribune.com/business/blue-sky/ct-giveforward-youcaring-acquisition-bsi-20170329-story.html.

Greene, Jay. "Amazon Values Same-Sex Equality, but Its Charitable-Giving Plan Clashes." *Seattle Times*, December 2, 2014, sec. Business. https://www.seattletimes.com/business/amazon-values-same-sex-equality-but-its-charitable-giving-plan-clashes-1/.

Greene, Jay, and Jeremy Merrill. "This Amazon Program Has Funneled Thousands to Anti-Vax Activists During the Pandemic." *Washington Post*, December 11, 2021. https://www.washingtonpost.com/technology/2021/12/11/amazon-anti-vaccine-charity/.

Grim, John A. "A Comparative Study in Native American Philanthropy." In *Philanthropy in the World's Traditions*, edited by Warren F. Ilchman, Stanley N. Katz, and Edward L. Queen II, 25–53. Bloomington: Indiana University Press, 1998.

Guy, Sam. "Access to Justice on the Market: An Empirical Case Study on the Dynamics of Crowdfunding Judicial Reviews." *Public Law*, no. 4 (October 2021): 678–87. https://doi.org/10.3316/agispt.20210930054184.

Harris, Ainsley. "How Crowdfunding Platform GoFundMe Has Created a $3 Billion Digital Safety Net." *Fast Company*, February 13, 2017. https://www.fastcompany.com/3067472/how-crowdfunding-platform-gofundme-has-created-a-3-billion-digital.

Hastings, Deborah. "N.J. Deli Owner Who Ignited Fury with 'White History Month' Goes out of Business." *New York Daily News*, April 17, 2015, sec. U.S. https://www.nydailynews.com/news/national/n-man-business-white-history-month-article-1.2189508.

Headworth, Spencer. *Policing Welfare: Punitive Adversarialism in Public Assistance.* Chicago: University of Chicago Press, 2021.

Heim, Maria. *Theories of the Gift in South Asia: Hindu, Buddhist, and Jain Reflections on Dana.* New York: Taylor & Francis Group, 2004. http://ebookcentral.proquest.com/lib/sfu-ebooks/detail.action?docID=183017.

Heller, Nathan. "The Hidden Cost of GoFundMe Health Care." *New Yorker*, June 24, 2019. https://www.newyorker.com/magazine/2019/07/01/the-perverse-logic-of-gofundme-health-care.

Hill, T. E. "Duties and Choices in Philanthropic Giving: Kantian Perspectives." In *The Ethics of Giving: Philosophers' Perspectives on Philanthropy*, edited by Paul Woodruff, 13–39. Oxford: Oxford University Press, 2018.

Hindle, Steve. "Dependency, Shame and Belonging: Badging the Deserving Poor, c. 1550–1750." *Cultural and Social History* 1, no. 1 (January 1, 2004): 6–35. https://doi.org/10.1191/1478003804cs0003oa.

Hollis, Aidan, and Arthur Sweetman. "The Life-Cycle of a Microfinance Institution: The Irish Loan Funds." *Journal of Economic Behavior & Organization* 46, no. 3 (2001): 291–311. https://doi.org/10.1016/S0167-2681(01)00179-2.

Hum, Peter. "Fundraiser Seeks to Feed Ottawa Front-Line Medical Staff with Restaurant Meals." *Ottawa Citizen*, January 12, 2022. https://ottawacitizen.com/news/local-news/fundraiser-seeks-to-feed-ottawa-front-line-medical-staff-with-restaurant-meals.

Hume, David. *An Enquiry Concerning the Principles of Morals*. Edited by Tom L. Beauchamp. Revised edition. Oxford/New York: Oxford University Press, 1998.

Humphreys, Robert. "Scientific Charity in Victorian London. Claims and Achievements of the Charity Organisation Society, 1869–1890." *London School of Economics and Political Science, Working Papers* 14 (1993): 1–38.

Hungerman, Daniel M. "Race and Charitable Church Activity." *Economic Inquiry* 46, no. 3 (2008): 380–400. https://doi.org/10.1111/j.1465-7295.2007.00104.x.

Husted, Bryan W., Dima Jamali, and Walid Saffar. "Near and Dear? The Role of Location in CSR Engagement." *Strategic Management Journal* 37, no. 10 (2016): 2050–70. https://doi.org/10.1002/smj.2437.

Igra, Mark. "Donor Financial Capacity Drives Racial Inequality in Medical Crowdsourced Funding." *Social Forces* 100, no. 4 (2022): 1856–83. https://doi.org/10.1093/sf/soab076.

Igra, Mark, Nora Kenworthy, Cadence Luchsinger, and Jin-Kyu Jung. "Crowdfunding as a Response to COVID-19: Increasing Inequities at a Time of Crisis." *Social Science & Medicine* 282 (2021): 114105. https://doi.org/10.1016/j.socscimed.2021.114105.

Ilinetsky, Gabi. "Save Yoel and Yael." gofundme.com. Accessed August 8, 2021. https://www.gofundme.com/f/cper2x-save-yoel-and-yael.

ImpactGuru. "About Us." ImpactGuru.com. Accessed March 24, 2022. https://www.impactguru.com/about-us.

ImpactGuru. "Donate Monthly to Support Patients with Critical Illness." ImpactGuru. Accessed April 27, 2022. https://www.impactguru.com/monthly/save-patients-with-critical-illness.

ImpactGuru. "Raise Funds for Covid Patients Online in India." ImpactGuru. Accessed February 22, 2022. https://www.impactguru.com/fight-covid.

Imperial Health Charity. "Support Our COVID-19 Relief Fund." JustGiving. Accessed February 22, 2022. https://www.justgiving.com/campaign/help-our-nhs.

Indiana University Lilly Family School of Philanthropy. "The Digital for Good: Brazil," May 2022. https://globalindices.iupui.edu/additional-research/Brazil.html.

Indiana University Lilly Family School of Philanthropy. "The Digital for Good: United Kingdom," May 2022. https://globalindices.iupui.edu/additional-research/united-kingdom.html.

Indiana University Lilly Family School of Philanthropy. "The Global Philanthropy Environment Index 2022," March 10, 2022. https://scholarworks.iupui.edu/handle/1805/28098.

Inman, Phillip. "Charities Go Online to Stay in the Running and Reach the Next Generation of Givers." *The Guardian*, March 25, 2008. https://www.theguardian.com/society/2008/mar/25/voluntarysector.charitablegiving.

Isaac, Mike, and Kellen Browning. "Fact-Checked on Facebook and Twitter, Conservatives Switch Their Apps." *New York Times*, November 11, 2020, sec. Technology. https://www.nytimes.com/2020/11/11/technology/parler-rumble-newsmax.html.

Jan Kamps, Haje. "GoFundMe Hits 25m Donors and $2b Raised on Its Giving Platform." *TechCrunch* (blog), May 10, 2016. https://social.techcrunch.com/2016/05/10/gofundme-2bn-raised/.

Jin, Pingyue. "Medical Crowdfunding in China: Empirics and Ethics." *Journal of Medical Ethics* 45, no. 8 (2019): 538–44.

JPost.com Staff. "Israeli Parents Crowd-Fund to Save Twin-Babies." *Jerusalem Post*, December 17, 2018. https://m.jpost.com/israel-news/israeli-parents-crowd-fund-to-save-twin-babies-574545/amp.

JustGiving. "About." JustGiving. Accessed March 24, 2022. https://justgiving.blackbaud.com/about.

JustGiving. "COVID-19." JustGiving. Accessed February 22, 2022. https://justgiving.blackbaud.com/inspiration/how-to-help/covid-19.

JustGiving. "I Have Concerns about a Crowdfunding Page, What Should I Do?" JustGiving. Accessed January 12, 2022. https://help.justgiving.com/hc/en-us/articles/20287160tmi2-I-have-concerns-about-a-Crowdfunding-Page-what-should-I-do-.

Kallman, Meghan Elizabeth. "Allocative Failures: Networks and Institutions in International Grantmaking Relationships." *VOLUNTAS: International Journal of Voluntary and Nonprofit Organizations* 28, no. 2 (April 1, 2017): 745–72. https://doi.org/10.1007/s11266-017-9827-3.

Kant, Immanuel. *Lectures on Ethics*. Edited by Peter Heath and J. B. Schneewind. Translated by Peter Heath. The Cambridge Edition of the Works of Immanuel Kant. Cambridge: Cambridge University Press, 1997. https://doi.org/10.1017/CBO9781107049512.

Katz, Michael B. *In the Shadow of the Poorhouse: A Social History of Welfare in America*. New York: Basic Books, 1996. http://hdl.handle.net/2027/mdp.39015040507918.

Katz, Michael B. *The Undeserving Poor: America's Enduring Confrontation with Poverty: Fully Updated and Revised*, 2nd edition. Oxford: Oxford University Press, 2013.

Kenworthy, Nora, Zhihang Dong, Anne Montgomery, Emily Fuller, and Lauren Berliner. "A Cross-Sectional Study of Social Inequities in Medical Crowdfunding Campaigns in the United States." *PLOS ONE* 15, no. 3 (March 5, 2020): e0229760. https://doi.org/10.1371/journal.pone.0229760.

Kenworthy, Nora J. "Crowdfunding and Global Health Disparities: An Exploratory Conceptual and Empirical Analysis." *Globalization and Health* 15, no. 1 (November 28, 2019): 71. https://doi.org/10.1186/s12992-019-0519-1.

Ketto. "Acknowledging Our Frontline COVID-19 Warriors on India's 75th Independence Day." Ketto, August 16, 2021. https://www.ketto.org/blog/acknowledging-our-frontline-covid-19-warriors-on-indias-75th-independence-day.

Ketto. "Charitable Donations as a Means of Tax Deduction." Ketto, July 6, 2021. https://www.ketto.org/blog/how-to-maximize-your-tax-deduction.

Ketto. "Disclaimer." Ketto. Accessed February 2, 2022. https://www.ketto.org/terms-of-use.php.

Ketto. "Ketto's Impact During the Coronavirus (COVID-19) Pandemic." Ketto, May 31, 2021. https://www.ketto.org/blog/kettos-impact-during-the-coronavirus-pandemic.

Ketto. "The Role of Crowdfunding in Pandemic," January 19, 2022. https://www.ketto.org/blog/role-of-crowdfunding-in-pandemic.

Kilikar, Divya. "How to Write a Medical Fundraising Story." ImpactGuru, March 19, 2018. https://www.impactguru.com/blog/donation-appeal-for-medical-fundraiser.

Kim, Jennifer G., Hwajung Hong, and Karrie Karahalios. "Understanding Identity Presentation in Medical Crowdfunding." In *Proceedings of the 2018 CHI Conference on Human Factors in Computing Systems*, 1–12, 2018.

Kim, Jennifer G., Ha Kyung Kong, Karrie Karahalios, Wai-Tat Fu, and Hwajung Hong. "The Power of Collective Endorsements: Credibility Factors in Medical Crowdfunding Campaigns." In *Proceedings of the 2016 CHI Conference on Human Factors in Computing Systems*, 4538–49, 2016.

Kim, Jennifer G., Kristen Vaccaro, Karrie Karahalios, and Hwajung Hong. "'Not by Money Alone' Social Support Opportunities in Medical Crowdfunding Campaigns." In *Proceedings of the 2017 ACM Conference on Computer Supported Cooperative Work and Social Computing*, 1997–2009, 2017.

Kinosian, Sarah. "Venezuelans Rely on the Kindness of Strangers to Pay for COVID-19 Treatment." *Reuters*, October 4, 2021, sec. Americas. https://www.reuters.com/world/americas/venezuelans-rely-kindness-strangers-pay-covid-19-treatment-2021-10-04/.

Klein, Michael. "Yelp Backs Down After Creating Restaurant GoFundMe Campaigns Without Consent." *Philadelphia Inquirer*, March 27, 2020, sec. Coronavirus, health, coronavirus. https://www.inquirer.com/health/coronavirus/yelp-gofundme-restaurants-contribution-campaign-unauthorized-automatic-20200327.html.

Kneese, Tamara. "Pay It Forward: Crowdfunding Is Not Mutual Aid." *Real Life*, June 22, 2020. https://reallifemag.com/pay-it-forward/.

Knowledge at Wharton Staff. "Can You Spare a Quarter? Crowdfunding Sites Turn Fans into Patrons of the Arts." Knowledge@Wharton, December 8, 2010. https://knowledge.wharton.upenn.edu/article/can-you-spare-a-quarter-crowdfunding-sites-turn-fans-into-patrons-of-the-arts/.

Knowlton, Thomas. "Exclusive Interview: Vancouver's FundRazr Raises the Bar with Monumental PayPal and Facebook Collaboration." *BrainStation* (blog), August 8, 2010. https://brainstation.io/magazine/exclusive-interview-vancouvers-fundrazr-raises-the-bar-with-monumental-paypal-and-facebook-collaboration.

Kochuyt, Thierry. "God, Gifts and Poor People: On Charity in Islam." *Social Compass* 56, no. 1 (March 1, 2009): 98–116. https://doi.org/10.1177/0037768608100345.

Kropotkin, Peter. *Mutual Aid: A Factor in Evolution*. London: McClure, Philips & Company, 1902.

Lake, Howard. "JustGiving Total Raised Passes $4 Billion." *UK Fundraising* (blog), June 6, 2016. https://fundraising.co.uk/2016/06/06/justgiving-total-raised-passes-4-billion/.

Lavin, Talia. "Crowdfunding Hate in the Name of Christ." *The Nation*, April 5, 2021. https://www.thenation.com/article/society/givesendgo-crowdfunding-extremism/.

Lawler, Ryan. "Crowdfunding Startup GoFundMe Launches Member Network Program, Now Sharing Revenue With Partners." *TechCrunch* (blog), September 25, 2012. https://social.techcrunch.com/2012/09/25/gofundme-partner-program/.

Lawler, Ryan. "Crowdfunding Startup GoFundMe, Which Is Like KickStarter for the Rest of Us, Is Pulling in $2 Million a Month." *TechCrunch* (blog), June 29, 2012. https://social.techcrunch.com/2012/06/29/gofundme/.

Lechterman, Theodore. *The Tyranny of Generosity: Why Philanthropy Corrupts Our Politics and How We Can Fix It.* New York: Oxford University Press, 2021.

LeClair, Mark S. *Philanthropy in Transition.* New York: Palgrave Macmillan US, 2014. https://doi.org/10.1057/9781137394484_1.

Lee, Dave. "GoFundMe: Hope, but No Solution, for the Needy." *BBC News*, February 12, 2019, sec. Technology. https://www.bbc.com/news/technology-47156142.

Lee, Sumin, and Vili Lehdonvirta. "New Digital Safety Net or Just More 'Friendfunding'? Institutional Analysis of Medical Crowdfunding in the United States." *Information, Communication & Society*, December 30, 2020, 1–25. https://doi.org/10.1080/13691 18X.2020.1850838.

Levy, Neil. "Against Philanthropy, Individual and Corporate." *Business & Professional Ethics Journal* 21, no. 3/4 (2002): 95–108.

Lewis-Kraus, Gideon. "Sam Bankman-Fried, Effective Altruism, and the Question of Complicity." *The New Yorker*, December 1, 2022. https://www.newyorker.com/news/annals-of-inquiry/sam-bankman-fried-effective-altruism-and-the-question-of-com plicity.

Lich, Tamara. "Freedom Convoy 2022." GoFundMe, January 20, 2022. https://web.arch ive.org/web/20220120205555/https://www.gofundme.com/f/taking-back-our-free dom-convoy-2022.

Lich, Tamara. "Taking Back Our Freedom Convoy 2022." GoFundMe, January 15, 2022. https://web.archive.org/web/20220115003941/https://www.gofundme.com/f/taking-back-our-freedom-convoy-2022.

Lilly Family School of Philanthropy. "Crowdfunding." Lilly Family School of Philanthropy. Accessed February 22, 2022. https://philanthropy.iupui.edu/research/covid/crowd funding.html.

Lorinc, Jacob. "The Big Business of GiveSendGo: U.S. Crowdfunding Site Earned at Least $735,000 on Ottawa Protests Alone, Leaked Data Shows." *Toronto Star*, February 25, 2022, sec. Business. https://www.thestar.com/business/2022/02/25/the-big-business-of-givesendgo-us-crowdfunding-site-earned-at-least-735000-on-ottawa-protests-alone-leaked-data-shows.html.

Loseke, Donileen R. "'The Whole Spirit of Modern Philanthropy': The Construction of the Idea of Charity, 1912–1992." *Social Problems* 44, no. 4 (1997): 425–44.

Loseke, Donileen R., and Kirsten Fawcett. "Appealing Appeals: Constructing Moral Worthiness, 1912–1917." *Sociological Quarterly* 36, no. 1 (1995): 61–77.

Lublóy, Ágnes. "Medical Crowdfunding in a Healthcare System with Universal Coverage: An Exploratory Study." *BMC Public Health* 20, no. 1 (November 9, 2020): 1672. https://doi.org/10.1186/s12889-020-09693-3.

Lucas, Evie. "Reinventing the Rattling Tin: How UK Charities Use Facebook in Fundraising." *International Journal of Nonprofit and Voluntary Sector Marketing* 22, no. 2 (2017): e1576. https://doi.org/10.1002/nvsm.1576.

Lukk, Martin, Erik Schneiderhan, and Joanne Soares. "Worthy? Crowdfunding the Canadian Health Care and Education Sectors." *Canadian Review of Sociology/Revue Canadienne de Sociologie* 55, no. 3 (2018): 404–24.

Lunden, Ingrid. "GoFundMe Acquires CrowdRise to Expand to Fundraising for Charities." *TechCrunch* (blog), January 10, 2017. https://social.techcrunch.com/2017/01/10/gofundme-buys-crowdrise-to-expand-to-fundraising-for-charities/.

Lunden, Ingrid. "GoFundMe Acquires YouCaring as Charitable Crowdfunding Continues to Consolidate." *TechCrunch* (blog), April 3, 2018. https://social.techcrunch.

com/2018/04/03/gofundme-acquires-youcaring-as-charitable-crowdfunding-contin ues-to-consolidate/.

Lunden, Ingrid. "GoFundMe, Now with $4B in Donations from 40M Donors, Plots Euro Expansion." *TechCrunch* (blog), June 9, 2017. https://social.techcrunch.com/2017/06/ 09/gofundme-europe-expansion/.

Lunden, Ingrid. "GoFundMe Passes $3B Raised on Its Platform, Adding $1B in Only the Last 5 Months." *TechCrunch* (blog), October 18, 2016. https://social.techcrunch. com/2016/10/18/gofundme-raises-3b-on-its-platform-raising-1b-in-only-the-last-5-months/.

Lunden, Ingrid. "GoFundMe Rebrands the Direct Impact Fund as GoFundMe.Org for Wider Charitable Giving." *TechCrunch* (blog), April 11, 2019. https://social.techcru nch.com/2019/04/11/gofundme-rebrands-the-direct-impact-fund-as-gofundme-org-for-wider-charitable-giving/.

Lunden, Ingrid, and Anthony Ha. "Yelp Pauses GoFundMe COVID-19 Fundraising After Opt-out Outcry." *TechCrunch* (blog), March 27, 2020. https://social.techcrunch.com/ 2020/03/27/yelp-pauses-gofundme-covid-19-fundraising-after-opt-out-outcry/.

Lyons, Kim. "Indiegogo Switches Gears to More Closely Screen Crowdfunding Campaigns." *The Verge* (blog), November 3, 2021. https://www.theverge.com/2021/11/ 3/22757421/indiegogo-crowdfunding-campaign-screening-fraud-gofundme.

Mackler, Aaron L. "Judaism, Justice, and Access to Health Care." *Kennedy Institute of Ethics Journal* 1, no. 2 (1991): 143–61.

Maclean, Mairi, Charles Harvey, Ruomei Yang, and Frank Mueller. "Elite Philanthropy in the United States and United Kingdom in the New Age of Inequalities." *International Journal of Management Reviews* 23, no. 3 (2021): 330–52. https://doi.org/10.1111/ ijmr.12247.

Madden, Mary, Michele Gilman, Karen Levy, and Alice Marwick. "Privacy, Poverty, and Big Data: A Matrix of Vulnerabilities for Poor Americans." *Washington University Law Review* 95, no. 1 (2017): 53–126.

Mak, Aaron. "The Lucrative Business of Stoking Vaccine Skepticism." *Slate*, August 6, 2021. https://slate.com/technology/2021/08/givesendgo-gofundme-vaccine-skeptics-covid-misinformation.html.

Marche, Stephen. "Go Fund Yourself." *Mother Jones*, February 2018. https://www.moth erjones.com/politics/2018/01/go-fund-yourself-health-care-popularity-contest/.

Marfatia, Jasmine. "Easy Ways to Raise Funds for Cancer Treatment in India." ImpactGuru, July 24, 2018. https://www.impactguru.com/blog/cancer-treatment-in-india.

Marler, Will. "'You Can Connect with Like, the World!': Social Platforms, Survival Support, and Digital Inequalities for People Experiencing Homelessness." *Journal of Computer-Mediated Communication* 27, no. 1 (January 1, 2022): 1–19. https://doi.org/ 10.1093/jcmc/zmab020.

Marquis, Christopher, Mary Ann Glynn, and Gerald F. Davis. "Community Isomorphism and Corporate Social Action." *Academy of Management Review* 32, no. 3 (2007): 925–45. https://doi.org/10.2307/20159342.

Masters, Blake. "Reclaiming Our Independence from Big Tech." *Wall Street Journal*, September 6, 2021, sec. Opinion. https://www.wsj.com/articles/big-tech-regulation-apple-google-facebook-twitter-amazon-addiction-antitrust-censorship-content-mod eration-section-230-11630959185.

Mauss, Marcel. *The Gift: The Form and Reason for Exchange in Archaic Societies.* New York: W. W. Norton & Company, 2000.

Max, Sarah. "A Plucky Startup Ditches 'Coin Piggy' Roots and Finds Its Mission." NBC News, July 1, 2013. https://www.nbcnews.com/id/wbna52363496.

McKechnie, Carolyn Victoria. "What Is a Crowdfunding Platform?" *Inside Philanthropy* (blog). Accessed March 28, 2022. https://www.insidephilanthropy.com/explainers/what-is-a-crowdfunding-platform.

McKitrick, Matthew, Nadine Schuurman, Valorie A. Crooks, and Jeremy Snyder. "Spatial and Temporal Patterns in Canadian COVID-19 Crowdfunding Campaigns." *PLOS ONE* 16, no. 8 (August 23, 2021): e0256204. https://doi.org/10.1371/journal.pone.0256204.

McLaughlin, Ross, and Espe Currie. "Donating Online? Here's How to Make Sure the Campaign Isn't Fake." *CTV News*, January 22, 2020. https://bc.ctvnews.ca/donating-online-here-s-how-to-make-sure-the-campaign-isn-t-fake-1.4772754.

McSheffrey, Elizabeth. "Here's How to Support B.C. Residents Impacted by Floods, Landslides." Global News, November 16, 2021. https://globalnews.ca/news/8378542/help-bc-residents-flooding-landslides/.

Mesch, Debra, Una Osili, Jacqueline Ackerman, and Elizabeth Dale. "How and Why Women Give: Current and Future Directions for Research on Women's Philanthropy." Working Paper. Indianapolis: Indiana University Lilly Family School of Philanthropy, May 2015. https://scholarworks.iupui.edu/handle/1805/6983.

Mesch, Debra, Una Osili, Jacqueline Ackerman, and Elizabeth Dale. "Where Do Men and Women Give? Gender Differences in the Motivations and Purposes for Charitable Giving." Working Paper. Indianapolis: Indiana University Lilly Family School of Philanthropy, September 2015. https://scholarworks.iupui.edu/handle/1805/6985.

Milaap. "COVID-19: The Only Way to Fight This, Is Together." Milaap. Accessed February 22, 2022. https://milaap.org/communities/covid-19.

Milaap. "Terms and Conditions of Milaap." Milaap, February 8, 2019. https://milaap.org/about-us/terms-and-conditions.

Milaap. "The Journey So Far of Crowdfunding in India." Milaap. Accessed March 22, 2022. https://milaap.org/about-us/overview.

Mill, John Stuart. *Utilitarianism*. Milton Park, UK: Routledge, 2016.

Milton, Chiara. "3 Life Lessons That Autistic Children Teach Us." ImpactGuru, July 17, 2021. https://www.impactguru.com/blog/3_lessons_to_learn_from_autistic_children_and_see_the_world_differently.

Milton, Diamond. "Kudos to These Kids For Putting Up a Brave Fight." ImpactGuru, July 28, 2021. https://www.impactguru.com/blog/How-These-Kids-Are-Putting-Up-A-Brave-Fight-Against-Cancer.

Moine, Alix, and Daphnée Papiasse. "Evidence from France: How Crowdfunding Is Being Used to Support the Response to COVID-19." *LSE European Politics and Policy (EUROPP) Blog* (blog), April 24, 2020. http://eprints.lse.ac.uk/105226/1/europpblog_2020_04_24_evidence_from_france_how_crowdfunding_is_being.pdf.

Mollat, Michel. *The Poor in the Middle Ages: An Essay in Social History*. New Haven: Yale University Press, 1986.

Monroe, Rachel. "When GoFundMe Gets Ugly." *The Atlantic*, November 2019. https://www.theatlantic.com/magazine/archive/2019/11/gofundme-nation/598369/.

Morgan Gore, Erin, and Breanna DiGiammarino. "Crowdfunding for Nonprofits." *Stanford Social Innovation Review*, May 22, 2014. https://ssir.org/articles/entry/crowdfunding_for_nonprofits.

Mottiar, Shauna, and Mvuselelo Ngcoya. "Indigenous Philanthropy: Challenging Western Preconceptions." In *The Routledge Companion to Philanthropy*, edited by Tobias Jung, Susan Phillips, and Jenny Harrow, 171–81. Milton Park, UK: Routledge, 2016.

Musu, Costanza, and Patrick Leblond. "How Authorities Are Targeting the 'Freedom Convoy' Money via the Emergencies Act." *The Conversation*. Accessed February 24, 2022. http://theconversation.com/how-authorities-are-targeting-the-freedom-convoy-money-via-the-emergencies-act-177204.

MyCause. "Your Essential Crowdfunding Page Checklist." MyCause, February 29, 2016. https://www.mycause.com.au/blog/your-essential-crowdfunding-page-checklist.

Nagel, Jonas, and Michael R. Waldmann. "Deconfounding Distance Effects in Judgments of Moral Obligation." *Journal of Experimental Psychology: Learning, Memory, and Cognition* 39, no. 1 (2013): 237–52.

Neuwelt-Kearns, Caitlin, Tom Baker, Octavia Calder-Dawe, Ann E. Bartos, and Susan Wardell. "Getting the Crowd to Care: Marketing Illness Through Health-Related Crowdfunding in Aotearoa New Zealand." *Environment and Planning A: Economy and Space*, April 23, 2021, 1–19. https://doi.org/10.1177/0308518X211009535.

Null, Clair. "Warm Glow, Information, and Inefficient Charitable Giving." *Journal of Public Economics*, Charitable Giving and Fundraising Special Issue, 95, no. 5 (2011): 455–65. https://doi.org/10.1016/j.jpubeco.2010.06.018.

Ohlheiser, Abby. "After GoFundMe Shuts down Christian Bakery Crowdfunding, It Bans 'Discriminatory' Campaigns." *Washington Post*, May 1, 2015. https://www.washingtonpost.com/news/acts-of-faith/wp/2015/05/01/after-gofundme-shuts-down-christian-bakery-crowdfunding-it-bans-discriminatory-fundraising-campaigns/.

Oommen, Paul. "Fake Fundraising Campaigns Tarnish Growing Crowdfunding Concept in India." *The News Minute*, August 3, 2021. https://www.thenewsminute.com/article/fake-fundraising-campaigns-tarnish-growing-crowdfunding-concept-india-153349.

Oorschot, Wim van. "Making the Difference in Social Europe: Deservingness Perceptions among Citizens of European Welfare States." *Journal of European Social Policy* 16, no. 1 (February 1, 2006): 23–42. https://doi.org/10.1177/0958928706059829.

O'Reilly, Nicole. "Burlington Woman Accused of Faking Rare Illness for Money." *InsideHalton.Com*, May 8, 2015. https://www.insidehalton.com/news-story/5607038-burlington-woman-accused-of-faking-rare-illness-for-money/.

Osili, Una, Jon Bergdoll, Andrea Pactor, Jacqueline Ackerman, and Peter Houston. "Charitable Crowdfunding: Who Gives, to What, and Why?" Working Paper. Indianapolis: Indiana University Lilly Family School of Philanthropy, March 31, 2021. https://scholarworks.iupui.edu/handle/1805/25515.

Osili, Una, Xiaonan Kou, Cathie Carrigan, Jon Bergdoll, Kinga Horvath, Carol Adelman, and Charles Sellen. "Global Philanthropy Tracker 2020." Working Paper, October 22, 2020. https://scholarworks.iupui.edu/handle/1805/24144.

Osili, Una, Sasha Zarins, Jonathan Bergdoll, Xionan Kou, Ted Grossnickle, Dan Schipp, Andy Canada, et al. "The Impact of Diversity: Understanding How Nonprofit Board Diversity Affects Philanthropy, Leadership, and Board Engagement." Indianapolis: Indiana University Lilly Family School of Philanthropy, February 20, 2018. https://scholarworks.iupui.edu/handle/1805/15239.

Palad, Varsha, and Jeremy Snyder. "'We Don't Want Him Worrying About How He Will Pay to Save His Life': Using Medical Crowdfunding to Explore Lived Experiences with Addiction Services in Canada." *International Journal of Drug Policy* 65 (March 1, 2019): 73–77. https://doi.org/10.1016/j.drugpo.2018.12.016.

Parent, W. A. "Privacy, Morality, and the Law." *Philosophy & Public Affairs* 12, no. 4 (1983): 269–88.

Pathi, Krutika, and Yirmiyan Arthur. "Pandemic Leaves Indians Mired in Massive Medical Debts." *US News & World Report*, July 26, 2021. //www.usnews.com/news/world/artic les/2021-07-26/pandemic-leaves-indians-mired-in-massive-medical-debts.

Paulus, Trena M., and Katherine R. Roberts. "Crowdfunding a 'Real-Life Superhero': The Construction of Worthy Bodies in Medical Campaign Narratives." *Discourse, Context & Media* 21 (2018): 64–72.

Paynter, Ben. "Can GoFundMe Be the Future of Philanthropy If the Alt-Right Uses It to Raise Funds?" *Fast Company*, January 20, 2017. https://www.fastcompany.com/3067 237/can-gofundme-be-the-future-of-philanthropy-if-the-alt-right-uses-it-r.

Paynter, Ben. "How Will the Rise of Crowdfunding Reshape How We Give to Charity?" *Fast Company*, March 13, 2017. https://www.fastcompany.com/3068534/how-will-the-rise-of-crowdfunding-reshape-how-we-give-to-charity-2.

Pellegrino, Edmund D. "The Relationship of Autonomy and Integrity in Medical Ethics." *Bulletin of the Pan American Health Organization* 24, no. 4 (1990): 361–71.

Penslar, Derek. "The Origins of Modern Jewish Philanthropy." In *Philanthropy in the World's Traditions*, edited by Warren F. Ilchman, Stanley N. Katz, and Edward L. Queen, 197–214. Bloomington: Indiana University Press, 1998.

Peshkar, Sushant. "Indians Embrace Crowdfunding to Help Covid-Related Campaigns." Ketto, September 8, 2020. https://www.ketto.org/blog/indians-embrace-crowdfund ing-to-help-covid-related-campaigns.

Pevnick, Ryan. "Democratizing the Nonprofit Sector." *Journal of Political Philosophy* 21, no. 3 (2013): 260–82. https://doi.org/10.1111/j.1467-9760.2011.00414.x.

Pew Charitable Trusts. "Harms Linked to Unapproved Stem Cell Interventions Highlight Need for Greater FDA Enforcement." The Pew Charitable Trusts, June 1, 2021. https:// pew.org/3fKASu5.

Pikora, Jillian. "Fake GoFundMe Removed as Community Rallies for School Bus Driver Dad Killed In I79 Crash." *Cumberland Daily Voice*, November 5, 2021. https://dailyvo ice.com/pennsylvania/cumberland/news/fake-gofundme-removed-as-community-rallies-for-school-bus-driver-dad-killed-in-i79-crash/819552/.

Pilkington, Ed. "Capitol Attack Insurrectionists Flock to Fundraising Websites to Raise Defense Funds." *The Guardian*, December 17, 2021, sec. US news. https://www.theg uardian.com/us-news/2021/dec/17/capitol-attack-insurrectionists-fundraising-defe nse-money.

Pol, Sarah J., Jeremy Snyder, and Samantha J. Anthony. "'Tremendous Financial Burden': Crowdfunding for Organ Transplantation Costs in Canada." *PLOS ONE* 14, no. 12 (December 20, 2019): e0226686. https://doi.org/10.1371/journal.pone.0226686.

Popper, Nathaniel, and Taylor Lorenz. "GoFundMe Confronts Coronavirus Demand." *New York Times*, March 26, 2020, sec. Style. https://www.nytimes.com/2020/03/26/ style/gofundme-coronavirus.html.

Rajwa, Pawel, Philip Hopen, Lin Mu, Andrzej Paradysz, Jakub Wojnarowicz, Cary P. Gross, and Michael S. Leapman. "Online Crowdfunding Response to Coronavirus Disease 2019." *Journal of General Internal Medicine* 35, no. 8 (August 1, 2020): 2482–84. https://doi.org/10.1007/s11606-020-05896-x.

Ray, Siladitya. "The Far-Right Is Flocking to These Alternate Social Media Apps: Not All of Them Are Thrilled." *Forbes*, January 14, 2021. https://www.forbes.com/sites/siladitya

ray/2021/01/14/the-far-right-is-flocking-to-these-alternate-social-media-apps---not-all-of-them-are-thrilled/.

Reed, Alex. "Subsidizing Hate: A Proposal to Reform the Internal Revenue Service's Methodology Test." *Fordham Journal of Corporate and Financial Law* 17, no. 3 (2012): 823–70.

Reich, Rob. *Just Giving: Why Philanthropy Is Failing Democracy and How It Can Do Better.* Princeton: Princeton University Press, 2018.

Reinstein, Julia, Rosie Gray, and Salvador Hernandez. "Former Top Trump Aide Stephen Bannon and 'Build the Wall' Founder Brian Kolfage Have Been Charged with Fraud." BuzzFeed News, August 20, 2020. https://www.buzzfeednews.com/article/juliareinst ein/stephen-bannon-brian-kolfage-wall-charged.

Reynolds, Christopher. "GoFundMe Withholding $4.7M from Trucker Convoy Until Plan Presented | CBC News." CBC, January 25, 2022. https://www.cbc.ca/news/can ada/manitoba/gofundme-withhold-millions-trucker-convoy-1.6327665.

Richard, Chad. "Yelp Teams Up with GoFundMe to Make It Easy for People to Support the Local Businesses They Love." *Yelp - Official Blog* (blog), March 24, 2020. https:// blog.yelp.com/news/yelp-teams-up-with-gofundme-to-make-it-easy-for-people-to-support-the-local-businesses-they-love/.

Ricketts, Andy. "Blackbaud Completes Its £95m Takeover of JustGiving." *Third Sector* (blog), October 4, 2017. https://www.thirdsector.co.uk/article/1446437?utm_source= website&utm_medium=social.

Rider, Gary. "Help Us Find Gabby." GoFundMe. Accessed June 15, 2022. https://www. gofundme.com/f/help-us-find-gabby.

Rife, Bradley. "How Internet Fundraisers Can Help You Cover Emergency Medical Bills." Oprah.com, December 2017. https://www.oprah.com/health_wellness/crowdfund ing-tips-for-emergency-medical-bills.

Rijn, Jordan van, Esteban J. Quiñones, and Bradford L. Barham. "Empathic Concern for Children and the Gender-Donations Gap." *Journal of Behavioral and Experimental Economics* 82 (October 1, 2019): 101462. https://doi.org/10.1016/j.socec.2019.101462.

Roberts, Michael. "Reshaping the Gift Relationship: The London Mendicity Society and the Suppression of Begging in England 1818–1869." *International Review of Social History* 36, no. 2 (August 1991): 201–31. https://doi.org/10.1017/S0020859000110508.

Roberts, Suzanne. "Contexts of Charity in the Middle Ages: Religious, Social, and Civic." In *Giving: Western Ideas of Philanthropy*, edited by Jerome B. Schneewind, 24–53. Bloomington: Indiana University Press, 1996.

Robinson, Ella, and Susan Wardell. "Effects of the COVID-19 Lockdown on the Healthcare Experiences of Medical Crowdfunders in Aotearoa New Zealand." University of Otago, December 23, 2020. https://ourarchive.otago.ac.nz/handle/10523/10615.

Roe, Susan J, and Ryan P. Smith. "Asking for Help: Restaurant Crowdfunding During COVID-19." *Journal of Foodservice Business Research* 26, no. 2 (2023): 164–85. https:// doi.org/10.1080/15378020.2021.2006038.

Romm, Cari. "Is It Fair to Ask the Internet to Pay Your Hospital Bill?" *The Atlantic*, March 12, 2015. https://www.theatlantic.com/health/archive/2015/03/is-it-fair-to-ask-the-internet-to-pay-your-hospital-bill/387577/.

Roose, Kevin. "How 'Save the Children' Is Keeping QAnon Alive." *New York Times*, September 28, 2020, sec. Technology. https://www.nytimes.com/2020/09/28/technol ogy/save-the-children-qanon.html.

Rouzé, Vincent. "Crowdsourcing and Crowdfunding: The Origins of a New System?" In *Cultural Crowdfunding: Platform Capitalism, Labour and Globalization*, edited by Vincent Rouze, 12: 15–33. London: University of Westminster Press, 2019.

Rubenstein, Jennifer C. "The Lessons of Effective Altruism." *Ethics & International Affairs* 30, no. 4 (2016): 511–26. https://doi.org/10.1017/S0892679416000484.

Saleh, Sameh Nagui, Christoph U. Lehmann, and Richard J. Medford. "Early Crowdfunding Response to the COVID-19 Pandemic: Cross-Sectional Study." *Journal of Medical Internet Research 23*, no. 2 (2021): e25429. https://doi.org/10.2196/25429.

Sanfilippo, Ana. *Crowdfunding Best Practices: Steps & Stories to Help You Launch a Successful Campaign*. Pennsauken: BookBaby, 2016.

Sarkar, Brinda. "Ketto Looks to Double Its Headcount in 2021." *Economic Times*, December 24, 2020. https://economictimes.indiatimes.com/tech/startups/ketto-looks-to-double-its-headcount-in-2021/articleshow/79940566.cms.

Saunders-Hastings, Emma. *Private Virtues, Public Vices: Philanthropy and Democratic Equality*. Chicago: University of Chicago Press, 2022. https://press.uchicago.edu/ucp/books/book/chicago/P/bo125362811.html.

Schneewind, J. B. "Philosophical Ideas of Charity: Some Historical Reflections." In *Giving: Western Ideas of Philanthropy*, edited by J. B Schneewind, 54–75. Bloomington: Indiana University Press, 1996.

Seneca, Lucius Annaeus. *On Benefits*. Translated by Miriam Griffin and Brad Inwood. Chicago: University of Chicago Press, 2011.

Sharma, Disha. "Crowdfunding Platform Impact Guru Gets Seed Funding." VCCircle, April 28, 2016. https://www.vccircle.com/crowdfunding-platform-impact-guru-gets-seed-funding.

Sherman, Carter. "Anti-LGTBQ 'Conversion Therapy' Fundraisers Are Still Alive and Well on GoFundMe." *Vice* (blog), September 4, 2020. https://www.vice.com/en/article/jgx9g7/gofundme-is-hosting-anti-lgbtq-conversion-therapy-fundraisers.

Siddiqui, Abdul Hameed, ed., *The Holy Qur'ān: English Translation and Explanatory Notes*. Chicago: Islamic Book Centre, 1977, 2: 83.

Sidel, Mark. "Philanthropy in Asia: Evolving Public Policy." In *The Routledge Companion to Philanthropy*, edited by Tobias Jung, Susan Phillips, and Jenny Harrow, 280–92. Milton Park, UK: Routledge, 2016.

Siegel, Daniel. *Charity and Condescension: Victorian Literature and the Dilemmas of Philanthropy*. Athens: Ohio University Press, 2012. http://muse.jhu.edu/book/13711.

Simmons, Robin. "Claims of Fake GoFundMe Accounts to Help Surfside Victims Prompt Call for Federal Probe." *7 News Miami*, October 19, 2021. https://wsvn.com/news/local/claims-of-fake-gofundme-accounts-to-help-surfside-victims-prompt-call-for-federal-probe/.

Singer, Amy. "Giving Practices in Islamic Societies." *Social Research: An International Quarterly* 80, no. 2 (2013): 341–58.

Singer, Peter. "Famine, Affluence, and Morality." *Philosophy & Public Affairs* 1, no. 3 (1972): 229–43.

Singer, Peter. *The Most Good You Can Do: How Effective Altruism Is Changing Ideas About Living Ethically*. New Haven: Yale University Press, 2015.

Singh, Akanksha. "Medical Crowdfunding Has Become Essential in India, but It's Leaving Many behind." Rest of World, August 4, 2021. https://restofworld.org/2021/crowdfunded-healthcare-in-india/.

Sisco, Matthew R., and Elke U. Weber. "Examining Charitable Giving in Real-World Online Donations." *Nature Communications* 10, no. 1 (September 3, 2019): 3968. https://doi.org/10.1038/s41467-019-11852-z.

Skiba, Katherine. "Beware of Phony Online Fundraisers on GoFundMe." *AARP* (blog), August 16, 2021. https://www.aarp.org/money/scams-fraud/info-2021/beware-of-phony-fundraisers-on-gofundme.html.

Skinner, Annie, and Nigel Thomas. "'A Pest to Society': The Charity Organisation Society's Domiciliary Assessments into the Circumstances of Poor Families and Children." *Children & Society* 32, no. 2 (2018): 133–44.

Skok, Deborah S. "Organized Almsgiving: Scientific Charity and the Society of St. Vincent de Paul in Chicago, 1871–1918." *U.S. Catholic Historian* 16, no. 4 (1998): 19–35.

Smith, David Horton, Sharon Eng, and Kelly Albertson. "The Darker Side of Philanthropy." In *The Routledge Companion to Philanthropy*, edited by Tobias Jung, Susan D. Phillips, and Jenny Harrow, 273–86. New York: Routledge, 2016. https://doi.org/10.4324/9781315740324.ch17.

Smith, Kelly Anne. "How Crowdfunding Changed These People's Lives." Forbes Advisor, December 19, 2020. https://www.forbes.com/advisor/personal-finance/how-crowdfunding-changed-these-peoples-lives/.

Smith, Michelle. "How a Kennedy Built an Anti-Vaccine Juggernaut amid COVID-19." *AP News*, December 15, 2021, sec. Coronavirus pandemic. https://apnews.com/article/how-rfk-jr-built-anti-vaccine-juggernaut-amid-covid-4997be1bcf591fe8b7f1f90d16c9321e.

Snow, Nancy E. "Neo-Aristotelian Virtue Ethics." In *The Oxford Handbook of Virtue*, 321–42. Oxford: Oxford University Press, 2018.

Snyder, Jeremy. "GoFundMe Is Becoming a Social Safety Net—an Inequitable One." Undark Magazine, April 8, 2021. https://undark.org/2021/04/08/gofundme-inequitable-social-safety-net/.

Snyder, Jeremy. "Is GoFundMe Violating Its Own Terms of Service on the 'Freedom Convoy?'" *The Conversation*, February 2, 2022. http://theconversation.com/is-gofundme-violating-its-own-terms-of-service-on-the-freedom-convoy-176147.

Snyder, Jeremy, and Timothy Caulfield. "Patients' Crowdfunding Campaigns for Alternative Cancer Treatments." *Lancet Oncology* 20, no. 1 (2019): 28–29.

Snyder, Jeremy, and Valorie A. Crooks. "Is There Room for Privacy in Medical Crowdfunding?" *Journal of Medical Ethics* 47, no. 12 (2021): e49.

Snyder, Jeremy, Valorie A. Crooks, Annalise Mathers, and Peter Chow-White. "Appealing to the Crowd: Ethical Justifications in Canadian Medical Crowdfunding Campaigns." *Journal of Medical Ethics* 43, no. 6 (June 1, 2017): 364–67. https://doi.org/10.1136/medethics-2016-103933.

Snyder, Jeremy, and Leigh Turner. "Crowdfunding for Stem Cell-Based Interventions to Treat Neurologic Diseases and Injuries." *Neurology* 93, no. 6 (2019): 252–58.

Snyder, Jeremy, and Leigh Turner. "Crowdfunding for Stem Cell-Based Interventions to Treat Neurologic Diseases and Injuries." *Neurology* 93, no. 6 (August 6, 2019): 252–58. https://doi.org/10.1212/WNL.0000000000007838.

Snyder, Jeremy, and Leigh Turner. "Crowdfunding, Stem Cell Interventions and Autism Spectrum Disorder: Comparing Campaigns Related to an International 'Stem Cell Clinic' and US Academic Medical Center." *Cytotherapy* 23, no. 3 (March 1, 2021): 198–202. https://doi.org/10.1016/j.jcyt.2020.09.002.

Snyder, Jeremy, Leigh Turner, and Valorie A. Crooks. "Crowdfunding for Unproven Stem Cell Procedures Spreads Misinformation." STAT, August 6, 2018. https://www.statn ews.com/2018/08/06/crowdfunding-for-unproven-stem-cell-procedures-wastes-money-and-spreads-misinformation/.

Snyder, Jeremy, Leigh Turner, and Valorie A. Crooks. "Crowdfunding for Unproven Stem Cell–Based Interventions." *Journal of the American Medical Association* 319, no. 18 (2018): 1935–36.

Snyder, Jeremy, Marco Zenone, and Timothy Caulfield. "Crowdfunding for Complementary and Alternative Medicine: What Are Cancer Patients Seeking?" *PLOS ONE* 15, no. 11 (November 20, 2020): e0242048. https://doi.org/10.1371/journal. pone.0242048.

Solomon, Rob. "GoFundMe CEO Rob Solomon on the Power of Social Fundraising." *BrainStation* (blog), November 10, 2017. https://brainstation.io/magazine/vanguards-gofundme-rob-solomon.

Solotke, Michael T., Nicole Brussel Faria, Hasna Karim, Shireen Roy, Joseph S. Ross, and Julia Cron. "Exploring Crowdfunding Campaigns for Abortion Services." *Contraception* 102, no. 1 (July 1, 2020): 18–22. https://doi.org/10.1016/j.contracept ion.2020.02.008.

Sonne, Lina, and Divya Chopra. "Global Philanthropy Tracker: India." Indianapolis: Indiana University Lilly Family School of Philanthropy, October 2020. https://scholarworks.iupui.edu/bitstream/handle/1805/24848/india-report21-1.pdf.

Soskis, Benjamin. "Norms and Narratives That Shape US Charitable and Philanthropic Giving." Washington, DC: Urban Institute, March 2021. https://www.urban.org/sites/ default/files/publication/103772/norms-and-narratives-that-shape-us-charitable-and-philanthropic-giving_0.pdf.

Spade, Dean. *Mutual Aid: Building Solidarity During This Crisis (and the Next).* New York: Verso Books, 2020.

Spires, Anthony J. "Organizational Homophily in International Grantmaking: US-Based Foundations and Their Grantees in China." *Journal of Civil Society* 7, no. 3 (September 1, 2011): 305–31. https://doi.org/10.1080/17448689.2011.605005.

Statt, Nick. "Yelp to Stop Auto-Creating Fundraisers After Outrage from Business Owners." The Verge, March 26, 2020. https://www.theverge.com/2020/3/26/21196446/ yelp-gofundme-coronavirus-automatic-opt-in-fundraiser-pause.

Stevenson, Seth. "The Dark Side of GoFundMe." *Slate*, December 9, 2020. https://slate. com/business/2020/12/gofundme-dark-side-fraud-social-media-health-care.html.

Stevenson, Seth. "The Tithes Are Turning: The GoFundMe Story." *Slate* (blog), June 7, 2022. https://slate.com/transcripts/K2wrN0tGYzFoNTlJZlRBa2tVTkE3STVoNGVo NHlKeUNOUkowY0MwenFlTT0=.

Tapasyananda, Swami. *Bhagavadgītā.* Sri Ramakrishna Math (1984), 17: 20–22.

Taqdees, Chiara. "Fundraisers You Should Start During Covid-19." Impact Guru, November 16, 2020. https://www.impactguru.com/blog/three-types-of-fundraisers-you-should-start-during-covid-19.

Tedder, Michael. "GoFundMe Helps Struggling Americans Raise Cash. It Also Has a Huge Fraud Problem." *Money*, January 25, 2021. https://money.com/fake-gofundme/.

TeKoltse, Rebecca. "Crowdfunding Research and Impact on the Philanthropic Sector." *Lilly Family School of Philanthropy* (blog), December 2, 2019. https://blog.philanthr opy.iupui.edu/2019/12/02/crowdfunding-research-and-impact-on-the-philanthro pic-sector/.

Tene, Omer, and Jules Polonetsky. "A Theory of Creepy: Technology, Privacy and Shifting Social Norms." *Yale Journal of Law and Technology* 16 (2013): 59–102.

Thomas, Hannah S., Austin W. Lee, Behnam Nabavizadeh, Nikan K. Namiri, Nizar Hakam, Patrick Martin-Tuite, Natalie Rios, Anthony Enriquez, Nnenaya A. Mmonu, and Andrew J. Cohen. "Characterizing Online Crowdfunding Campaigns for Patients with Kidney Cancer." *Cancer Medicine* 10, no. 13 (2021): 4564–74.

Thompson, Elizabeth. "Crowdfunding Platforms Now Required to Report Transactions, After Truck Convoy Protests." CBC, May 4, 2022. https://www.cbc.ca/news/politics/convoy-finance-crowdfunding-fintrac-1.6440671.

Thompson, Elizabeth, Roberto Rocha, and Albert Leung. "Hacked Convoy Data Shows More than Half of Donations Came from U.S." CBC, February 14, 2022. https://www.cbc.ca/news/politics/convoy-protest-donations-data-1.6351292.

Thompson, Haschal. "Vaccine Police." GiveSendGo. Accessed February 23, 2022. http://givesendgo.com/vaccinepolicenews.

Trevelyan, Charles E. *Three Letters from Sir Charles Trevelyan to "The Times" on London Pauperism: With the Leading Article upon Them and Extracts from "How to Relieve the Poor of Edinburgh and Other Great Cities, without Increasing Pauperism: A Tried Successful, and Economical Plan, 1867" and from the "Report on the Condition of the Poorer Classes of Edinburgh, and of Their Dwellings, Neighbourhoods, and Families, 1868." Talbot Collection of British Pamphlets.* London: Longmans, Green, and Co., 1870. http://www.archive.org/details/threelettersfrom00trev.

Truth and Reconciliation Commission of Canada. *Canada's Residential Schools: The Final Report of the Truth and Reconciliation Commission of Canada.* Montreal/Kingston: McGill-Queen's Press, 2015.

Tunney, Catharine. "GoFundMe Has Released $1M of More than $6M Raised for Protest Convoy." CBC, January 27, 2022. https://www.cbc.ca/news/politics/gofundme-money-released-convoy-1.6328029.

Turgot, Anne Robert Jacques. *The Turgot Collection.* Edited by David Gordon. Auburn, AL: Mises Institute, 2011. https://mises.org/library/turgot-collection.

United Nations Development Programme China Poverty, Equity, and Governance. "Internet Philanthropy in China." Beijing: United Nations Development Programme, 2016.

Van Grove, Jennifer. "GoFundMe Founders Get Big Payday." *San Diego Union-Tribune,* August 24, 2016. https://www.sandiegouniontribune.com/sdut-gofundme-founders-sell-company-to-investors-2015jun24-story.html.

Van Leeuwen, Marco H. D., Elise van Nederveen Meerkerk, and Lex Heerma van Voss. "Provisions for the Elderly in North-Western Europe: An International Comparison of Almshouses, Sixteenth–Twentieth Centuries." *Scandinavian Economic History Review* 62, no. 1 (2014): 1–16.

Vassell, Anika. *Medical Crowdfunding and the Communication of Health-Related Financial Needs in Digital Environments.* Simon Fraser University, 2019. Accessed May 30, 2023, https://summit.sfu.ca/item/19937.

Vassell, Anika, Valorie A. Crooks, and Jeremy Snyder. "What Was Lost, Missing, Sought and Hoped for: Qualitatively Exploring Medical Crowdfunding Campaign Narratives for Lyme Disease." *Health* 25, no. 6 (November 1, 2021): 707–21. https://doi.org/10.1177/1363459320912808.

Villegas, Paulina, and Reis Thebault. "Frozen out of GoFundMe, Canadian Protest Convoy Raises Millions on Christian Site." *Washington Post*, February 7, 2022. https://www.washingtonpost.com/world/2022/02/07/canada-protesters-fundraising-platform/.

Vox, Ford, Kelly McBride Folkers, Angela Turi, and Arthur L. Caplan. "Medical Crowdfunding for Scientifically Unsupported or Potentially Dangerous Treatments." *Journal of the American Medical Association* 320, no. 16 (2018): 1705–6.

Wade, Matthew. "'The Giving Layer of the Internet': A Critical History of GoFundMe's Reputation Management, Platform Governance, and Communication Strategies in Capturing Peer-to-Peer and Charitable Giving Markets." *Journal of Philanthropy and Marketing* e1777 (November 14, 2022). https://doi.org/10.26181/21547116.v1.

Wardell, Susan. "To Wish You Well: The Biopolitical Subjectivities of Medical Crowdfunders During and After Aotearoa New Zealand's COVID-19 Lockdown." *BioSocieties*, September 22, 2021. https://doi.org/10.1057/s41292-021-00251-7.

Warren, Rossalyn. "Meet the Lawyer-Turned-Tech Entrepreneur Trying to Make Justice Available to All." *The Guardian*, August 29, 2019, sec. Guardian Careers. https://www.theguardian.com/careers/2019/aug/29/meet-the-lawyer-turned-tech-entrepreneur-trying-to-make-justice-available-to-all.

Warren, Samuel D., and Louis D. Brandeis. "The Right to Privacy." *Harvard Law Review* 4, no. 5 (1890): 193–220.

Watkins-Hayes, Celeste, and Elyse Kovalsky. "The Discourse of Deservingness: Morality and the Dilemmas of Poverty Relief in Debate and Practice." In *The Oxford Handbook of the Social Science of Poverty*, edited by David Brady and Linda Burton, 193–220. New York: Oxford University Press, 2016.

Watsi. "FAQ." Watsi. Accessed April 27, 2022. https://watsi.org/faq.

Whitmore, Bobby. "It's Time to Act: Help American Families Struggling to Make Ends Meet." *GoFundMe Stories* (blog), December 21, 2020. https://medium.com/gofundme-stories/its-time-to-act-help-american-families-struggling-to-make-ends-meet-fdc19dbd1992.

Wilde, Oscar. "The Soul of Man Under Socialism." In *The Spirit of the Age*, edited by Gertrude Himmelfarb, 294–310. New Haven: Yale University Press, 2007.

Willer, Robb, Christopher Wimer, and Lindsay A. Owens. "What Drives the Gender Gap in Charitable Giving? Lower Empathy Leads Men to Give Less to Poverty Relief." *Social Science Research* 52 (July 1, 2015): 83–98. https://doi.org/10.1016/j.ssresearch.2014.12.014.

Willgress, Lydia. "JustGiving Accused of Taking £20m from Donations While Paying Staff up to £200,000." *The Telegraph*, February 7, 2017. https://www.telegraph.co.uk/news/2017/02/07/justgiving-accused-taking-20m-donations-paying-staff-200000/.

William-Ross, Lindsay. "'We Are Going to Survive This Closure': Customers Pitch in over $21k to Save Vancouver Restaurant." Vancouver Is Awesome, April 20, 2021. https://www.vancouverisawesome.com/food-and-drink/we-are-going-to-survive-this-closure-customers-pitch-in-over-21k-to-save-vancouver-restaurant-3648681.

Wolpert, Julian. "Redistributional Effects of America's Private Foundations." In *The Legitimacy of Philanthropic Foundations: United States and European Perspectives*, edited by Kenneth Prewitt, Mattei Dogan, Steven Heydemann, and Stefan Toepler, 123–49. New York: Russell Sage Foundation, 2006.

Woodward, Jon. "Ontario Government Staffer out of a Job After $100 Donation to Ottawa Blockade, Others Under Scrutiny." CTV News, February 16, 2022. https://toronto.ctvn

ews.ca/ontario-government-staffer-out-of-a-job-after-100-donation-to-ottawa-block ade-others-under-scrutiny-1.5784390.

WXYZ. "More Families Relying on Crowdfunding for Funeral Costs amid COVID-19 Pandemic." *WXYZ*, October 11, 2021. https://www.wxyz.com/news/more-families-relying-on-crowdfunding-for-funeral-costs-amid-covid-19-pandemic.

Zenone, Marco Antonio, and Jeremy Snyder. "Crowdfunding Abortion: An Exploratory Thematic Analysis of Fundraising for a Stigmatized Medical Procedure." *BMC Women's Health* 20, no. 90 (May 4, 2020). https://doi.org/10.1186/s12905-020-00938-2.

Zenone, Marco, and Jeremy Snyder. "Fraud in Medical Crowdfunding: A Typology of Publicized Cases and Policy Recommendations." *Policy & Internet* 11, no. 2 (2019): 215–34. https://doi.org/10.1002/poi3.188.

Zenone, Marco, Jeremy Snyder, and Timothy Caulfield. "Crowdfunding Cannabidiol (CBD) for Cancer: Hype and Misinformation on GoFundMe." *American Journal of Public Health* 110, no. S3 (October 1, 2020): S294–99. https://doi.org/10.2105/AJPH.2020.305768.

Zhang, Fuguo, Bingyu Xue, Yiran Li, Hui Li, and Qihua Liu. "Effect of Textual Features on the Success of Medical Crowdfunding: Model Development and Econometric Analysis from the Tencent Charity Platform." *Journal of Medical Internet Research* 23, no. 6 (June 11, 2021): e22395. https://doi.org/10.2196/22395.

Zhao, Kexin, Lina Zhou, and Xia Zhao. "Multi-Modal Emotion Expression and Online Charity Crowdfunding Success." *Decision Support Systems*, July 22, 2022, 113842. https://doi.org/10.1016/j.dss.2022.113842.

Index